CLARENDON MEDIEVAL AND
TUDOR SERIES

General Editor

J. A. W. BENNETT

CLARENDON MEDIEVAL AND TUDOR SERIES

Quhill at the last, he saw quhair Lowrence lay
Ane bow he bent, ane flane with fedderis gray
He haillit to the heid, and or he steird,
The fox he prikkit fast vnto the eird.

Now (quod the fox) allace and wellaway,
Gorrit I am, and may na forther gang.
Me think na man may may speik ane word in play,
Bot now on ernis, in ernist it is tane.
He faulit him, and out he drew his flane.
And sloe his kid, and vther violence,
He tuke his skyn, and maid ane recompence.

❧ Moralitas.

THis suddand deith, and vnprouysit end,
   Of this fals Tod, without prouisioun,
Exempill is exhortand folk to amend.
For dreid of sic ane lyke confusioun,
For mony now hes gude professioun,
zit not repentis, nor for thair sinnis greit,
Becaus thay think thair lustie lyfe sa sweit.

Sum bene also throw consuetude and ryte,
Vincust with carnall sensualitie,
Suppose thay be as for the tyme contryte,
Can not forbeir, nor fra thair sinnis fle.
Vse drawis Nature swa in propertie,
Of beist and man, that neidlingis thay man do,
As thay of lang tyme hes bene hantit to.

Page 34 of the Bassandyne Print of Henryson's *Morall Fabillis*,
Edinburgh, 1571

ROBERT HENRYSON

Poems

Selected and edited
with an Introduction, Notes, and
Glossary by
CHARLES ELLIOTT

SECOND EDITION

OXFORD
AT THE CLARENDON PRESS
1974

Oxford University Press, Ely House, London W. 1

GLASGOW NEW YORK TORONTO MELBOURNE WELLINGTON
CAPE TOWN IBADAN NAIROBI DAR ES SALAAM LUSAKA ADDIS ABABA
DELHI BOMBAY CALCUTTA MADRAS KARACHI LAHORE DACCA
KUALA LUMPUR SINGAPORE HONG KONG TOKYO

CASEBOUND ISBN 0 19 871091 7

PAPERBACK ISBN 0 19 871092 5

© *Oxford University Press 1963, 1974*

First edition 1963
Second edition 1974

*Printed in Great Britain
at the University Press, Oxford
by Vivian Ridler
Printer to the University*

CONTENTS

LIST OF FABLES

The Morall Fabillis of Esope the Phrygian

INTRODUCTION

'CHAUCERIANISM' in the sense of those essential qualities associated with Chaucer's poetry is something easily recognized and responded to. Yet the expression stands for an amalgam of things: a capacity for humour, urbanity, and sympathy held in near-perfect balance for most of the time; a fluent narrative art using a variety of measures and manipulated by a changing yet always identifiable *persona*; a faculty for juxtaposition (whether for immediate effect or to carry broad thematic points); an ability to produce rich patterns of responses (manifested sometimes in piquant lexical complexities, but more often in the handling of the *sentence* itself).

The loose expression 'Scottish Chaucerians' brings in another facet of 'Chaucerianism', namely influence upon succeeding poets. Indirectly, the expression suggests that these Chaucerians are distinguishable from writers who are more self-sufficingly 'Scottish'. Among these last is John Barbour, whose *The Actes and Life of Robert Bruce* (1375) initiates, with its celebration of traditional history, a narrative genre. And there is Andrew Wyntoun (prior of Lochleven until 1422) whose *Orygynale Chronykil of Scotland* emphasizes that country's right to independence, but expresses it without Barbour's rhetorical finesse. There is, too, Blind Harry, who gives in *The Actis and Deidis of Schir William Wallace* (? *c*. 1460) a free-ranging treatment, with bravado-touches, of a national hero. The line is returned to in the next century by Sir David Lindsay's *The Historie of Squyer Meldrum* (*c*. 1550), a romantic biography of the 'vmquhyle Laird of Clesche and Bynnis' in which easy room is given to Englishmen found wanting when compared with Scots.

As for the so-called 'Scottish Chaucerians', while there seems to be good reason for accepting James I (1394–1437) as the author of *The Kingis Quair*,[1] the argument that it fits better into

[1] See J. Norton-Smith (ed.), *The Kingis Quair*, pp. xix–xx (Clarendon Medieval and Tudor Series, Oxford, 1971).

the English tradition is not open to serious doubt.[1] And the
'Chaucerianism' of Sir Richard Holland is something odd and
not a little crabbed. His *The Buke of the Howlat* (*c.* 1450) has some
debt to *The Parlement of Foules*, but its alliterative rhymed
stanzas are heavily un-Chaucerian, while the allegorical pane-
gyric on the Douglas family labours under a maze of sub-plots.
Possibly next in time comes Henryson, and after him William
Dunbar (*c.* 1456–*c.* 1515) and then Gavin Douglas (*c.* 1475–
1522). And it is these last three, chronologically central in the
late medieval scene and producing, apparently, all their work
within a period of about fifty years, who would seem to have
strongest claim to the title 'Scottish Chaucerians'.

Undoubtedly in Henryson's poetry there is something
stronger than reminiscence of the English poet. As regards tone
(the writer's attitude towards his audience) there is, in Henry-
son's work generally, a Chaucer-like protrusion of a personality.
The author–hearer context may be vivified in a variety of ways.
In some cases, direct address gains this effect; see *Fabillis*,
ll. 1220–2, and cp. Chaucer's *The Frankeleyns Tale*, ll. 1493–6.
In others, obliqueness is employed, as in *Fabillis*, ll. 2969–72,
Testament, l. 252; cp. *Sir Thopas*, ll. 926–8, which make up an
ironic comment on the quality of the interrupted tale. Yet other
cases show a direct broadening of the area of reference. Thus in
'Ane Prayer for the Pest', the recurring use of 'we', 'us', and
'our' yokes the suffering ones being described with the audience
itself; cp. *The Pardoners Tale*, ll. 919 ff., where the specimen offer
of corrupt pardons is 'realistically' made to the surrounding
pilgrims, but rejected by Bailly on their behalf and, by some-
thing stronger than inference, on behalf of the laity at large.
Again, the *persona* can be realized by means of a statement of
ignorance; see *Orpheus and Erudices*, ll. 240–2, and cp. *The
Frankeleyns Tale*, ll. 1264–84, where the poet, disclaiming know-
ledge of astrological terms, provides them. As regards feeling
(the writer's attitude towards his material) there is again a
Chaucerian resemblance. Thus narrative may be used for ends

[1] See D. Pearsall, pp. 226–8 in D. S. Brewer (ed.), *Chaucer and Chaucerians*
(1966). Pearsall discusses the poem in a chapter entitled 'The English Chaucerians'.
For the southern nature of its language, see Sir William Craigie, *Essays and Studies*,
xxv (1939), 22–38.

other than narrative, as in the *Fabillis* retrospectively evaluated by the *moralitas* sections. Similarly, Bailly's comment on *The Tale of the Man of Law*, 'This was a thrifty tale' (l. 1165), suggests that Custance can be interpreted as a figure of fortitude. Description may be functionally employed; in 'The Thre Deid-Pollis' temporal splendour points a moral; cp. Chaucer's *The House of Fame*, in which the eagle's description of sound-laws suggests a 'scientific' credence for the Palace of Fame as the destination of 'every speche'. There is, too, the capacity to overturn traditional associations, as in 'Robene and Makyne', where pastoral conventions are translated into psychological realism; cp. *The Knyghtes Tale*, l. 2169 where Chaucer momentarily belittles the chivalric grandeur of Emetrius, who has 'a fewe frakenes in his face yspreynd'. As well, there is the faculty of transposing viewpoints; in *Fabillis*, ll. 2313–14 a man's hand is reduced to the level of a tod's tail, in ll. 2331–3 it is implied that chicken-stealing is an offence against all-seeing God, and in ll. 2893–5 a dying mouse calls for a priest. Compare *The Nonnes Preestes Tale*, ll. 3221–9, where Iscariot, Ganelon, and Sinon are linked by the term 'homycides' to a cock-stalking fox. And pathos and humour can be juxtaposed so as to yield irony; see *Fabillis*, ll. 761–71, 2896–2906, and cp., in *The Bok of the Duchesse*, the Dreamer's attitude of excessive *naïveté* which interacts with the pathos of the Knight's circumstance to produce, apart from the main 'elegiac' result, an ironic comment on the doctrinaire principles of *amour courtois*.

In the matter of expression, Henryson shows a sureness of diction and of metrical touch akin to Chaucer's. Choice of word is generally decorous and functional (the aureate style concluding 'Ane Prayer for the Pest' is a set exercise and unrepresentative). A single stanza of the *Fabillis* (ll. 1825–31) succinctly describes flax-preparation; ll. 887–919 mingle a static appeal, coming from the numerous substantive ideas, with an active one deriving from the kinetic verbs. Occasionally there is a lexical complexity reminiscent of Chaucer's; thus in the *Testament*, l. 483, 'rank' suggests both 'loathsome' and 'complete'; in 'Deid-Pollis', l. 3, 'gaistly' has active and passive connotations. Compare l. 628 of *The Prologe of the Wyves Tale of Bathe*, where 'hende' can signify 'amiable', 'gentle', 'courteous', or 'to hand'. In places rhetoric is used in effective contrast to adjacent areas of the direct or even colloquial, as in Cresseid's 'Complaint' or in the *moralitas* portions of the *Fabillis* (cp. *Troilus and Criseyde*, ii. 904–10, a stanza beginning with the rhetorical figure of *interpretatio* and progressing to an evocative simplicity).

Like most of the 'makaris', Henryson is attracted more to Chaucerian stanza-forms than to the heroic couplet (though the latter form is used in the *Orpheus moralitas*). While not showing Dunbar's range and virtuosity in these, he works with a competent variety. 'The Garmont of Gud Ladeis' decorously uses ballad-metre; the four-lined stanzas distinguish the lesser entities within the over-all unity of the 'garmont', and the three-foot alternate lines in each admit a quiet qualification of the ideas being expressed. In 'The Bludy Serk' and 'Robene and Makyne' the double pattern of this metre is employed; in the former, the expanded form unobtrusively meets the slight narrative needs, while in the second an ironic mutation is achieved—the piece is entrenched within the ballad-world and yet disrupts that world. Most of the *Fabillis*, *Testament*, and *Orpheus* is in freely flowing *Troilus* verse adapted to diverse contexts. The eight-line moralizing stanzas of 'Deid-Pollis', 'Nerar Hevynnis Blyss', and most of the 'Pest' take their sanction from Chaucer's *An ABC*, and the use of one metrical mode for the three does not prevent a differentiated expression of tension, resolution, and direct address respectively. Cresseid's 'Complaint' (in nine-lined stanzas; the form is eked out to ten by an extra rhyme in Orpheus' 'mone') has metrical forebear in parts of Chaucer's 'The Compleynt of feire Anelida and fals Arcite'; and here the slow measured rhythms and intricate rhyme-patterns contrast with the sharp modulations and direct sound-groupings employed in the description of Saturn, the active punisher of Cresseid. 'The Annunciation' (in stanzas of twelve lines and of two rhymes only) is fittingly segmented into areas of contemplation, while the identical weak rhyme in all its three-foot lines unifies the whole with its regular cadence.

Henryson's autonomy and distinctiveness are best illustrated from the *Fabillis*, the *Testament*, and *Orpheus and Erudices*.

The genealogy of the *Fabillis* has no real place for Chaucer,[1] while the treatment is hardly Chaucerian. The over-all method shows a dichotomy. The fables take in the broad tradition of the beast-story, and are self-sufficient. Preoccupation with narrative details yields its own reward in spite of the ever-present equating of animal with man for man's behoof. The account of the two mice is vivified by the minutiae of rusticity and urbanity kept at a 'tim'rous' level. The trial of the fox is rooted in the world of animals by the cataloguing of *all forfuttit beistis in eird*. The proem to 'The Preiching of the Swallow' is almost cosmic in its sweep through Godhead, firmament, air, fire, earth, water, and seasons; man is indeed momentarily elevated (ll. 1668–74), but the subsequent action is played out in a world of swallows, seeds, and nets. In the two fables of fox, wolf, and cadgear (carter), and fox, wolf, and husbandman, the interplay of 'character' is so manipulated as to 'realize' the animals and make puppets of the humans. The narrative line of the tale of paddock and mouse merely follows a cursive sequence of hesitation, convincing, deception, and disaster.

The dichotomy is due to the unfailing *moralitas*. Henryson exploits the narrative potential of his material so that it becomes independent and satisfying in 'literary' terms. From this the *sentence* is deliberately detached. The direct and blatant 'teaching' has no counterpart in Chaucer. Henryson's tale of cock and fox and Chaucer's *The Nonnes Preestes Tale* ostensibly have the same narrative base. In the former, the traditional story-line of sparse-living widow, grand bird deceived and captured and then freed through counter-deception, is refreshingly vivified by the hen's disquisition on the cock as chivalric lover, as one cold and dry as a mate, and as a creature loose and lecherous. Such augments the smooth, economical story-telling and the manifest skill in dialogue. Everything is reared and kept on a dung-hill. The *moralitas* points the obvious lesson: for cockerel read proud men, for fox read flatterers. Yet in the articulation of the didacticism, the significance of the hens is not realized, with the result that neither part of the fable is entirely satisfactory. We respond to the subtlety with which the hen-attitudes are expressed and we take the

[1] See pp. 144–5.

point about pride and flattery; yet what of that subtlety in a moralistic context? Chaucer's narrator declares that his story will be 'of a cok', but simply that it certainly is not. And the potential *sentence* is both hinted at and unobtrusively directed towards a moral and ethical area by means of light touches. In ll. 3187–8 there is allusion to the creation of the world, in ll. 3226 ff. a reference to Christ's betrayer, in ll. 3257–9 one to the loss of Paradise, and in l. 3341 one to the Friday—the Long Friday which is Good Friday. From dung-hill happenings emerges comment on something more than secular pride, one on the old Adam in human-kind. And that comment is generated from the narrative details.

Henryson's art is impressively varied, assured and modulated in narrative terms, and it works effectively in expressing a grave yet enterprising moralizing mind. But from the very manner of the poet's procedure, our response cannot easily be a unified one. Of course, it would be false to imply that at all times Chaucer wears his moral conscience lightly, that hint and innuendo amid narrative will do for him. He possesses 'high seriousness' indeed; we remember the palinode to *Troilus and Criseyde*, the praise of 'gentilesse' put into *The Wyves Tale of Bathe*, and the bold exemplum which is *The Clerkes Tale* and which blunts the charge of 'cold inhumanity' sometimes made against that tale, since the story is not 'realistically' intended. But such are hardly ever at one point Chaucer's sole concern. The palinode forces one to reassess the earlier extended celebration of secular love, the estimations of 'gentilesse' add unexpected depth to a hitherto 'animal' characterization, while the Clerk's moral tale is, at another level, a rejoinder to the 'secte' of Bath.

It is, perhaps, simply a case of difference in sensibility. Henryson accepts, and assumes in his audience, the medieval ethos. The paths of right and wrong, towards bliss or bale, are clear and distinct. Awareness of felicity beyond the grave compels him to regard this life as being compounded of fleeting pleasures and perilous temptations. Even his so-called 'humanitarianism', his frequent concern for the *sempill folk*, the *pure pepill*, the *commounis* oppressed by *tirrane men*, is not unmixed condemnation of social ills, but is again a subordinating of temporal to eternal values. The existence of the wronged one is *half ane Purgatorie*, and the oppressors suppose

> this present lyfe suld ever lest;
> Bot all begylit thay will in schort tyme end,
> And efter deith to lestand panis wend. (ll. 1262–4.)

By means of succinct astronomical periphrasis (l. 5) *The Testament of Cresseid* is set in a bleak season. The beginning is both functional and decorous. The poet discards the dream framework (here is no February trance or May 'sweven'), and is able neatly to motivate the action (cold drives him indoors and to his *quair*). The allusion to the early spring reminds one that April was conventionally the month of Venus, the arbitress of Cresseid's fate. In retrospect, the theme of *mortall neid and greit penuritie* is seen to be prefigured by the opening touch of coldness. The hour is after sunset (ll. 8–14), the beginning is in darkness, and in what follows, brilliance and light are not experienced but remembered only, in the *ubi sunt* 'Complaint' uttered by Cresseid. By abandoning his intention to pray favour of Venus the poet appears to slight the Queen of Love; later Cresseid is to show explicit and greater disrespect, but the essential nature of the 'gery goddess' is underlined—the man can go to his warming hearth, while the woman must make her way to the lazar-house. In such ways these early elements interrelate and provide a fitting proem.

The obvious links with *Troilus and Criseyde* are Chaucer's four protagonists who reappear not radically altered. In Diomeid, Henryson swiftly stresses the same double unscrupulousness: the seduction is recapitulated (ll. 71–2) and the further act of supplanting referred to (l. 73). The character of Calchas is modified and developed. He is now priest of Venus and not of Apollo, a change making for obvious dramatic unity, since Venus blasphemed gives him a leprous daughter. Furthermore, his 'priestly' task of receiving and succouring a lazar permits the poet to articulate situations of greater intimacy and pathos.[1] Troilus retains generally the attributes of the courtly lover: grief, pallor, easy tears, febrile activity, and extreme emotions. He is true, noble, worthy, *gentill and fre*, the ideal warrior, successful and charitable (see ll. 519–22, 603–9). For Cresseid, Henryson shows

[1] See note to ll. 372–7.

more than Chaucer's sympathy, and he indicates Fortune as the cause of her disaster in love (ll. 85–91). Again, there is a strong echo of Chaucer's emphasis upon fear as one of her dominant traits; when her second 'wal of stele' falls, demoralization follows, and part of her outcry is a desire for life ordered by someone else (l. 131). She too is given traditional epithets (*bricht of hew*, *flour and A per se*, *cristall*, etc.), and she shows some concern for the properties of the courtly system (*royall ring*, *rubie reid*, *drowrie*, *broche and belt*) and experiences intense feelings.

Cresseid's initial offence is linked to yet another courtly concept, that of a contract between lover and love's deities. The notion is epitomized in Gower's *Confessio Amantis*:

> The god of love is favorable
> To hem that ben in love stable. (iv. 443–4.)

That an agreement has existed is apparent from ll. 124–8, 134–8; but the contract is now broken. Her mood of self-pity (ll. 129–33) implies that she is the injured partner and that the gods have done a spiteful hurt; yet it hides the fact that as long as she remained faithful in love the gods continued beneficent. There is no hint of self-accusation, no understanding that she is being fittingly punished by Love. Her unequivocal denunciation (ll. 134–5) reveals the sin of Pride, while the attitude of presumption is expressed in the language of Anger (ll. 124–5, 352). Here is the significant transition from courtly to moral theme.

Cresseid is doomed by a *parliament* of the gods. The poet dwells on their astrological qualities. Thus the yoking of Saturn and Cynthia to pronounce leprosy represents an association of unlikes, the former being masculine, diurnal, of black colour, and the slowest-motioned, the other feminine, nocturnal, white, and the swiftest. This evokes ideas of legality, and of the cosmic nature of Cresseid's offence. Further, each of the pair was popularly associated with the onset of leprosy, and so their conjoining implies the inevitability of that affliction. The *parliament* also takes account of traditional, mythological rivalries; thus Saturn has little respect for Cupid, the son of his enemy Venus. Yet the figures are humanized in a way that has no direct counterpart in

Chaucer; all seven go into committee and elect Mercury as their
'chairman' (*foirspeikar*), while Saturn is delegated to implement
their decision. Such touches make them, and what they deliberate
on and judge, measurable by mortal standards.

Cupid convenes the assembly

> ringand ane silver bell,
> Quhilk men micht heir fra hevin unto hell.   (ll. 144-5.)

This simple allusion to the poles of Christian thinking furthers
the process by which the theme is taken out of the context of
amour courtois, and the sustained prominence given to Cupid
continues the movement. He recapitulates the offence, and he is
throughout single-minded over the trespass (ll. 285-7). He is
arranger and arraigner, superior in his one-ness to the manifold-
ness of the others, who merely share a transmitted wisdom (l.
289). There is in this at least reminiscence of the Boethian scheme
as propounded in *De Consolatione Philosophiae*. Cupid's function
is analogous to that of Providence, whereby the Divine Intelli-
gence conceives the universe as a timeless whole. The convened
gods resemble the blind destinal forces, and are yet without the
attributes of Fortune, that apparently capricious agency more
remote than they from Divine one-ness. For they reason and
observe procedure; Saturn and Cynthia pronounce sentence only
after reflection (l. 303). And so the earlier allusion to Fortune
(ll. 89-90) appears to be restricted to the ethos of courtly love,
and thereby Cresseid's courtly and moral failings are differ-
entiated. Her Pride and Anger are considered and punished
against a background of powers similar to those of Providence
and Destiny, both of which are nearer Divine Reason than is
Fortune.

The *pane* is the affliction of leprosy, popularly regarded as
expiation for sin. At the seclusion-ceremony for one so afflicted,
'The priest then with the spade casts earth on each of his feet,
saying: "Be thou dead to the world, but alive again unto God."
. . . The priest must lead him to the Church, from the Church to
his house as a dead man.'[1]

In her 'Complaint', Cresseid is still occupied with Self. The

[1] R. M. Clay, *The Mediaeval Hospitals of England* (1909), p. 274.

second-person pronouns of the first four stanzas reflect no objectivity; she has come out of herself only to regard herself more acutely. Sorrow is mingled with bewilderment, and her conclusion is still an arraignment of Fortune. To her, the suffering appears unwarranted and capriciously inflicted. Regret is for loss (of things physical, sensuous, and abstract) and not for trespass. Her cry is a *chydand*, a sorrowful indignation, still embracing Pride and Anger.

The resolution follows from the last meeting of Troilus and Cresseid. Recovering from her swoon, she is a transformed creature. Self-knowledge and self-condemnation have replaced self-pity. Her suffering now takes on the hue of purgation, and the gulfs between self-deception and self-awareness, blasphemy and repentance, pride and humility, have been crossed. The leprous Cresseid, 'dead to the world', becomes 'alive again unto God'. With presumption departs resentment, and it is a resigned person who writes out her bequeathings. The body is made over to worms, and earthly possessions are made over to others (ll. 579–80, 582–4). The Cresseid once with *fleschelie lust sa maculait* can assign her spirit to Diana, goddess of chastity. Troilus is central in the transformation. He enters the poem as courtly lover, and now he re-enters it as the power through which Cresseid achieves spiritual regeneration.

Both Chaucer and Henryson refer to their poems as 'tragedies'. For Chaucer, the tragedy connotes something secular, for it embraces the brittle nature of earthly love, which can bring disaster to friend and kin. It points as well to the ineffectiveness of 'trouthe' in the human situation. Troilus holds on to his 'trouthe'; but that is no proof against lack of 'trouthe' in others— Criseyde is unstable in character and Pandarus unstable in action. For Henryson too the tragedy is secular and limited, and it signifies the 'temporal' suffering of Cresseid through which she gains her own 'trouthe', self-knowledge. The *sentence* is immutably part of the structure of the poem. Henryson here achieves a satisfying artistic unity, something lacking in the *Fabillis* and something which Chaucer achieves more disjunctively by use of the palinode.

The theme of regeneration is universal and timeless. Yet some of the machinery used to articulate it is traditional (introductory season-motif, 'vision', astrological material, etc.). And some aspects of the expression are common property (repetition in balanced fashion, ll. 232–8, 316–22; apostrophe, *passim* in the 'Complaint'; the time-honoured and Lydgatian simile of l. 176; the well-worn Chaucerian gnome of l. 478). However, indication of season is functional (the unnatural cold of the spring accords with the theme of dispossession), while the vision-device is truly objectified—the poet relates and does not experience the dream. And there is no prolixity. The 'recognition-scene' has no extended, mawkish moralizing, and there is no parallel to Troilus' soliloquy on predestination.

In *Orpheus and Erudices* Henryson works in a deceptively simple way. The staple of the narrative is faithful to old materials deriving from Ovid and Virgil, and refurbished somewhat by Boethius. Orpheus is begotten, weds Eurydice, and for a while lives in happiness with her. A serpent-bite destroys her and she is taken to the underworld. He searches for her, and eventually finds her under the dominion of Pluto and Persephone. His music vanquishes these, and Eurydice is conditionally released to him. But he fails the condition; he looks behind to her, whereupon she is lost to him for ever.

In the *moralitas*, the narrative details are made to yield their precise *sentence* through a close following of Nicholas Trevet's commentary on Boethius' *De Consolatione*.

However, by use of a method different from that of the *Fabillis*, here story and didacticism coexist and are not merely juxtaposed. The marks of this method are certain individual emphases which Henryson applies in the narrative section.

The first significant change is the inclusion of the explicit account of the genealogy of Orpheus. Jupiter and Mnemosyne beget the muses, and the chief of these, Calliope, is made queen by Phebus and their offspring is Orpheus. In such a genealogy intellect is dominant. Jupiter, the highest of the gods and subject only to the decrees of fate, transmits divine intelligence.[1] Mne-

---

[1] Jupiter is, of course, the Greek Zeus, identified in Stoic philosophy with its highest principle, fire, which is at the same time the Reason which animates the world.

mosyne (Memoria) represents a power obviously cogitative, while Phebus is the god of reason, of light. Calliope, traditionally the muse of heroic poetry, is here invested with primacy in music; she is *of all musik mastress* (l. 44), the *fyndar of all ermonye* (l. 67), and she sustains the infant Orpheus with the *sweit licour of all musike perfyte* (l. 70). From a union of divine intellect and sovereign skill in music Orpheus achieves life; and, by simple poetic inference, he should partake of the qualities of his be-getters.

Admitting another new emphasis, the poet shows those virtues to be dormant in Orpheus. Eurydice responds to his noble fame (l. 73), and nothing is said of his music. Indeed, as long as he possesses her, he creates no music of any kind. To-wards her Orpheus is shown as being neutral and passive; he is not cogitative. The initiative in the wooing and wedding is entirely with Eurydice; he is 'required' to take her as wife, l. 77, and he agrees. Further, she is given certain secular and sensual touches; she is *haboundand in riches* (l. 75), and feels no shame (which suggests emotion raised above reason) in offering to Orpheus *wordis sweit and blenkis amorus* (l. 81). If he has some claim to intellect by descent, she implies the appetitive, and he becomes king and lord (and then only with some limitation—*In this province*, l. 83) by her consent. Here is the apparent harmony: the 'intellectif' with the appetitive.

Aristaeus is *pastor* in Virgil; but Henryson gives him the vague function of beast-keeper (l. 98). Here too a change of narrative detail seems to work thematically. A domestic, 'pastoral' role is replaced by one much vaguer. Allegorically, beasts are the sensual passions, and here such types of carnality are governed, 'kept', by Aristaeus. The narrative innovation serves the *sentence*. Aristaeus exercises moral virtue, regulation of passions. He sees Eurydice as his fit prey, and this implies some criticism of her union with Orpheus. She is the appetitive in need of restraint, Orpheus partakes of divine intellect but is unable to govern her. The point is swiftly made; Eurydice flees moral virtue and ex-poses herself to sensuality, which is the serpent's sting.

With her loss, Orpheus becomes active. To begin, he is *rampand as ane lyoun ravenus* (l. 121), which again suggests a restricted operation of reason. Then, in his 'mone' (ll. 134–83) for the first time he invokes his skill in music. But that skill, of divine origin, has been debased by the 'effectioun' of the world. It cannot work for Orpheus, and while it can operate somewhat upon irrational creation (ll. 144–7), the result is *all in vane* (l. 148). The music and the music-maker have not full potency.

Henryson is expansive in his account of Orpheus' search for Eurydice. Certainly there is not an equivalent depth of detail in Ovid or Virgil, while the bare statements of Boethius are now given a fresh extended poetic life. Thus the report of the journey to the heavens greatly fills out Boethius' declaration that 'he pleynid hym of the hevene goddis' (Chaucer's translation). In this section it is perhaps significant that the only planet-deity addressed directly is Venus. Orpheus' only *rapport* is with the goddess of sensual love, and it is her reply alone that provides him with any guiding information (see ll. 205–11). It is as if like and part-like can communicate because of their common element of sensuality; and this is further implied criticism of the decayed Orpheus. But, in another accretion to the stock account, the poet tells now Orpheus, in his search among the planets, gains knowledge of different musical skills, controlled, patterned, and intellectual (see ll. 219–39).[1] The fallen faculty has been regenerated. On reaching the gate of Hell, Orpheus has opportunity to prove this different music, and here the legends concerning Ixion, Tantalus, and Tityus neatly take their place in the evolving *sentence*. These figures represent respectively abuse of appetite in carnality, conscience, and knowledge, and appetite is satisfied through the intellectual music. *At hiddowis hellis hous* itself, Orpheus encounters further exemplars, all of which again point to appetite uncontrolled. Here are types of forceful mastery and dominion (kings and queens, Hector, Priam, Alexander, Caesar, Pharaoh), of fleshly greed (Antiochus, Herod), of covetousness (Naboth, Jezebel), of selfish dictates (Saul, Pilate), and of sacred office abused (pope to abbot stained by simony and nepotism). To these *mortal* shades that music is not offered; it has been effectively proffered to the 'immortal' Ixion, Tantalus, and Tityus, and it is later successful against the dread ones

[1] Also note to ll. 226–39.

themselves, Pluto and Persephone. In all this there seems to be implied criticism of man's state; it is a fallen one, and therefore a *vane* object of divine intellect symbolized by the new music.

At the moment of repossession, Orpheus becomes

> with inward luf replet,
> So . . . blyndit in gret effectioun.   (ll. 387–8.)

He looks back, and Eurydice is lost to him. The climax of the legend is the climax of the moral. It is not that intellect and appetite *may* fail to achieve harmony, but rather that failure is inevitable, part of the human situation. Man's intelligence is, at best, decayed; hence the intermittent criticism of Orpheus in the poem. His intellect, divinely given, is tarnished in the act of being transmitted. True harmony with the appetitive is an illusion, and even divine contemplation, represented by the new music and which gives man 'a second chance', is corrupted by desire in all mankind.

In these ways, artistic unity is brought about. Henryson is to some degree derivative in both story and *moralitas*. His treatment of the former, however, is original in certain important respects, and the originality permits the story to fit easily into the didacticism. Without the confines of narrative ever being broken, the legend is subtly moved towards a moral plane, the *moralitas* fully realizes the subtlety and still finds room for legend—in the accounts of Ixion, Tantalus, and Tityus. The dichotomy, so real in the *Fabillis* and quite absent from the *Testament*, is here only apparent.

If the expression 'Scottish Chaucerian' is to be applied to Henryson, it must connote qualities of control and urbanity, an impressively fluent narrative technique, ironic juxtaposing, assurance of metre and diction, and the engaging presence of a *persona* fully conscious of an audience. But that *persona* is different from Chaucer's. Its dominant trait is gravity, and this is expressed in varying ways, sometimes disjunctively, sometimes more subtly, but always with sincerity and independence. He impresses less immediately than Dunbar and puts on far fewer masks. He is by no means as 'occasional', not as bewilderingly varied in style and diction. But we are in no doubt about the man and the mind behind the poetry, which is something we perhaps cannot say of Dunbar. And though Henryson may lack the vigour and passion of Douglas, he is more succinct, employs a richer range of poetic sensibility and techniques, and is less blatantly 'allegorical'.

BIOGRAPHICAL AND TEXTUAL NOTE

INFORMATION concerning the life and person of Robert Henryson is limited and vague, taking on the nature of inference rather than of evidence.[1] There is no unequivocal 'historical' allusion in his poetry. In places the *Morall Fabillis* apparently reveal some influence from Caxton's *Reynard the Fox*, a translation (1481) of the Dutch version of the Reynard cycle. This mere general indication of chronology can be eked out by a reference in Dunbar's 'Lament: quhen he wes sek':

> In Dunfermelyne he hes done roune
> With Maister Robert Henrisoun.

Here *he* signifies Death, and *hes done roune* literally 'talked' but figuratively 'had dealings', &c. The poem was probably written *c.* 1505;[2] it is earliest found among the so-called Chepman and Myllar Prints presumably produced *c.* 1508–9. The allusion does no more than provide a reasonable *terminus ad quem* for Henryson. Even less satisfying is a reference in the introductory note given by Sir Francis Kinaston to the Latin version (together with an English text similar to that printed by Thynne) of Henryson's *Testament*. The piece follows Kinaston's Latin translation of Chaucer's *Troilus and Criseyde*, and both are found in a single manuscript begun in 1639. Part of the note reads: 'I haue very sufficiently bin informed by Sʳ Tho Eriskin late earle of Kelly & diuers aged schollers of the Scottish nation, that it was made & written by one Mʳ Robert Henderson sometimes cheife schoole master in Dunfermling much about the time that Chaucer was first printed & dedicated to king Henry the 8ᵗʰ by Mʳ Thinne which was neere the end of his raigne.' (The Thynne print appeared in 1532.) He continues: 'about or a little after his time the most famous of the Scottish poets Gawen Douglas made his learned & excellent translation of Virgils

---

[1] For full discussion of such matters see D. Laing's edn., pp. ix–xxi, xxxvii–lx.
[2] J. W. Baxter, *William Dunbar* (Edinburgh, 1952), pp. 134, 178–80.

Ænids.' (Douglas had completed this work by 22 July 1513.) Kinaston then goes on to say of Henryson that 'being very old he dyed'. The rather confused chronology inspires no great faith in this reference to the poet's advanced age. If he were dead by *c.* 1505, and if he had died 'very old', all that can be added reasonably is that he flourished during the reign of the Scottish James III (1460–88), a period of general unrest under the weak king finally murdered, and during that of James IV (1488–1513), a time of greater order and prosperity.

The poet is repeatedly referred to as 'Master Robert Henryson' (in the Dunbar and Kinaston allusions; also by Douglas in glossing the word 'Muse' in his *Eneados*, and in many of the ascriptions to Henryson of the various poems). The customary sense of 'Master' during this period, and particularly in Scotland, was *Magister*: yet the registers of the universities of St. Andrews and Glasgow do not unequivocally link this title with a Robert Henryson. The poet may have graduated at a continental university; the medieval Scot frequently studied abroad. In the fourteenth century there was particular attraction to Paris, where the Scots College had been founded in 1326. Early in the next century, because of the conciliar controversy and the generally disturbed condition of France, the number of Scots students at Paris decreased; those of papalist sympathies turned towards Louvain, those of other tendencies towards Cologne. But apparently no record of a fifteenth-century Robert Henryson is to be found at any of these universities.[1] Possibly the title 'Master' is used of Henryson more neutrally to indicate approbation of learning and a general esteem, a sense common in the late Middle Ages, and one reasonably justified by the general impression of the poet's writings. Possibly the appellation simply denotes one teaching and in charge of children. That the title in Henryson's case has some technical significance seems probable from the persistent association of him with the calling of schoolmaster in Dunfermline (in the above quotation from Kinaston, on the title-pages of several of the versions of the *Fabillis*, &c.). Dunfermline possessed a Benedictine abbey founded, apparently, by

[1] I here acknowledge helpful communications from the librarians at Louvain and Cologne, and from the Keeper of Manuscripts, Bibliothèque Nationale.

David I in 1128. That schools were established and supervised
through the initiative residing in the Scottish abbeys is clear
enough.[1] And that Dunfermline Abbey embraced such a school
is evident from a complaint placed before the Lords of the
Privy Council on 13 October 1573, part of which goes as fol-
lows: 'Johne Henrysoun Mr of the Grammer Schole within the
Abbay of Dunfermling . . . he and his predecessouris hes con-
tinewit maisteris and teichearis of the youth in letters and doctrine
to thair grit commoditie within the said Schole past memor of
man admittit thairto be the Abbottis of Dunfermling for the
tyme as havand the vndoubtit richt and privilege to that effect
be virtew of the foundation of the said Abbay.'[2] Robert Henry-
son may well have been such a 'maister and teichear'.

The link of the poet with Dunfermline is perhaps further
strengthened by certain textual details. Thus the alliterative
expression 'fra lawdian to lundin' (i.e. from Lothian south of the
Firth of Forth to Lundian north of it) occurring in 'Sum Prac-
tysis of Medecyne' has an appropriateness for Dunfermline,
situated, broadly speaking, between these two locations. In the
Testament the leprous woman leaves by a gate for a spittal-house
in a nearby village, and it has been suggested that these physical
features can be associated with those of present-day Dunfermline;
see note on the *Testament*, ll. 382, 388, 390, 391. The Asloan MS.
includes in its list of contents 'maister Robert Hendersonnis
Dreme On fut by forth' (i.e. the Firth of Forth); the poem has
not survived, but the location fits a dweller in Dunfermline.

It is not possible to establish the Henryson canon definitively.
However, there is unambiguous ascription to the poet of one
long work, two fairly extended ones, and twelve short pieces.
A thirteenth short poem shows ascription to Henryson and to
Patrick Johnstoun.[3]

The poems survive in a number of manuscripts and prints.
The Makculloch MS., properly a collection of Latin notes on
logic but with vernacular pieces on blank pages, is dated 1477

---

[1] See J. Edgar, *History of Early Scottish Education* (1893), pp. 65–83; also J. Mac-
Queen, pp. 7–15.
[2] See Laing's edn., pp. lv–lvii. For the cultural and educational prominence of
Dunfermline in this period, see MacQueen, pp. 16–17.   [3] See note on pp. 178–9.

and is now in the library of Edinburgh University;[1] it includes
'The Ressoning betuix Aige and Yowth', 'Nerar Hevynnis Blyss',
and a little of the *Fabillis*. The Gray MS., written *c.* 1500 and now
in the National Library of Scotland,[2] provides the only text of
'The Annunciation'. The Asloan MS. dates from the early six-
teenth century and was acquired in 1966 by the National Library
of Scotland; it has a text of *Orpheus and Erudices* and part of
the *Fabillis*. The Bannatyne MS., compiled in 1568 and pre-
served in the National Library of Scotland,[4] has texts of the
Fabillis, *Orpheus and Erudices*, and all but one of the shorter
pieces, being the only source for 'Robene and Makyne', 'Ane
Prayer for the Pest', 'The Garmont of Gud Ladeis', 'The Bludy
Serk', 'Sum Practysis of Medecyne', and 'The Ressoning betwixt
Deth and Man'. The Maitland Folio MS., compiled between
1570 and 1585, is in the Pepysian Library, Magdalene College,
Cambridge;[5] it contains texts of 'The Ressoning betuix Aige and
Yowth', 'The Thre Deid-Pollis', 'Aganis Haisty Credence of
Titlaris', and 'The Abbay Walk'. Harleian MS. 3865 (dated 1571;
British Museum) gives a text of the *Fabillis*. Two manuscripts of
the *Testament* exist: the Kinaston[6] (Bodleian) and a version
(? sixteenth-century) following a fifteenth-century copy of
Chaucer's *Troilus* (St. John's College, Cambridge). The first
three stanzas of the *Testament* are found on fol. 301ᵛ of the
Ruthven MS. of Gavin Douglas's *Eneados* in Edinburgh Univer-
sity Library.[7]

The Chepman and Myllar Prints[8] contain texts of *Orpheus
and Erudices*, 'Nerar Hevynnis Blyss', and 'The Want of Wyse
Men'. Four early prints of the *Fabillis* survive: the Charteris
(Edinburgh, 1570; now in the British Museum), the Bassandyne
(Edinburgh, 1571), that produced by Richard Smith (London,
1577) and that put out by Andro Hart (Edinburgh, 1621). All

[1] Scottish Text Society, 1918.   [2] S.T.S., 1918.
[3] S.T.S., 2 vols., 1923–5. On loan since 1923 to the British Museum.
[4] S.T.S., 4 vols., 1928–34. The earlier section of the manuscript is by way of
being a first draft; most of its pieces are repeated with variations in the main part.
[5] S.T.S., 2 vols., 1919–27.
[6] Reproduced in G. Gregory Smith's ed. of Henryson, i. ciii–clx.
[7] See E. Bennett, *MLR*, xxxiii. 403.
[8] S.T.S., 1918. W. Beattie's photograph facsimile appeared in 1950.

four are extant in apparently unique copies, and the last three are now in the National Library of Scotland. The earliest print of the *Testament* is that following *Troilus and Criseyde* in William Thynne's edition of Chaucer (London, 1532); it is similarly located in the virtual reprints of Thynne by John Stow (London, 1561) and Thomas Speght (London, 1598). The most satisfactory text is that printed by Henry Charteris (Edinburgh, 1593), the only known copy being now in the British Museum. A print deriving generally from Charteris, dated 1663 and usually accepted as the work of the Glasgow printer A. Anderson, survives in a single copy in the library of Trinity College, Cambridge.[1]

The present edition excludes 'Sum Practysis of Medecyne' (it shows chiefly an esoteric verbal dexterity), 'The Abbay Walk' (a meditation in one key on the text 'Obey and thank thy God of all'), 'The Ressoning betuix Aige and Yowth' (a theme more succinctly treated in 'Nerar Hevynnis Blyss'), 'Aganis Haisty Credence of Titlaris' and 'The Want of Wyse Men' (both committed to rather conventional social denigration), and 'The Ressoning betwixt Deth and Man' (similar thoughts are more evocatively expressed in 'The Thre Deid-Pollis'). All the other poems are included in full.

All relevant textual sources have been examined afresh, either directly or with the help of microfilm, photostat, and facsimile. Where a poem survives in more than one version, generally that combining accuracy, consistency, intelligibility, and relative earliness in time has been chosen. The manuscripts and prints have been closely followed, but initial *ff* is shown as *F* or *f*, *þ* as *th*, *з* as *y*, and *z* (for scribal *з*) also as *y*. Where *y* follows normalized *з* or *z*, it is printed as *i*. The use of *i*, *j*, *u*, *w*, and of frequent final scribal *ß* is generally adapted to modern conventions. Purely scribal devices are suppressed, contractions (including ampersand) expanded silently, and numerals given word-values. Capitalization and word-division are modern, and punctuation is editorial. Emendations and lacunae are put in square brackets.

[1] The print is fully discussed by D. Fox in *Studies in Scottish Literature*, Oct. 1970, 75–96.

The stanzas reproduced as frontispiece illustrate the two printing types used in the Bassandyne version of the *Fabillis*: 'lettres de civilité' for the narrative, Roman for the *moralitas* sections.

The editor gratefully acknowledges help and advice given by Professor J. A. W. Bennett, Professor J. Kinsley, Professor E. C. Llewellyn, Professor R. G. Thomas, and the staffs of the National Library of Scotland, Edinburgh University Library, and the Library, University College, Cardiff.

SELECT BIBLIOGRAPHY

Scottish Text Society volumes (shown as 'S.T.S.') are published at
Edinburgh. In the following entries, as in all bibliographical references
elsewhere, place of publication is London unless otherwise stated.

HISTORICAL BACKGROUND

Dickson, W. C., *Scotland from the Earliest Times to 1603*, vol. i of *A New
History of Scotland*, 2nd edn., Edinburgh, 1965.
Mackie, J. D., *A History of Scotland*, 1964.

II. LITERARY HISTORY

Fox, D., 'The Scottish Chaucerians', pp. 164–200 in *Chaucer and Chaucer-
ians*, ed. D. S. Brewer, 1966.
Speirs, J., *The Scots Literary Tradition*, rev. edn., 1962.
Wittig, K., *The Scottish Tradition in Literature*, 1958.

III. LANGUAGE

Aitken, A. J., 'Completing the Record of Middle Scots', *Scottish Studies*,
viii (1964), 129–40.
Gregory Smith, G., *Specimens of Middle Scots*, Edinburgh, 1902.

IV. EDITED HENRYSON TEXTS

(i) *Complete*: Gregory Smith, G., S.T.S., 3 vols., 1906–14; Laing, D.,
Edinburgh, 1865; Harvey Wood, H., 1933, 1958.
(ii) *Selected*: Kinghorn, A. M., in his *The Middle Scots Poets*, 1970;
Murison, D., Edinburgh, 1952; Murray, H. M. R., 1930.
(iii) *The Testament of Cresseid*: Dickins, B., Edinburgh, 1925; Fox, D.,
1968.

SELECT BIBLIOGRAPHY

V. HENRYSON STUDIES

(i) *General*

MacQueen, J., *Robert Henryson: a Study of the Major Narrative Poems*, Oxford, 1967.

Stearns, M. W., *Robert Henryson*, New York, 1949.

(ii) *Particular*

Bauman, R., 'The Folktale and Oral Tradition in the Fables of Robert Henryson', *Fabula*, vi (1965), 108–24.

Duncan, D., 'Henryson's *Testament of Cresseid*', *Essays in Criticism*, ii (1961), 128–35.

Fox, D., 'Henryson's *Fables*', *ELH* xxix (1962), 337–56.

Fox, D., 'Henryson and Caxton', *JEGP* lxvii (1968), 586–93.

Kinghorn, A. M., 'The Minor Poems of Robert Henryson', *Studies in Scottish Literature*, iii (1965), 30–40.

MacDonald, D., 'Narrative Art in Henryson's *Fables*', *Studies in Scottish Literature*, iii (1965), 101–13.

Rowlands, M. E., 'Robert Henryson and the Scottish Courts of Law', *Aberdeen University Review*, xxxix (1962), 219–26.

Spearing, A. C., 'Conciseness and The Testament of Cresseid'; ch. vi of his *Criticism and Medieval Poetry*, 1964.

Stevens, J., 'Devotion and Wit in Henryson's "The Annunciation" ', *English Studies*, li (1970), 323–31.

Tillyard, E. M. W., *Poetry and its Background*, 1955; first published as *Five Poems: 1470–1870*, 1948. Discusses *Cresseid*.

Toliver, H. E., 'Robert Henryson: from *Moralitas* to Irony', *English Studies*, xlvi (1965), 300–9.

Wright, D. A., 'Henryson's *Orpheus and Eurydice* and the Tradition of the Muses', *Medium Aevum*, xl (1971), 41–7.

THE MORALL FABILLIS OF ESOPE THE PHRYGIAN

The Prolog

THOCHT feinyeit fabils of ald poetre
Be not al grunded upon truth, yit than
Thair polite termes of sweit rhetore
Richt plesand ar unto the eir of man;
And als the caus that thay first began   5
Wes to repreif the haill misleving
Off man be figure of ane uther thing.

In lyke maner as throw the bustious eird,
Swa it be laubourit with grit diligence,
Springis the flouris and the corne abreird,   10
Hailsum and gude to mannis sustenence,
Sa dois spring ane morall sweit sentence
Oute of the subtell dyte of poetry,
To gude purpois quha culd it weill apply.

The nuttis schell, thocht it be hard and teuch,   15
[H]aldis the kirnill and is delectabill;
Sa lyis thair ane doctrine wyse aneuch
And full of frute under ane fenyeit fabill;
And clerkis sayis it is richt profitabill
Amangis ernist to ming ane merie sport,   20
To light the spreit and gar the tyme be schort.

Forthermair, ane bow that is ay bent
Worthis unsmart and dullis on the string;
Sa dois the mynd that is ay diligent
In ernistfull thochtis and in studying: 25
With sad materis sum merines to ming
Accordis weill: thus Esope said, iwis:
'*Dulcius arrident seria picta Iocis.*'

Of this authour, my maisteris, with your leif,
Submitting me in your correctioun,   30
In mother-toung of Latyng I wald preif
To mak ane maner of translatioun—
Nocht of myself, for vane presumptioun,
Bot be requeist and precept of ane lord,
Of quhome the name it neidis not record.   35

In hamelie language and in termis rude
Me neidis wryte, forquhy of eloquence
Nor rethorike I never understude.
Thairfoir meiklie I pray your reverence,
Gif that ye find it throw my negligence   40
Be deminute, or yit superfluous,
Correct it at your willis gratious.

My author in his fabillis tellis how
That brutal beistis spak, and understude
Into gude purpois dispute and argow,   45
Ane sillogisme propone, and eik conclude;
Put in exempill and similitude
How mony men in operatioun
Ar like to beistis in conditioun.

Na mervell is ane man be lyke ane beist,   50
Quhilk lufis ay carnall and foull delyte;
That schame can not him renye nor arreist,
Bot takis all the lust and appetyte,
And that throw custum and daylie ryte;
Syne in thair myndis sa fast is radicate   55
That thay in brutal beistis ar transformate.

This nobill clerk Esope, as I haif tauld,
In gay metir, as poete lawriate,
Be figure wrait his buke; for he nocht wald
Lak the disdane off hie nor low estate.   60
And to begin, first of ane cok he wrate,
Seikand his meit, quhilk fand ane jolie stone,
Of quhome the fabill ye sall heir anone.

2

The Taill of the Cok and the Jasp

ANE cok, sum tyme, with feddram fresch and gay,
Richt cant and crous, albeit he was bot pure,   65
Fleu furth upon ane dunghill sone be day;
To get his dennar set was al his cure.
Scraipand amang the as, be aventure
He fand ane jolie jasp, richt precious,
Wes castin furth in sweping of the hous.   70

As damisellis wantoun and insolent,
That fane wald play and on the streit be sene,
To swoping of the hous thay tak na tent;
Thay cair nathing swa that the flure be clene;
Jowellis ar tint, as oftymis hes bene sene,   75
Upon the flure, and swopit furth anone—
Peradventure sa wes the samin stone.

Sa mervelland upon the stane, quod he:
'O gentill jasp! O riche and nobill thing!
Thocht I the find, thow ganis not for me;   80
Thow art ane jouell for ane lord or king;
Pietie it wer thow suld ly in this mydding,
Be buryit thus amang this muke on mold,
And thow so fair and worth sa mekill gold.

'It is pietie I suld the find, forquhy   85
Thy grit vertew, nor yit thy cullour cleir,
It may me nouther extoll nor magnify;
And thow to me may mak bot lyttill cheir;
To grit lordis thocht thow be leif and deir,
I lufe fer better thing of les availl,   90
As draf or corne, to fill my tume intraill.

'I had lever [haif] scrapit heir with my naillis
Amangis this mow, and luke my lifys fude,
As draf or corne, small wormis or snaillis,

3

Or ony meit wald do my stomok gude,   95
Than of jaspis ane mekill multitude;
And thow agane, upon the samin wyis,
For les availl may me as now dispyis.

'Thow hes na corne, and thairof haif I neid;
Thy cullour dois bot confort to the sicht,   100
And that is not aneuch my wame to feid;
For wyfis sayis lukand werkis ar licht.
I wald have sum meit, get it geve I micht,
For houngrie men may not leve on lukis;
Had I dry breid, I compt not for na cukis.   105

'Quhar suld thow mak thy habitatioun?
Quhar suld thow duell bot in ane royall tour?
Quhar suld thow sit bot on ane kingis croun,
Exaltit in worschip and in grit honour?
Rise gentill jasp, of all stanis the flour,   110
Out of this midding, and pas quhar thow suld be;
Thow ganis not for me, nor I for the.'

Levand this jowell law upon the ground,
To seik his meit this cok his wayis went;
Bot quhen or how or quhome be it wes found,   115
As now I set to hald na argument:
Bot of the inward sentence and intent
Of this, as myne author dois write,
I sall reheirs in rude and hamelie dite.

Moralitas

This jolie jasp had properteis sevin: 120
The first—of cullour it was mervelous,
Part lyke the fyre and part lyke to the hevin—
It makis ane man stark and victorious,
Preservis als fra cacis perrillous:
Quha hes this stane sall have gude hap to speid,   125
Or fyre nor water him neidis not to dreid.

4

This gentill jasp, richt different of hew,
Betakinnis perfite prudence and cunning,
Ornate with mony deidis of vertew,
Mair excellent than ony eirthly thing,   130
Quhilk makis men in honour for to ring,
Happie, and stark to wyn the victorie
Of all vicis and spirituall enemie.

Quha may be hardie, riche, and gratious?
Quha can eschew perrell and aventure?   135
Quha can governe ane realme, cietie or hous
Without science? No man, I yow assure.
It is riches that ever sall indure,
Quhilk maith, nor moist, nor uther rust can screit;
To mannis saull it is eternall meit.   140

This cok, desyrand mair the sempill corne
Than ony jasp, may till ane fule be peir,
Quhilk at science makis bot ane moik and scorne,
And na gude can; als lytill will he leir;
His hart wammillis wyse argument to heir,   145
As dois ane sow, to quhome men for the nanis
In hir draf-troich wald saw precious stanis.

Quha is enemie to science and cunning
Bot ignorants that understandis nocht?
Quhilk is sa nobill, sa precious and sa ding,   150
That it may not with eirdlie thing be bocht?
Weill wer that man over all uther that mocht
All his lyfe-dayis in perfite studie wair
To get science; for him neidis na mair.

Bot now, allace, this jasp is tynt and hid;   155
We seik it nocht, nor preis it for to find.
Haif we richis, na better lyfe we bid,
Of science thocht the saull be bair and blind.
Of this mater to speik it wer bot wind;
Thairfore I ceis and will na forther say: 160
Ga seik the jasp quha will, for thair it lay.

5

The Taill of the Uponlandis Mous and the Burges Mous

Esope myne authour makis mentioun
Of twa myis, and thay wer sisteris deir,
Of quham the eldest duelt in ane borous-toun,
The uther wynnit uponland weill neir,   165
Soliter, quhyle under busk, quhyle under breir,
Quhilis in the corne, and uther mennis skaith,
As owtlawis dois and levis on thair waith.

This rurall mous into the wynter-tyde
Had hunger, cauld, and tholit grit distres;   170
The uther mous that in the burgh can byde,
Was gild-brother and made ane fre burges—
Toll-fre als, but custum mair or les,
And fredome had to ga quhairever scho list,
Amang the cheis in ark, and meill in kist.   175

Ane tyme quhen scho wes full and unfutesair,
Scho tuke in mynd hir sister uponland,
And langit for to heir of hir weilfair,
To se quhat lyfe scho had under the wand:
Bairfute, allone, with pykestaf in hir hand,   180
As pure pylgryme scho passit owt off town,
To seik hir sister baith oure daill and down.

Furth mony wilsum wayis can scho walk;
Throw mosse and mure, throw bankis, busk and breir,
Scho ran cryand quhill scho come to a balk: 185
'Cum furth to me, my awin sister deir;
Cry peip anis!' With that the mous culd heir,
And knew hir voce, as kinnisman will do,
Be verray kynd; and furth scho come hir to.

The hartlie joy God geve ye had sene   190
Beis kith quhen that thir sisteris met!
And grit kyndnes wes schawin thame betuene,

For quhylis thay leuch, and quhylis for joy thay gret,
Quhyle kissit sweit, quhylis in armis plet;
And thus thay fure quhill soberit wes thair mude,   195
Syne fute for fute unto the chalmer yude.

As I hard say, it was ane sober wane,
Off fog and farne full febilie wes maid—
Ane sillie scheill under ane steidfast stane,
Off quhilk the entres wes not hie nor braid;   200
And in the samin thay went but mair abaid,
Without fyre or candill birnand bricht,
For comonly sic pykeris luffis not lycht.

Quhen thay wer lugit thus, thir sely myse,
The youngest sister into hir butterie glyde,   205
And brocht furth nuttis and candill insteid off spyce;
Giff this wes gude fair, I do it on thame besyde.
The burges-mous prompit forth in pryde,
And said: 'Sister, is this your dayly fude?'
'Quhy not?' quod scho. 'Is not this meit rycht gude?'   210

'Na, be my saull, I think it bot ane scorne.'
'Madame,' quod scho, 'ye be the mair to blame;
My mother sayd, sister, quhen we wer borne,
That I and ye lay baith within ane wame:
I keip the rate and custome off my dame,   215
And off my leving into povertie,
For landis have we nane in propertie.'

'My fair sister,' quod scho, 'have me excusit—
This rude dyat and I can not accord;
To tender meit my stomok is ay usit,   220
For quhylis I fair als weill as ony lord;
Thir wydderit peis and nuttis, or thay be bord,
Wil brek my teith, and mak my wame ful sklender,
Quhilk wes before usit to meitis tender.'

7

'Weil, weil, sister,' quod the rurall mous,   225
'Geve it pleis yow, sic thing as ye se heir,
Baith meit and dreink, harberie and hous,
Sal be your awin, will ye remane al yeir;
Ye sall it have wyth blyith and mery cheir—
And that suld mak the maissis that ar rude,   230
Amang freindis, richt tender and wonder gude.

'Quhat plesure is in the feistis delicate,
The quhilkis ar gevin with ane glowmand brow?
Ane gentill hart is better recreate
With blyith curage, than seith to him ane kow;   235
Ane modicum is mair for till allow,
Swa that gude will be kerver at the dais,
Than thrawin vult and mony spycit mais.'

For all hir mery exhortatioun,
This burges-mous had littill will to sing;   240
Bot hevilie scho kest hir browis doun
For all the daynteis that scho culd hir bring.
Yit at the last scho said, halff in hething:
'Sister, this victuall and your royall feist
May weill suffice unto ane rurall beist.   245

'Lat be this hole, and cum into my place;
I sall to yow schaw be experience
My Gude Friday is better nor your Pace;
My dische-likingis is worth your haill expence.
I have housis anew off grit defence;   250
Off cat nor fall-trap I have na dreid.'
'I grant,' quod scho; and on togidder thay yeid.

In stubbill array throw gers and corne,
And under buskis prevelie couth thay creip—
The eldest wes the gyde and went beforne,   255
The younger to hir wayis tuke gude keip;
On nicht thay ran, and on the day can sleip,
Quhill in the morning, or the laverok sang,
Thay fand the town, and in blythlie couth gang.

8

Not fer fra thyne unto ane worthie wane,   260
This burges brocht thame sone quhare thay suld be;
Withowt 'God speid!' thair herberie wes tane,
Into ane spence with vittell grit plentie;
Baith cheis and butter upon thair skelfis hie,
And flesche and fische aneuch, baith fresche and salt,   265
And sekkis full off meill and eik off malt.

Eftir quhen thay disposit wer to dyne,
Withowtin grace thay wesche and went to meit,
With all coursis that cukis culd devyne—
Muttoun and beif, strikin in tailyeis greit;   270
Ane lordis fair thus couth thay counterfeit—
Except ane thing—thay drank the watter cleir
Insteid off wyne: bot yit thay maid gude cheir.

With blyith upcast and merie countenance,
The eldest sister sperit at hir gest   275
Giff that scho be ressone fand difference
Betuix that chalmer and hir sarie nest.
'Ye, dame,' quod scho, 'how lang will this lest?'
'For evermair, I wait, and langer to.'
'Giff it be swa, ye ar at eis,' quod scho.   280

Till eik thair cheir ane subcharge furth scho brocht—
Ane plait off grottis, and ane dische full off meill;
Thraf-caikkis als I trow scho spairit nocht
Aboundantlie about hir for to deill;
And [mane full fyne] scho brocht insteid off geill,   285
And ane quhyte candill owt off ane coffer stall,
Insteid off spyce to gust thair mouth withall.

This maid thay merie quhill thay micht na mair,
And 'Haill, Yule! Haill!' cryit upon hie.
Yit efter joy oftymes cummis cair,   290
And troubill efter grit prosperitie:
Thus as thay sat in all thair jolitie,
The spenser come with keyis in his hand,
Oppinnit the dure, and thame at denner fand.

Thay taryit not to wesche, as I suppose,   295
Bot on to ga quha that micht formest win.
The burges had ane hole, and in scho gois;
Hir sister had na hole to hyde hir in:
To se that selie mous it wes grit sin,
So desolate and will off ane gude reid;   300
For verray dreid scho fell in swoun neir deid.

Bot as God wald, it fell ane happie cace;
The spenser had na laser for to byde,
Nowther to seik nor serche, to sker nor chace;
Bot on he went, and left the dure up wyde.   305
The bald burges his passing weill hes spyde;
Out off hir hole scho come and cryit on hie:
'How fair ye sister? Cry peip quhairever ye be!'

This rurall mous lay flatling on the ground,
And for the deith scho wes full sair dredand,   310
For till hir hart straik mony wofull stound;
As in ane fever scho trimbillit fute and hand.
And quhan hir sister in sic ply hir fand,
For verray pietie scho began to greit,
Syne confort hir with wordis hunny-sweit.   315

'Quhy ly ye thus? Ryse up, my sister deir!
Cum to your meit; this perrell is overpast.'
The uther answerit hir with hevie cheir:
'I may not eit, sa sair I am agast!
I had lever thir fourty dayis fast,   320
With watter-caill, and to gnaw benis or peis,
Than all your feist in this dreid and diseis.'

With fair tretie yit scho gart hir upryse,
And to the burde thay went and togidder sat;
And scantlie had thay drunkin anis or twyse,   325
Quhen in come Gib Hunter, our jolie cat,
And bad 'God speid!' The burges up with that
And till hir hole scho went as fyre on flint;
Bawdronis the uther be the bak hes hint.

Fra fute to fute he kest hir to and fra,   330
Quhylis up, quhylis doun, als cant as ony kid;
Quhylis wald he lat hir rin under the stra,
Quhylis wald he wink, and play with hir buk-heid.
Thus to the selie mous grit pane he did,
Quhill at the last, throw fortune and gude hap,   335
Betwix ane burde and the wall scho crap.

And up in haist behind ane parraling
Scho clam so hie that Gilbert micht not get hir—
Syne be the cluke thair craftelie can hing
Till he wes gane; hir cheir wes all the better;   340
Syne doun scho lap quhen thair wes nane to let hir,
And to the burges-mous loud can scho cry:
'Fairweill, sister, thy feist heir I defy!

'Thy mangerie is mingit all with cair—
Thy guse is gude, thy gansell sour as gall;   345
The subcharge off thy service is bot sair—
Sa sall thow find heir efterwart na fall.
I thank yone courtyne and yone perpall wall
Off my defence now fra yone crewell beist.
Almichtie God keip me fra sic ane feist!   350

'Wer I into the kith that I come fra,
For weill nor wo suld I never cum agane.'
With that scho tuke hir leif and furth can ga,
Quhylis throw the corne, and quhylis throw the plane:
Quhen scho wes furth and fre, scho wes full fane,   355
And merilie markit unto the mure.
I can not tell how weill thairefter scho fure.

Bot I hard say scho passit to hir den,
Als warme as woll, suppose it wes not greit,
Full beinly stuffit, baith but and ben,   360
Off beinis, and nuttis, peis, ry and quheit;
Quhenever scho list, scho had aneuch to eit,
In quyet and eis, withoutin ony dreid;
Bot to hir sisteris feist na mair scho yeid.

11

Freindis, ye may find, and ye will tak heid,   365
Into this fabill ane gude moralitie:
As fitchis myngit ar with nobill seid,
Swa interminglit is adversitie
With eirdlie joy, swa that na estate is frie,
Without trubill and sum vexatioun—   370
And namelie thay quhilk clymmis up maist hie,
That ar not content with small possessioun.

Blissed be sempill lyfe withoutin dreid;
Blissed be sober feist in quietie:
Quha hes aneuch, of na mair hes he neid,   375
Thocht it be littill into quantatie.
Grit aboundance and blind prosperitie
Oftymes makis ane evill conclusioun;
The sweitest lyfe, thairfoir, in this cuntrie,
Is sickernes with small possessioun.   380

O wantoun man, that usis for to feid
Thy wambe, and makis it a god to be,
[Luke] to thy self! I warne the weill; but dreid
The cat cummis, and to the mous hes ee.
Quhat vaillis than thy feist and royaltie   385
With dreidfull hart and tribulatioun?
Best thing in eird, thairfoir, I say for me,
Is blyithnes in hart, with small possessioun.

Thy awin fyre, my freind, sa it be bot ane gleid,
It warmis weill, and is worth gold to the;   390
And Solomon sayis, gif that thow will reid:
'Under the hevin thair can not better be
Than ay be blyith and leif in honestie.'
Quhairfoir I may conclude be this ressoun:
Of eirthly joy it beiris maist degre,   395
Blyithnes in hart, with small possessioun.

The Taill of Schir Chantecleir
and the Foxe

Thocht brutall beistis be irrationall,
That is to say wantand discretioun,
Yit ilk ane in thair kynd naturall
Hes mony divers inclinatioun: 400
The bair busteous, the wolff, the wylde lyoun,
The fox fenyeit, craftie and cawtelows,
The dog to bark on nicht and keip the hows.

Sa different thay ar in properteis,
Unknawin to man, and sa infinite,   405
In kynd havand sa fell diversiteis,
My cunning is excludit for to dyte.
Forthy as now I purpose for to wryte
Ane cais I fand, quhilk fell this ather yeir
Betwix ane fox and ane gentill chantecleir.   410

Ane wedow dwelt intill ane drop thay dayis,
Quhilk wan hir fude off spinning on hir rok;
And na mair had forsuth, as the fabill sayis,
Except off hennis scho had ane lyttill flok;
And thame to keip scho had ane jolie cok,   415
Richt curageous, that to this wedow ay .
Devydit nicht, and crew befoir the day.

Ane lyttill fra this foirsaid wedowis hows,
Ane thornie schaw thair wes off grit defence,
Quhairin ane foxe, craftie and cautelous,   420
Maid his repair and daylie residence:
Quhilk to this wedow did grit violence
In pyking off pultrie baith day and nicht;
And na way be revengit on him scho micht.

This wylie tod, quhen that the lark couth sing,   425
Full sair hungrie unto the toun him drest,
Quhair Chantecleir into the gray dawing,
Werie for nicht, wes flowen fra his nest.
Lowrence this saw, and in his mynd he kest
The jeperdie, the wayis, and the wyle,   430
Be quhat menis he micht this cok begyle.

Dissimuland into countenance and cheir,
On kneis fell, and simuland thus he said:
'Gude morne, my maister, gentill Chantecleir!'
With that the cok start bakwart in ane braid.   435
'Schir, be my saull, ye neid not be effraid,
Nor yit for me to start nor fle abak;
I come bot heir service to yow to mak.

'Wald I not serve to yow, it wer bot blame,
As I have done to yowr progenitouris: 440
Your father full oft fillit hes my wame,
And send me meit fra midding to the muris:
And at his end I did my besie curis
To hald his heid and gif him drinkis warme:
Syne at the last the sweit swelt in my arme.'   445

'Knew ye my father?' quod the cok, and leuch.
'Yea, my fair sone, I held up his heid
Quhen that he deit under ane birkin beuch,
Syne said the Dirigie quhen that he wes deid.
Betuix us twa how suld thair be ane feid?   450
Quhame suld ye traist bot me, your servitour,
That to your father did sa grit honour?

'Quhen I behald your fedderis fair and gent,
Your beik, your breist, your hekill and your kame,
Schir, be my saull and the Blissit Sacrament,   455
My hart is warme; me think I am at hame:
To mak yow blyith I wald creip on my wame
In froist and snaw in wedder wan and weit,
And lay my lyart loikkis under your feit.'

14

This fenyeit foxe, fals and dissimulate,   460
Maid to this cok ane cavillatioun:
'Ye ar, me think, changit and degenerate
Fra your father off his conditioun;
Off craftie crawing he micht beir the croun,
For he wald on his tais stand and craw;   465
This wes na le; I stude beside and saw.'

With that the cok upon his tais hie
Kest up his beik and sang with all his micht.
Quod Schir Lowrence: 'Weill said, sa mot I the!
Ye ar your fatheris sone and air upricht: 470
Bot off his cunning yit ye want ane slicht:
For,' quod the tod, 'he wald—and haif na dout—
Baith wink and craw and turne him thryis about.'

The cok infect with wind and fals vanegloir,
That mony puttis unto confusioun,   475
Traisting to win ane grit worschip thairfoir,
Unwarlie winkand, wawland up and doun,
And syne to chant and craw he maid him boun.
And suddandlie, be he had crawin ane note,
The foxe wes war and hint him be the throte.   480

Syne to the woid but tarie with him hyit,
Off that cryme haifand bot lytill dout.
With that Pertok, Sprutok and Toppok cryit;
The wedow hard and with ane cry come out;
Seand the cace scho sichit and gaif ane schout: 485
'How! Murther! Hay!'—with ane hiddeous beir—
'Allace, now lost is gentill Chantecleir!'

As scho wer woid, with mony yell and cry,
Ryvand hir hair, upon hir breist can beit;
Syne paill of hew, half in ane extasy,   490
Fell doun for cair in swoning and in sweit.
With that the selie hennis left thair meit,
And quhill this wyfe wes lyand thus in swoun,
Fell in that cace in disputatioun.

15

'Allace,' quod Pertok makand sair murning,   495
With teiris grit attour hir cheikis fell,
'Yone wes our drowrie and our dayis darling,
Our nichtingall and als our orloge-bell,
Our walkryfe watche, us for to warne and tell
Quhen that Aurora with hir curcheis gray   500
Put up hir heid betuix the nicht and day.

'Quha sall our lemman be? Quha sall us leid?
Quhen we ar sad, quha sall unto us sing?
With his sweit bill he wald brek us the breid:
In all this warld wes thair ane kynder thing?   505
In paramouris he wald do us plesing
At his power as nature did him geif;
Now efter him, allace, how sall we leif?'

Quod Sprutok than: 'Ceis, sister, of your sorrow;
Ye be to mad for him sic murning mais: 510
We sall fair weill; I find, Sanct Johne to borrow,
The proverb sayis "Als gude lufe cummis as gais".
I will put on my halydayis clais
And mak me fresch agane this jolie May,
Syne chant this sang: "Wes never wedow sa gay!"   515

'He wes angry and held us ay in aw,
And woundit with the speir off jelowsy;
Off chalmerglew, Pertok, full weill ye knaw
Waistit he wes, off nature cauld and dry.
Sen he is gone, thairfoir, sister, say I,   520
Be blyith in baill, for that is best remeid:
Let quik to quik, and deid ga to the deid.'

Than Pertok spak with feinyeit faith befoir:
'In lust but lufe he set all his delyte;
Sister, ye wait, off sic as him ane scoir   525
Wald not suffice to slaik our appetyte.
I hecht be my hand, sen he is quyte,
Within ane oulk, for schame and I durst speik,
To get ane berne suld better claw oure breik.'

16

Than Toppok lyke ane curate spak full crous: 530
'Yone wes ane verray vengeance from the hevin;
He wes sa lous and sa lecherous;
He had,' quod scho, 'kittokis ma than sevin;
Bot rychteous God, haldand the balandis evin,
Smytis rycht sair, thocht He be patient,   535
For adulterie that will thame not repent.

'Prydefull he wes, and joyit off his sin,
And comptit not for Goddis favour nor feid,
Bot traistit ay to rax and sa to rin,
Quhill at the last his sinnis can him leid   540
To schamefull end and to yone suddand deid:
Thairfoir it is the verray hand off God
That causit him be werryit with the tod.'

Quhen this wes said, this wedow fra hir swoun
Start up on fute and on hir kennettis cryde: 545
'How! Berk! Berrie, Bawsie Broun,
Rype Schaw, Rin Weil, Curtes, Nuttie Clyde—
Togidder all but grunching furth ye glyde!
Reskew my nobill cok or he be slane,
Or ellis to me se ye cum never agane!'   550

With that, but baid thay braidet over the bent;
As fyre off flint thay over the feildis flaw,
Full wichtlie thay throw wood and wateris went,
And ceissit not Schir Lourence quhill thay saw.
Bot quhen he saw the kennettis cum on raw,   555
Unto the cok in mynd he said: 'God sen
That I and thow wer fairlie in my den!'

Then said the cok, with sum gude spirit inspyrit,
'Do my counsall and I sall warrand the;
Hungrie thow art, and for grit travell tyrit,   560
Richt faint off force, and may not ferther fle:
Swyith turne agane, and say that I and ye
Freindis ar maid and fellowis for ane yeir;
Than will thay stint—I stand for it—and not steir.'

17   D

This tod, thocht he wes fals and frivolus,   565
And had frawdis his querrell to defend,
Desavit wes be menis richt mervelous;
For falset failyeis ay at the latter end.
He start about and cryit as he wes kend;
With that the cok he braid out off the bewch: 570
Now juge ye all quhairat Schir Lowrence lewch.

Begylit thus, the tod under the tre
On kneis fell, and said: 'Gude Chantecleir,
Cum doun agane, and I, but meit or fe,
Sal be your man and servand for ane yeir.'   575
'Na, fals theif and revar, stand not me neir;
My bludy hekill and my nek sa bla
Hes partit freindschip for ever betwene us twa.

'I wes unwyse that winkit at thy will,
Quhairthrow almaist I loissit had my heid.'   580
'I wes mair fule,' quod he, 'to be sa still,
Quhairthrow to put my pray into pleid.'
'Fair on fals theif; God keip me fra thy feid!'
With that the cok over the feildis tuke his flicht,
And in at the wedowis lewer couth he licht.   585

Moralitas

Now, worthie folk, suppose this be ane fabill,
And overheillit wyth typis figurall,
Yit may ye find ane sentence richt agreabill
Under thir fenyeit termis textuall:
To our purpose this cok weill may we call   590
Nyse proud men, woid and vaneglorious
Of kin and blude, quhilk ar presumpteous.

Fy, puft-up pryde! Thow is full poysonabill!
Quha favoris the on force man haif ane fall:
Thy strenth is nocht, thy stule standis unstabill;   595
Tak witnes of the feyndis infernall,

18

Quhilk houndit doun wes fra that hevinlie hall
To hellis hole, and to that hiddeous hous,
Because in pryde thay wer presumpteous.

This fenyeit foxe may weill be figurate   600
To flatteraris with plesand wordis quhyte,
With fals mening and mynd maist toxicate,
To loif and le that settis thair haill delyte.
All worthie folk at sic suld haif despyte;
For quhair is thair mair perrellous pestilence   605
Nor gif to learis haistelie credence?

The wickit mynd and adullatioun,
Of sucker sweit haifand the similitude,
Bitter as gall, and full of poysoun
To taist it is, quha cleirlie understude.   610
Forthy as now schortlie to conclude,
Thir twa sinnis, flatterie and vaneglore,
Ar vennomous; gude folk, fle thame thairfoir!

4

*The Taill how this foirsaid Tod maid his Confessioun
to Freir Wolf Waitskaith*

Leif we this wedow glaid I yow assure,
Off Chantecleir mair blyith than I can tell,   615
And speik we off the subtell aventure
And destenie that to this foxe befell,
Quhilk durst na mair with waitting intermell
Als lang as leme or licht wes off the day,
Bot bydand nicht full styll lurkand he lay   620

Quhill that [Thetes] the Goddes off the flude
Phebus had callit to the harbery,
And Hesperous put up his cluddie hude,

19

Schawand his lustie visage in the sky.
Than Lourence luikit up, quhair he couth ly,   625
And kest his hand upon his ee on hicht,
Merie and glade that cummit wes the nicht.

Out off the wod unto ane hill he went,
Quhair he micht se the tuinkling sternis cleir,
And all the planetis off the firmament,   630
Thair cours and eik thair moving in the spheir,
Sum retrograde and sum stationeir,
And off the zodiak in quhat degre
Thay wer ilk ane, as Lowrence leirnit me.

Than Saturne auld wes enterit in Capricorne,   635
And Juppiter movit in Sagittarie,
And Mars up in the Rammis heid wes borne,
And Phebus in the Lyoun furth can carie;
Venus the Crab, the Mone wes in Aquarie;
Mercurius, the god off eloquence,   640
Into the Virgyn maid his residence.

But astrolab, quadrant or almanak,
Teichit off nature be instructioun,
The moving off the hevin this tod can tak,
Quhat influence and constellatioun   645
Wes lyke to fall upon the eirth adoun;
And to himself he said, withoutin mair:
'Weill worth my father, that send me to the lair!

'My destenie and eik my weird I ken;
My aventure is cleirlie to me kend;   650
With mischeif myngit is my mortall men,
My misleving the soner bot gif I mend;
It is reward off sin ane schamefull end:
Thairfoir I will ga seik sum confessour,
And schryiff me clene off my sinnis to this hour.   655

'Allace,' quod he, 'richt waryit ar we thevis!
Our lyifis set ilk nicht in aventure;
Our cursit craft full mony man mischevis;
For ever we steill and ever ar lyke pure;
In dreid and schame our dayis we indure;   660
Syne "Widdi-nek" and "Craik-raip" callit als,
And till our hyre hangit up be the hals.'

Accusand thus his cankerit conscience,
Into ane craig he kest about his ee;
So saw he cummand ane lyttill than frome hence   665
Ane worthie Doctour in Divinitie;
Freir Wolff Waitskaith, in science wonder sle,
To preiche and pray wes new cummit fra the closter,
With beidis in hand, sayand his Pater Noster.

Seand this wolff, this wylie tratour tod   670
On kneis fell, with hude into his nek.
'Welcome, my gostlie father under God!'
Quod he with mony binge and mony bek.
'Ha!' quod the wolff, 'Schir Tod, for quhat effek
Mak ye sic feir? Ryse up! Put on your hude.'   675
'Father,' quod he, 'I haif grit cause to dude.

'Ye ar mirrour, lanterne and sicker way
Suld gyde sic sempill folk as me to grace:
Your bair feit and your russet coull off gray,
Your lene cheik, your paill, pietious face,   680
Schawis to me your perfite halines;
For weill wer him that anis in his lyve
Had hap to yow his sinnis for to schryve.'

'Na, selie Lowrence,' quod the wolff, and leuch.
'It plesis me that ye ar penitent.'   685
'Off reif and stouth, schir, I can tell aneuch;
That causis me full sair for to repent:
Bot father, byde still heir upon the bent,
I yow beseik, and heir me to declair
My conscience that prikkis me sa sair.'   690

21

'Weill,' quod the wolff, 'sit doun upon thy kne.'
And he doun bairheid sat full humilly
And syne began with 'Benedicitie!'.
Quhen I this saw, I drew ane lytill by,
For it effeiris nouther to heir, nor spy,   695
Nor to reveill thing said under that seill:
Unto the tod this-gait the wolf couth kneill.

'Art thow contrite and sorie in thy spreit
For thy trespas?' 'Na schir, I can not duid:
Me think that hennis ar sa honie-sweit,   700
And lambes flesche that new ar lettin bluid;
For to repent my mynd can not concluid
Bot off this thing—that I haif slane sa few.'
'Weill,' quod the wolff, 'in faith, thow art ane schrew.

'Sen thow can not forthink thy wickitnes,   705
Will thow forbeir in tyme to cum, and mend?'
'And I forbeir, how sall I leif, allace,
Haifand nane uther craft me to defend?
Neid causis me to steill quhairever I wend:
I eschame to thig; I can not wirk, ye wait;   710
Yit wald I fane pretend to gentill stait.'

'Weill,' quod the wolff, 'thow wantis pointis twa
Belangand to perfyte Confessioun;
To the thrid part off Penitence let us ga:
Will thow tak pane for thy transgressioun?'   715
'Na schir; considder my complexioun,
Selie and waik, and off my nature tender;
Lo, will ye se, I am baith lene and sklender.

'Yit nevertheles, I wald, swa it wer licht,
Schort and not grevand to my tendernes,   720
Tak part off pane—fulfill it gif I micht—
To set my selie saull in way off grace.'
'Thow sall,' quod he, 'forbeir flesch untill Pasche,
To tame this corps, that cursit carioun;
And heir I reik the full remissioun.'   725

22

'I grant thairto, swa ye will giff me leif
To eit puddingis, or laip ane lyttill blude,
Or heid or feit or paynchis let me preif
In cace I fall no flesch unto my fude.'
'For grit mister I gif the leif to dude   730
Twyse in the oulk, for neid may haif na law.'
'God yeild yow schir, for that text weill I knaw.'

Quhen this wes said, the wolff his wayis went.
The foxe on fute he fure unto the flude—
To fang him fisch haillelie wes his intent;   735
Bot quhen he saw the watter and wallis woude,
Astonist all still into ane stair he stude
And said: 'Better that I had biddin at hame
Nor bene ane fischar in the devillis name.

'Now man I scraip my meit out off the sand,   740
And I haif nouther boittis, [net nor bait].'
As he wes thus for falt off meit murnand,
Lukand about his leving for to lait,
Under ane tre he saw ane trip off gait;
Than wes he blyith, and in ane hewch him hid,   745
And fra the gait he stall ane lytill kid.

Syne over the heuch unto the see he hyis,
And tuke the kid be the hornis twane,
And in the watter outher twyis or thryis
He dowkit him, and till him can he sayne: 750
'Ga doun Schir Kid, cum up Schir Salmond agane!'
Quhill he wes deid; syne to the land him drewch,
And off that new-maid salmond eit anewch.

Thus fynelie fillit with young tender meit,
Unto ane derne for dreid he him addrest;   755
Under ane busk, quhair that the sone can beit,
To beik his breist and bellie he thocht best;
And rekleslie he said quhair he did rest,
Straikand his wame aganis the sonis heit:
'Upon this wame set wer ane bolt full meit.'   760

23

Quhen this wes said, the keipar off the gait,
Cairfull in hart his kid wes stollen away,
On everilk syde full warlie couth he wait;
Quhill at the last he saw quhair Lowrence lay:
Ane bow he bent, ane flane with fedderis gray   765
He haillit to the heid, and or he steird,
The foxe he prikkit fast unto the eird.

'Now,' quod the foxe, 'allace and wellaway!
Gorrit I am and may na forther gang;
Me think na man may speik ane word in play,   770
Bot nowondayis in ernist it is tane.'
He harlit him, and out he drew his flane;
And for his kid, and uther violence,
He tuke his skyn and maid ane recompence.

Moralitas

This suddand deith and unprovysit end   775
Of this fals tod, without provisioun,
Exempill is exhortand folk to amend,
For dreid of sic ane lyke confusioun;
For mony now hes gude professioun,
Yit not repentis nor for thair sinnis greit,   780
Because thay think thair lustie lyfe sa sweit.

Sum bene also, throw consuetude and ryte,
Vincust with carnall sensualitie;
Suppose thay be as for the tyme contryte,
Can not forbeir, nor fra thair sinnis fle;   785
Use drawis nature swa in propertie
Of beist and man, that neidlingis thay man do
As thay of lang tyme hes bene hantit to.

Be war gude folke, and feir this suddand schoit,
Quhilk smytis sair withoutin resistence: 790
Attend wyislie, and in your hartis be noit;

24

Aganis deith may na man mak defence;
Ceis of your sin, remord your conscience;
Obey unto your God, and ye sall wend
Efter your deith to blis withouttin end.   795

5

The Taill of the Sone and Air of the foirsaid
Foxe, callit Father Wer: Alswa the Parliament
of fourfuttit Beistis, haldin be the Lyoun

This foirsaid foxe, that deit for his misdeid,
Had not ane barne wes gottin richteouslie,
Till airschip be law that micht succeid,
Except ane sone quhilk in adulterie
He gottin had in purches privelie;   800
And till his name wes callit Father War,
That luifit weill with pultrie to tig and tar.

It followis weill be ressoun naturall,
And gre be gre of richt comparisoun,
Off evill cummis war, off war cummis werst of all;   805
Off wrangus geir cummis fals successioun.
This foxe, bastard of generatioun,
Off verray kynde behuifit to be fals;
Swa wes his father and his grandschir als.

As nature will, seikand his meit be sent,   810
Off cace he fand his fatheris carioun,
Nakit, new-slane; and till him hes he went,
Tuke up his heid, and on his kne fell doun,
Thankand grit God off that conclusioun,
And said: 'Now sall I bruke, sen I am air,   815
The boundis quhair thow wes wont for to repair.'

Fy! Couetice unkynd and venemous!
The sone wes fane he fand his father deid,
Be suddand schot for deidis odious,
That he micht ringe and raxe intill his steid,   820
Dreidand nathing the samin lyfe to leid,
In thift and reif, as did his father befoir;
Bot to the end attent he tuke no moir.

Yit nevertheles, throw naturall pietie
The carioun upon his bak he tais.   825
'Now find I weill this proverb trew,' quod he,
' "Ay rinnis the foxe als lang as he fute hais." '
Syne with the corps unto ane peit-poit gais,
Off watter full, and kest him in the deip,
And to the devill he gaif his banis to keip.   830

O fulische man plungit in wardlynes,
To conqueis wardlie gude and gold and rent,
To put thy saull in pane or hevines
To riche thy air, quhilk efter thow art went,
Have he thy gude, he takis bot small tent   835
To execute, to do, to satisfie
Thy letter will, thy det and legacie!

This tod to rest him he passit to ane craig,
And thair he hard ane buisteous bugill blaw,
Quhilk, as he thocht, maid all the warld to waig.   840
Ane unicorne come lansand over ane law:
Than start he up quhen he this hard and saw;
With horne in hand, ane bill in [buste] he bure—
Ane pursephant semelie, I yow assure.

Unto ane bank, quhair he micht se about   845
On everilk syde, in haist he culd him hy,
Schot out his voce full schyll and gaif ane schout,
And on this wyis twyse or thryse did cry.
With that the beistis in the feild thairby,
All mervelland quhat sic ane thing suld mene,   850
Gritlie agast, thay gaderit on ane grene.

26

Out off ane [bust] ane bull sone can be braid,
And red the text withoutin tarying:
Commandand silence, sadlie thus he said:
'The Nobill Lyoun, off all beistis the King:—   855
Greting to God, helth everlestyng
To brutall beistis and irrationall
I send, as to my subjectis grit and small.

'My celsitude and hie magnificence
Lattis yow to wit, that evin incontinent,   860
Thinkis the morne with royall deligence,
Upon this hill to hald ane parliament:
Straitlie thairfoir I gif commandement
For to compeir befoir my tribunall,
Under all pane and perrell that may fall.'   865

The morrow come and Phebus with his bemis
Consumit had the mistie cluddis gray;
The ground wes grene and als as gold it glemis,
With gers growand gudelie, grit and gay;
The spyce thay spred to spring on everilk spray;   870
The lark, the maveis and the merll full hie,
Sweitlie can sing, creippand fra tre to tre.

The leopardis come with croun off massie gold—
Beirand thay brocht unto that hillis hicht,
With jaspis jonit, and royall rubeis rold,   875
And mony diveris dyamontis dicht;
With towis proud ane palyeoun doun thay picht;
And in that throne thair sat ane wild lyoun,
In rob royall, with sceptour, swerd and croun.

Efter the tennour off the cry befoir,   880
That gais on all fourfuttit beistis in eird,
As thay commandit wer, withoutin moir,
Befoir thair lord the lyoun thay appeird:
And quhat thay wer, to me as Lowrence leird,
I sall reheirs ane part off everilk kynd,   885
Als fer as now occurris to my mynd.

27

The Minotaur, ane monster mervelous;
Bellerophont, that beist of bastardrie;
The warwolff, and the Pegase perillous
Transformit be assent of sorcerie;   890
The linx; the tiger full off tiranie;
The elephant, and eik the dromedarie;
The cameill with his cran nek furth can carie.

The leopard, as I haif tauld beforne;
The anteloip the sparth furth couth speid;   895
The peyntit pantheir, and the unicorne;
The rayndeir ran throw reveir, rone and reid;
The jolie gillet, and the gentill steid;
The asse, the mule, the hors of everilk kynd;
The da, the ra, the hornit hart, the hynd.   900

The bull, the beir, the bugill and the bair,
The tame cat, wild cat and the wild wod-swyne,
The hard-bakkit hurcheoun and the hirpland hair,
Baith otter and aip and pennit porcupyne,
The gukit gait, the selie scheip, the swyne,   905
The wylde once, the buk, the welterand brok,
The fowmart with the fibert furth can flok.

The gray grewhound with slewthound furth can slyde,
With doggis all divers and different;
The rattoun ran—the glebard furth can glyde,   910
The quhrynand quhitret with the quhasill went,
The feitho that hes furrit mony fent,
The mertrik, with the cunning and the con—
The [bow ran bane]—and eik the lerion.

The marmisset the mowdewart couth leid,   915
Because that nature denyit had hir sicht;
Thus dressit thay all furth for dreid off deid;
The musk; the lytill mous with all hir micht
With haist scho haikit unto that hill of hicht;
And mony kynd off beistis I couth not knaw   920
Befoir thair lord the lyoun thay loutit law.

28

Seing thir beistis all at his bidding boun,
He gaif ane braid, and luikit him about;
Than flatlingis to his feit thay fell all doun—
For dreid off deith thay droupit all in dout.   925
He lukit quhen that he saw thame lout,
And bad thame, with ane countenance full sweit:
'Be not efferit, bot stand up on your feit.

'I lat yow wit my micht is merciabill,
And steiris nane that ar to me prostrait;   930
Angrie, austerne and als unamyabill
To all that standfray ar to myne estait:
I rug, I reif all beistys that makis debait
Aganis the micht off my magnyficence:
Se nane pretend to pryde in my presence.   935

'My celsitude and my hie majestie
With micht and mercie myngit sall be ay;
The lawest heir I can full sone up hie,
And mak him maister over yow all I may;
The dromedarie giff he will mak deray,   940
The grit camell thocht he wer never sa crous,
I can him law als lytill as ane mous.

'Se neir be twentie mylis quhair I am
The kid ga saiflie be the gaittis syde,
The tod Lowrie luke not to the lam,   945
Na revand beistis nouther ryn nor ryde.'
Thay couchit all efter that this wes cryde;
The justice bad the court for to gar fence,
The sutis callit, and foirfalt all absence.

The panther, with his payntit coit-armour,   950
Fensit the court, as off the law effeird;
Than Tod Lowrie luikit quhair he couth lour,
And start on fute, all stonist and all steird;
Ryifand his hair he cryit with ane reird,
Quaikand for dreid and sichand couth he say: 955
'Allace this hour! Allace this dulefull day!

'I wait this suddand semblie that I se,
Haifand the pointis off ane parliament,
Is maid to mar sic misdoars as me;
Thairfoir geve I me schaw, I will be schent—
I will be socht, and I be red absent;
To byde or fle it makis no remeid;
All is alyke—thair followis not bot deid!'

Perplexit thus in his hart can he mene
Throw falset how he micht himself defend;
His hude he drew laich attoure his ene,
And winkand with ane eye furth he wend;
Clinscheand he come, that he micht not be kend,
And for dreddour that he suld bene arreist,
He playit buk-hude behind fra beist to beist.

O fylit spreit and cankerit conscience!
Befoir ane roy renyeit with richteousnes,
Blakinnit cheikis and schamefull countenance!
Fairweill thy fame! Now gone is all thy grace!
The phisnomie—the favour off thy face—
For thy defence is foull and disfigurate,
Brocht to the licht, basit, blunt and blait.

Be thow atteichit with thift or with tressoun,
For thy misdeid wrangous and wickit fay
Thy cheir changis, Lowrence; thow man luke doun;
Thy worschip of this warld is went away.
Luke to this tod, how he wes in effray,
And fle the filth of falset, I the reid,
Quhairthrow thair fallowis syn and schamefull deid.

Compeirand thus befoir thair lord and king,
In ordour set as to thair estait effeird,
Of everilk kynd he gart ane part furth bring,
And awfullie he spak and at thame speird
Geve there wes ony kynd of beistis in eird
Absent, and thairto gart thame deiplie sweir;
And thay said: 'Nane, except ane stude gray meir.'

960

965

970

975

980

985

990

30

'Ga, mak ane message sone unto that stude!'
The court than cryit: 'Now see; quha sall it be?'
'Cum furth Lowrie, lurkand under thy hude!'
'Aa schir! Mercie! Lo, I have bot ane ee!   995
Hurt in the hoche and cruikit as ye may se;
The wolff is better in ambassatry,
And mair cunning in clergie fer than I.'

Rampand he said: 'Ga furth, brybouris baith!'
And thay to ga withowtin tarying;   1000
Over ron and rute thay ran togidder raith
And fand the meir at hir meit in the morning.
'Now,' quod the tod, 'madame, cum to the king;
The court is callit and ye ar contumax.'
'Let be, Lowrence,' quod scho, 'your cowrtlie knax.'   1005

'Maistres,' quod he, 'cum to the court ye mon;
The lyoun hes commandit so indeid.'
'Schir Tod, tak ye the flyrdome and the fon;
I have respite ane yeir—and ye will reid.'
'I can not spell,' quod he, 'sa God me speid!   1010
Heir is the wolff, ane nobill clerk at all,
And of this message is maid principall.

'He is autentik and ane man of age,
And hes grit practik of the chanceliary;
Let him ga luke and reid your privilage,   1015
And I sall stand and beir witnes yow by.'
'Quhair is thy respite?' quod the wolff in hy.
'Schir, it is heir, under my hufe weill hid.'
'Hald up thy heill!' quod he; and so scho did.

Thocht he wes blindit with pryde, yit he presumis   1020
To luke doun law quhair that hir letter lay:
With that the meir gird him upon the gumis
And straik the [hattrell] off his heid away:
Halff out off lyif thair lenand doun he lay:
'Allace!' quod Lowrence, 'Lupus, thow art loist!'   1025
'His cunning,' quod the meir, 'wes worth sum coist!'

'Lowrence,' quod scho, 'will thow luke on my letter,
Sen that the wolff nathing thairoff can wyn?'
'Na, be Sanct Bryde!' quod he. 'Me think it better
To sleip in haill nor in ane hurt skyn.   1030
Ane skrow I fand, and this wes writtin in—
For fyve schillingis I wald not anis forfaut him—
"*Felix quem faciunt aliena pericula cautum*".'

With brokin skap and bludie cheikis reid,
This wretchit wolff weipand thus on he went,   1035
Off his menye markand to get remeid;
To tell the king the cace wes his intent.
'Schir,' quod the tod, 'byde still upon this bent
And fra your browis wesche away the blude,
And tak ane drink, for it will do yow gude.'   1040

To fetche watter this fraudfull foxe furth fure;
Sydelingis abak he socht unto ane syke;
On cace he meittis, cummand fra the mure,
Ane trip off lambis dansand on ane dyke:
This tratour tod, this tirrant and this tyke,   1045
The fattest off this flock he fellit hais,
And eit his fill; syne to the wolff he gais.

Thay drank togidder and syne thair journey takis;
Befoir the king syne kneillit on thair kne.
'Quhair is yone meir, Schir Tod, wes contumax?'   1050
Than Lowrence said: 'My lord, speir not at me!
Speir at your Doctour off Divinitie,
With his reid cap can tell yow weill aneuch.'
With that the lyoun and all the laif thay leuch.

'Tell on the cais now, Lowrence; let us heir!'   1055
'This wittie wolff,' quod he, 'this clerk off age,
On your behalff he bad the meir compeir;
And scho allegit to ane privilage:
"Cum neir and se, and ye sall haiff your wage!"
Because he red [hir] rispite plane and weill,   1060
Yone reid bonat scho raucht him with hir heill.'

32

The lyoun said: 'Be yone reid cap I ken
This taill is trew, quha tent unto it takis;
The greitest clerkis ar not the wysest men;
The hurt off ane happie the uther makis.'   1065
As thay wer carpand in this cais with knakis,
And all the court in merines and in gam,
Swa come the yow, the mother off the lam.

Befoir the justice on hir kneis fell,
Put out hir playnt on this wyis wofully: 1070
'This harlet huresone and this hound off hell,
Devorit hes my lamb full doggitly,
Within ane myle, in contrair to your cry.
For Goddis lufe, my lord, gif me the law
Off this lurker!' With that Lowrence let draw.   1075

'Byde!' quod the lyoun. 'Lymmer, let us se
Giff it be suthe the selie yow hes said.'
'Aa, soverane lord, saif your mercie!' quod he.
'My purpois wes with him for to haif plaid;
Causles he fled, as he had bene effraid;   1080
For dreid off deith he duschit over ane dyke
And brak his nek.' 'Thow leis,' quod scho, 'fals tyke!

'His deith be practik may be previt eith:
Thy gorrie gumis and thy bludie snout,
The woll, the flesche, yit stikkis on thy teith;   1085
And that is evidence aneuch, but dout!'
The justice bad ga cheis ane assyis about:
And so thay did, and fand that he wes fals
Off murther, thift, pyking and tressoun als.

Thay band him fast; the justice bad belyif   1090
To gif the dome and tak off all his claıs,
The wolff, that new-maid Doctour, couth him schrif,
Syne furth him led, and to the gallous gais,
And at the ledder-fute his leif he tais:
The aip was bowcher, and bad him sone ascend,   1095
And hangit him; and thus he maid his end.

Richt as the mynour in his minorall
Fair gold with fyre may fra the leid weill wyn,
Richt so under ane fabill figurall
Sad sentence men may seik, and efter [fyne]—   1100
As daylie dois the Doctouris of Devyne,
That to our leving full weill can apply
And paynt thair mater furth be poetry.

The lyoun is the warld be liknes,
To quhome loutis baith empriour and king,   1105
And thinkis of this warld to get incres,
Thinkand daylie to get mair leving:
Sum for to reull, and sum to raxe and ring;
Sum gadderis geir, sum gold, sum uther gude;
To wyn this warld sum wirkis as thay wer wod.   1110

The meir is men of gude conditioun,
As pilgrymes walkand in this wildernes,
Approvand that for richt religioun,
Thair God onlie to pleis in everilk place;
Abstractit from this warldis wretchitnes,   1115
Fechtand with lust, presumptioun and pryde,
And fra this warld in mynd ar mortyfyde.

This wolf I likkin to sensualitie,
As quhen lyke brutall beistis we accord
Our mynd all to this warldis vanitie,   1120
Lyking to tak and loif him as our lord:
Fle fast thairfra gif thow will richt remord;
Than sall ressoun ryse, rax and ring,
And for thy saull thair is na better thing.

Hir hufe I likkin to the thocht of deid: 1125
Will thow remember, man, that thow man de?
Thow may brek sensualiteis heid,
And fleschlie lust away fra the sall fle,

34

Fra thow begin thy mynd to mortifie;
Salomonis saying thow may persaif heirin: 1130
'Think on thy end, thow sall not glaidlie sin.'

This tod I likkin to temptationis,
Beirand to mynd mony thochtis vane,
Assaultand men with sweit perswasionis,
Ay reddie for to trap thame in ane trayne;   1135
Yit gif thay se sensualitie neir slane,
And suddand deith draw neir with panis sore,
Thay go abak and temptis thame no more.

O Mediatour mercifull and meik,
Thow soveraigne Lord and King celestiall,   1140
Thy celsitude maist humillie we beseik
Us to defend fra pane and perrellis all!
And help us up unto Thy hevinlie hall,
In gloir quhair we may se the face of God!
And thus endis the talking of the tod.   1145

6

The Taill of the Scheip and the Doig

Esope ane taill puttis in memorie
How that ane doig, because that he wes pure,
Callit ane scheip to the consistorie,
Ane certane breid fra him for to recure.
Ane fraudfull wolff wes juge that tyme, and bure   1150
Authoritie and jurisdictioun,
And on the scheip send furth ane strait summoun.

For by the use and cours and commoun style,
On this maner maid his citatioun:
'I, Maister Wolff, partles off fraud and gyle,   1155
Under the panis off Hie Suspensioun,
Off Grit Cursing and Interdictioun,
Schir Scheip, I charge the for to compeir,
And answer to ane doig befoir me heir.'

Schir Corbie Ravin wes maid apparitour,   1160
Quha pykit had full mony scheipis ee;
The charge hes tane and on the letteris bure;
Summonit the scheip befoir the wolff, that he
Peremptourlie, within twa dayis or thre,
Compeir under the panis in this bill,   1165
'To heir quhat perrie doig will say the till.'

This summondis maid befoir witnes anew
The ravin—as to his office weill effeird;
Indorsat hes the write, and on he flew;
The selie scheip durst lay na mouth on eird   1170
Till he befoir the awfull juge appeird,
The oure off cause quhilk that the juge usit than,
Quhen Hesperus to schaw his face began.

The foxe wes clerk and noter in the cause;
The gled, the graip, at the bar couth stand;   1175
As advocatis expert into the lawis
The doggis pley togidder tuke on hand,
Quhilk wer confidderit straitlie in ane band
Aganis the scheip to procure the sentence;
Thocht it wes fals thay had na conscience.   1180

The clerk callit the scheip, and he wes thair;
The advocatis on this wyse couth propone:
'Ane certane breid worth fyve schilling or mair
Thow aw the doig, off quhilk the terme is gone.'
Off his awin heid, but advocate, allone,   1185
The scheip avysitlie gaif answer in the cace:
'Heir I declyne the juge, the tyme, the place.

'This is my cause, in motive and effect:
The law sayis it is richt perrillous
Till enter in pley befoir ane juge suspect;   1190
And ye, Schir Wolff, hes bene richt odious
To me, for with your tuskis ravenous
Hes slane full mony kinnismen off myne:
Thairfoir juge as suspect I yow declyne.

36

'And schortlie, of this court ye memberis all,   1195
Baith assessouris, clerk and advocate,
To me and myne ar ennemies mortall,
And ay hes bene, as mony scheipheird wate;
The place is fer, the tyme is feriate;
Quhairfoir na juge suld sit in consistory   1200
Sa lait at evin; I yow accuse forthy.'

Quhen that the juge in this wyse wes accusit,
He bad the parteis cheis with ane assent
Twa arbeteris, as in the law is usit,
For to declair and gif arbitriment   1205
Quhidder the scheip suld answer in jugement
Befoir the wolff; and so thay did but weir,
Off quhome the namis efterwart ye sall heir.

The beir, the brok, the mater tuke on hand,
For to discyde gif this exceptioun   1210
Wes off na strenth nor lauchfully mycht stand;
And thairupon as jugis thay sat doun
And held ane lang quhyle disputatioun,
Seikand full mony decreitis off the law,
And glosis als, the veritie to knaw.   1215

Of civile law volumis full mony thay revolve,
The codies and digestis new and ald;
[Contra and pro, strait] argumentis thay resolve,
Sum objecting and sum can hald;
For prayer or price trow ye that thay wald fald?   1220
Bot hald the glose and text of the decreis
As trew jugis; I beschrew thame ay that leis.

Schortlie to mak ane end off this debait:
The arbiteris than sweirand plane,
The sentence gave and proces fulminait: 1225
The scheip suld pas befoir the wolff agane
And end his pley. Than wes he nathing fane,
For fra thair sentence couth he not appeill.
On clerkis I do it gif this sentence wes leill.

37

The scheip agane befoir the wolff derenyeit,   1230
But advocate abasitlie couth stand.
Up rais the doig and on the scheip thus plenyeit:
'Ane soume I payit have befoir-the-hand
For certane breid.' Thairto ane borrow he fand
That wrangouslie the scheip did hald the breid—   1235
Quhilk he denyit: and thair began the pleid.

And quhen the scheip this stryif had contestait,
The justice in the cause furth can proceid;
Lowrence the actis and the proces wrait,
And thus the pley unto the end thay speid.   1240
This cursit court, corruptit all for meid,
Aganis gude faith, law and eik conscience,
For this fals doig pronuncit the sentence.

And it till put to executioun
The wolff chargit the scheip, without delay,   1245
Under the panis off interdictioun,
The soume off silver or the breid to pay.
Off this sentence, allace, quhat sall I say,
Quhilk dampnit hes the selie innocent
And justifyit the wrangous jugement?   1250

The scheip dreidand mair the executioun,
Obeyand to the sentence, he couth tak
His way unto ane merchand off the toun,
And sauld the woll that he bure on his bak,
Syne bocht the breid and to the doig couth mak   1255
Reddie payment, as it commandit was;
Naikit and bair syne to the feild couth pas.

Moralitas

This selie scheip may present the figure
Of pure commounis that daylie ar opprest
Be tirrane men, quhilkis settis all thair cure   1260

38

Be fals meinis to mak ane wrang conquest,
In hope this present lyfe suld ever lest;
Bot all begylit thay will in schort tyme end,
And efter deith to lestand panis wend.

This wolf I likkin to ane schiref stout   1265
Quhilk byis ane forfalt at the kingis hand,
And hes with him ane cursit assyis about,
And dytis all the pure men upon land;
Fra the crownar haif laid on him his wand,
Thocht he wer trew as ever wes Sanct Johne,   1270
Slane sall he be, or with the juge compone.

This ravin I likkin to ane fals crownair
Quhilk hes ane portioun of the inditement,
And passis furth befoir the justice air,
All misdoaris to bring to jugement;   1275
Bot luke gif he wes of ane trew intent
To scraip out Johne and wryte in Will or Wat,
And tak ane bud at boith the parteis tat.

Of this fals tod, of quhilk I spak befoir,
And of this gled, quhat thay micht signify   1280
Of thair nature, as now I speik no moir:
Bot of this scheip and of his cairfull cry
I sall reheirs; for as I passit by
Quhair that he lay, on cais I lukit doun,
And hard him mak sair lamentatioun.   1285

'Allace,' quod he, 'this cursit consistorie
In middis of the winter now is maid,
Quhen Boreas with blastis bitterlie
And hard froistes thir flouris doun can faid!
On bankis bair now may I mak na baid!'   1290
And with that word into ane coif he crap,
Fra sair wedder and froistis him to hap.

Quaikand for cauld, sair murnand ay amang,
Kest up his ee unto the hevinnis hicht
And said: 'Lord God, quhy sleipis Thow sa lang? 1295

39

Walk and discerne my cause groundit on richt;
Se how I am be fraud, maistrie and slicht
Peillit full bair!' And so is mony one
Now in this warld richt wonder wo begone!

Se how this cursit sone of covetice   1300
Loist hes baith lawtie and eik law.
Now few or nane will execute justice,
In fault of quhome the pure man is overthraw.
The veritie, suppois the juge it knaw,
He is so blindit with affectioun,   1305
But dreid, for micht he lettis the richt go doun.

Seis Thow not, Lord, this warld overturnit is,
As quha wald change gude gold in leid or tyn?
The pure is peillit; the lord may do na mis;
And simonie is haldin for na syn;   1310
Now is he blyith with okker maist may wyn;
Gentrice is slane and pietie is ago;
Allace, gude Lord, quhy tholis Thow it so?

Thow tholis this evin for our grit offence;
Thow sendis us troubill and plaigis soir,   1315
As hunger, derth, grit weir or pestilence;
Bot few amendis now thair lyfe thairfoir:
We pure pepill as now may do no moir
Bot pray to The; sen that we ar opprest
Into this eirth, grant us in hevin gude rest!   1320

7

The Taill of the Lyoun and the Mous

In middis of June, that sweit seasoun,
Quhen that fair Phebus with his bemis bricht
Had dryit up the dew fra daill and doun
And all the land maid with his bemis licht,
In ane mornyng betuix midday and nicht,   1325
I rais and put all sleuth and sleip asyde
And to ane wod I went allone but gyde.

40

Sweit wes the smell off flouris quhyte and reid,
The noyes off birdis richt delitious;
The bewis braid blomit abone my heid,   1330
The ground growand with gers gratious;
Off all plesance that place wes plenteous,
With sweit odouris and birdis harmony;
The mornyng myld—my mirth wes mair forthy.

The rosis reid arrayit on rone and ryce,   1335
The prymeros and the purpour violat bla;
To heir it wes ane poynt off Paradice,
Sic mirth the mavis and the merle couth ma;
The blossummis blythe brak upon bank and bra;
The smell off herbis and off fowlis cry,   1340
Contending quha suld have the victory.

Me to conserve than fra the sonis heit,
Under the schaddow off ane hawthorne grene
I lenit doun amang the flouris sweit,
Syne cled my heid and closit baith my ene: 1345
On sleip I fell amang thir bewis bene,
And in my dreme me thocht come throw the schaw
The fairest man that ever befoir I saw.

His gowne wes off ane claith als quhyte as milk;
His chemeis wes off chambelate purpour broun;   1350
His hude off scarlet, bordowrit weill with silk,
On hekillit-wyis untill his girdill doun;
His bonat round and off the auld fassoun;
His beird wes quhyte; his ene wes grit and gray;
With lokker hair quhilk over his schulderis lay.   1355

Ane roll off paper in his hand he bair;
Ane swannis pen stikand under his eir;
Ane inkhorne with ane prettie gilt pennair,
Ane bag off silk—all at his belt can beir:
Thus wes he gudelie grathit in his geir.   1360
Off stature large and with ane feirfull face:
Evin quhair I lay he come ane sturdie pace,

And said: 'God speid, my sone!' And I wes fane
Off that couth word and off his cumpany;
With reverence I salusit him agane: 1365
'Welcome, father'—and he sat doun me by—
'Displeis yow not, my gude maister, thocht I
Demand your birth, your facultye and name,
Quhy ye come heir or quhair ye dwell at hame.'

'My sone,' said he, 'I am off gentill blude;   1370
My native land is Rome withoutin nay,
And in that towne first to the sculis I yude,
In civile law studyit full mony ane day;
And now my winning is in hevin for ay:
Esope I hecht; my writing and my werk   1375
Is couth and kend to mony cunning clerk.'

'O Maister Esope, poet lawriate,
God wait, ye ar full deir welcum to me!
Ar ye not he that all thir fabillis wrate,
Quhilk in effect, suppois thay fenyeit be,   1380
Ar full off prudence and moralitie?'
'Fair sone,' said he, 'I am the samin man.'
God wait gif that my hert wes merie than!

I said: 'Esope, my maister venerabill,
I yow beseik hartlie for cheritie   1385
Ye wald not disdayne to tell ane prettie fabill
Concludand with ane gude moralitie!'
Schaikand his heid he said: 'My sone lat be;
For quhat is it worth to tell ane fenyeit taill
Quhen haly preiching may nathing availl?   1390

'Now in this warld, me think, richt few or nane
To Goddis word that hes devotioun;
The eir is deif, the hart is hard as stane;
Now oppin sin without correctioun,
The hart inclynand to the eirth ay doun;   1395
Sa roustit is the warld with canker blak
That now my taillis may lytill succour mak.'

42

'[Yit] gentill schir,' said I, 'for my requeist,
Not to displeis your fatherheid, I pray
Under the figure off ane brutall beist   1400
Ane morall fabill ye wald denye to say:
Quha wait nor I may leir and beir away
Sum thing thairby heirefter may availl?'
'I grant,' quod he: and thus begouth ane taill:

Ane lyoun at his pray [verray] foir-run,   1405
To recreat his limmis and to rest,
Beikand his breist and belly at the sun,
Under ane tre lay in the fair forest:
Swa come ane trip off myis out off thair nest,
Richt tait and trig, all dansand in ane gyis,   1410
And over the lyoun lansit twyis or thryis.

He lay so still, the myis wes not effeird,
Bot to and fro out over him tuke thair trace;
Sum tirlit at the campis off his beird,
Sum spairit not to claw him on the face: 1415
Merie and glaid thus dansit thay ane space,
Till at the last the nobill lyoun woke,
And with his pow the maister mous he tuke.

Scho gave ane cry, and all the laif, agast,
Thair dansing left and hid thame sone alquhair: 1420
Scho that wes tane cryit and weipit fast
And said: Allace oftymes that scho come thair:
'Now am I tane ane wofull presonair,
And for my gilt traistis incontinent
Off lyfe and deith to thoill the jugement.'   1425

Than spak the lyoun to that cairfull mous:.
'Thow cative wretche and vile unworthie thing,
Over-malapart and eik presumpteous
Thow wes to mak out over me thy tripping:
Knew thow not weill I wes baith lord and king   1430
Off beistis all?' 'Yes,' quod the mous, 'I knaw;
Bot I misknew because ye lay so law.

43

'Lord, I beseik thy kinglie royaltie,
Heir quhat I say, and tak in patience;
Considder first my simple povertie,   1435
And syne thy mychtie, hie magnyfycence;
Se als how thingis done off neglygence—
Nouther off malice nor of presumptioun,
The rather suld have grace and remissioun.

'We wer repleit and had grit aboundance   1440
Off alkin thingis sic as to us effeird;
The sweit sesoun provokit us to dance
And mak sic mirth as nature to us leird:
Ye lay so still and law upon the eird
That, be my sawll, we weind ye had bene deid—   1445
Elles wald we not have dancit over your heid.'

'Thy fals excuse,' the lyoun said agane,
'Sall not availl ane myte, I underta;
I put the cace I had bene deid or slane,
And syne my skyn bene stoppit full off stra—   1450
Thocht thow had found my figure lyand swa,
Because it bare the prent off my persoun
Thow suld for feir on kneis have fallin doun.

'For thy trespas thow can mak na defence,
My nobill persoun thus to vilipend;   1455
Off thy feiris nor thy awin negligence
For to excuse thow can na cause pretend;
Thairfoir thow suffer sall ane schamefull end
And deith sic as to tressoun is decreit—
Upon the gallous harlit be the feit.'   1460

'Na! Mercie, lord, at thy gentrice I ase!
As thow art king off beistis coronate,
Sober thy wraith and let it overpas
And mak thy mynd to mercy inclynate;
I grant offence is done to thyne estate,   1465
Quhairfoir I worthie am to suffer deid
Bot gif thy kinglie mercie reik remeid.

44

'In everie juge mercy and reuth suld be,
As assessouris and collaterall;
Without mercie justice is crueltie,   1470
As said is in the lawis speciall:
Quhen rigour sittis in the tribunall
The equitie off law quha may sustene?
Richt few or nane but mercie gang betwene.

'Alswa ye knaw the honour triumphall   1475
Off all victour upon the strenth dependis
Off his conqueist, quhilk manlie in battell
Throw jeopardie of weir lang defendis:
Quhat pryce or loving, quhen the battell endis,
Is said off him that overcummis ane man   1480
Him to defend quhilk nouther may nor can?

'Ane thowsand myis to kill and eik devoir
Is lytill manheid to ane strang lyoun;
Full lytill worschip have ye wyn thairfoir,
To qwhais strenth is na comparisoun;   1485
It will degraid sum part off your renoun
To sla ane mous quhilk may mak na defence,
Bot askand mercie at your excellence.

'Also it semis not your celsitude,
Quhilk usis daylie meittis delitious,   1490
To fyle your teith or lippis with my blude,
Quhilk to your stomok is contagious;
Unhailsum meit is of ane sarie mous—
And that namelie untill ane strang lyoun
Wont till be fed with gentill vennesoun.   1495

'My lyfe is lytill worth, my deith is les;
Yit and I leif, I may peradventure
Supple your hienes beand in distres:
For oft is sene ane man off small stature
Reskewit hes ane lord off hie honour,   1500
Keipit that wes in poynt to be overthrawin
Throw misfortoun: sic cace may be your awin.'

Quhen this wes said, the lyoun his language
Paissit and thocht according to ressoun,
And gart mercie his cruell ire asswage,   1505
And to the mous grantit remissioun:
Oppinnit his pow and scho on kneis fell doun
And baith hir handis unto the hevin upheild,
Cryand: 'Almichty God mot yow foryeild!'

Quhen scho wes gone the lyoun held to hunt,   1510
For he had nocht, bot levit on his pray,
And slew baith tayme and wyld as he wes wont,
And in the cuntrie maid ane grit deray:
Till at the last the pepill fand the way
This cruell lyoun how that thay mycht tak: 1515
Off hempyn cordis strang nettis couth thay mak.

And in ane rod quhair he wes wont to ryn,
With raipis rude fra tre to tre it band;
Syne kest ane range on raw the wod within,
With hornis blast and kennettis fast calland: 1520
The lyoun fled, and throw the ron rynnand,
Fell in the net and hankit fute and heid;
For all his strenth he couth mak na remeid.

Welterand about with hiddeous rummissing,
Quhyle to, quhyle fra, quhill he mycht succour get; 1525
Bot all in vane—it vailyeit him nathing;
The mair he flang the faster wes the net;
The raipis rude wes sa about him plet
On everilk syde that succour saw he nane;
Bot styll lyand and murnand maid his mane.   1530

'O lamit lyoun liggand heir sa law,
Quhair is the mycht off thy magnyfycence,
Off quhome all brutall beist in eird stude aw
And dred to luke upon thy excellence?
But hoip or help, but succour or defence,   1535
In bandis strang heir man I ly—allace!—
Till I be slane: I se nane uther grace.

'Thair is na wy that will my harmis wreik,
Nor creature do confort.to my croun:
Quha sall me bute? Quha sall my bandis breik?   1540
Quha sall me put fra pane off this presoun?'
Be he had maid this lamentatioun,
Throw aventure, the lytill mous come neir,
And off the lyoun hard the pietuous beir.

And suddanlie it come intill hir mynd   1545
That it suld be the lyoun did hir grace;
And said: 'Now wer I fals and richt unkynd
Bot gif I quit sum part off thy gentrace
Thow did to me.' And on this way scho gais
To hir fellowis and on thame fast can cry: 1550
'Cum help! Cum help!' And thay come all in hy.

'Lo,' quod the mous, 'this is the samin lyoun
That grantit grace to me quhen I wes tane—
And now is fast heir bundin in presoun,
Brekand his hart with sair murning and mane!   1555
Bot we him help, off souccour wait he nane;
Cum help to quyte ane gude turne for ane-uther;
Go, lous him sone!' And thay said: 'Ye, gude brother!'

Thay tuke na knyfe—thair teith wes scharpe anewch:
To se that sicht forsuith it wes grit wounder—   1560
How that thay ran amang the rapis tewch;
Befoir, behind sum yeid about, sum under,
And schuir the raipis off the net in-schunder;
Syne bad him ryse; and he start up anone
And thankit thame; syne on his way is gone.   1565

Now is the lyoun fre off all danger,
Lows and delyverit to his libertie
Be lytill beistis off ane small power,
As ye have hard, because he had pietie.
Quod I: 'Maister, is thair ane moralitie   1570
In this fabill?' 'Yea, sone,' he said, 'richt gude.'
'I pray yow, schir,' quod I, 'ye wald conclude.'

47

As I suppois, this mychtie gay lyoun
May signifie ane prince or empriour,
Ane potestate or yit ane king with croun—   1575
Quhilk suld be walkrife gyde and governour
Of his pepill—that takis na labour
To reule and steir the land and justice keip,
Bot lyis still in lustis, sleuth and sleip.

The fair forest with levis lowne and le,   1580
With foulis sang and flouris ferlie sweit,
Is bot the warld and his prosperitie,
As fals plesance myngit with cair repleit:
Richt as the rois with froist and wynter weit
Faidis, swa dois the warld, and thame desavis   1585
Quhilk in thair lustis maist confidence havis.

Thir lytill myis ar bot the commountie,
Wantoun, unwyse, without correctioun:
Thair lordis and princis quhen that thay se
Of justice mak nane executioun,   1590
Thay dreid nathing to mak rebellioun
And disobey, forquhy thay stand nane aw—
That garris thame thair soveranis misknaw.

Be this fabill ye lordis of prudence
May considder the vertew of pietie,   1595
And to remit sumtyme ane grit offence,
And mitigate with mercy crueltie:
Oftymis is sene ane man of small degre
Hes quit ane kinbute baith of gude and ill,
As lord hes done rigour or grace him till.   1600

Quha wait how sone ane lord of grit renoun,
Rolland in wardlie lust and vane plesance,
May be overthrawin, destroyit and put doun
Throw fals fortoun—quhilk of all variance

48

Is haill maistres, and leidar of the dance   1605
Till injust men, and blindis thame so soir
That thay na perrell can provyde befoir?

Thir rurall men that stentit hes the net
In quhilk the lyoun suddandlie wes tane,
Waittit alway amendis for to get—   1610
For hurt men wrytis in the marbill stane.
Mair till expound as now I lett allane—
Bot king and lord may weill wit quhat I mene:
Figure heirof oftymis hes bene sene.

Quhen this wes said, quod Esope: 'My fair child   1615
I the beseik and all men for to pray
That tressoun of this cuntrie be exyld,
And justice regne, and lordis keip thair fay
Unto thair soverane king baith nycht and day.'
And with that word he vanist and I woke;   1620
Syne throw the schaw my journey hamewart tuke.

8

The Preiching of the Swallow

The hie prudence and wirking mervelous,
The profound wit off God omnipotent,
Is sa perfyte and sa ingenious,
Excellent far all mannis jugement: 1625
Forquhy to Him all thing is ay present,
Rycht as it is or ony tyme sall be,
Befoir the sicht off His Divinitie.

Thairfoir our saull with sensualitie
So fetterit is in presoun corporall,   1630
We may not cleirlie understand nor se
God as He is nor thingis celestiall;
Our mirk and deidlie corps naturall
Blindis the spirituall operatioun—
Lyke as ane man wer bundin in presoun.   1635

49   F

In Metaphisik Aristotell sayis
That mannis saull is lyke ane bakkis ee
Quhilk lurkis still als lang as licht off day is,
And in the gloming cummis furth to fle;
Hir ene ar waik, the sone scho may not se: 1640
Sa is our saull with fantasie opprest
To knaw the thingis in nature manifest.

For God is in His power infinite,
And mannis saull is febill and over-small,
Off understanding waik and unperfite,   1645
To comprehend Him That contenis all:
Nane suld presume be ressoun naturall
To seirche the secreitis off the Trinitie,
Bot trow fermelie and lat all ressoun be.

Yit nevertheles we may haif knawlegeing   1650
Off God Almychtie be His creatouris
That he is gude, fair, wyis and bening:
Exempill tak be thir jolie flouris
Rycht sweit off smell and plesant off colouris,
Sum grene, sum blew, sum purpour, quhyte and reid, 1655
Thus distribute be gift off His Godheid.

The firmament payntit with sternis cleir,
From eist to west rolland in cirkill round,
And everilk planet in his proper spheir,
In moving makand harmonie and sound;   1660
The fyre, the air, the watter and the ground—
Till understand it is aneuch, iwis,
That God in all His werkis wittie is.

Luke weill the fische that swimmis in the se;
Luke weill in eirth all kynd off bestiall;   1665
The foulis fair sa forcelie thay fle,
Scheddand the air with pennis grit and small;
Syne luke to man, that He maid last off all,
Lyke to His image and His similitude:
Be thir we knaw that God is fair and gude.   1670

All creature He maid for the behufe
Off man and to his supportatioun
Into this eirth, baith under and abufe,
In number, wecht and dew proportioun;
The difference off tyme and ilk seasoun   1675
Concorddand till our opurtunitie,
As daylie be experience we may se.

The somer with his jolie mantill off grene,
With flouris fair furrit on everilk fent,
Quhilk Flora Goddes, off the flouris quene,   1680
Hes to that lord as for his seasoun lent,
And Phebus with his goldin bemis gent
Hes purfellit and payntit plesandly
With heit and moysture stilland from the sky.

Syne harvest hait, quhen Ceres that goddes   1685
Hir barnis benit hes with abundance;
And Bachus, god off wyne, renewit hes
The tume pyipis in Italie and France
With wynis wicht and liquour off plesance;
And Copia Temporis to fill hir horne,   1690
That never wes full off quheit nor uther corne.

Syne wynter wan, quhen austerne Eolus,
God off the wynd, with blastis boreall
The grene garment off somer glorious
Hes all to-rent and revin in pecis small;   1695
Than flouris fair faidit with froist man fall,
And birdis blyith changit thair noitis sweit
In styll murning, neir slane with snaw and sleit.

Thir dalis deip with dubbis drounit is,
Baith hill and holt heillit with frostis hair;   1700
And bewis bene laifit bair off blis
Be wickit windis off the winter wair;
All wyld beistis than from the bentis bair
Drawis for dreid unto thair dennis deip,
Coucheand for cauld in coifis thame to keip.   1705

Syne cummis ver, quhen winter is away,
The secretar off somer with his sell,
Quhen columbie up-keikis throw the clay,
Quhilk fleit wes befoir with froistes fell;
The mavis and the merle beginnis to mell;   1710
The lark onloft with uther birdis haill
Than drawis furth fra derne over doun and daill.

That samin seasoun, into ane soft morning,
Rycht blyth that bitter blastis wer ago,
Unto the wod, to se the flouris spring   1715
And heir the mavis sing and birdis mo,
I passit furth, syne lukit to and fro
To se the soill that wes richt sessonabill,
Sappie and to resave all seidis abill.

Moving thus-gait grit myrth I tuke in mynd   1720
Off lauboraris to se the besines—
Sum makand dyke and sum the pleuch can wynd,
Sum sawand seidis fast frome place to place,
The harrowis hoppand in the saweris trace:
It wes grit joy to him that luifit corne   1725
To se thame laubour baith at evin and morne.

And as I baid under ane bank full bene,
In hart gritlie rejosit off that sicht,
Unto ane hedge, under ane hawthorne grene,
Off small birdis thair come ane ferlie flicht,   1730
And doun belyif can on the leifis licht
On everilk syde about me quhair I stude—
Rycht mervellous—ane mekill multitude.

Amang the quhilks ane swallow loud couth cry,
On that hawthorne hie in the croip sittand: 1735
'O ye birdis on bewis heir me by,
Ye sall weill knaw and wyislie understand
Quhair danger is or perrell appeirand;
It is grit wisedome to provyde befoir,
It to devoyd—for dreid it hurt yow moir.'   1740

'Schir Swallow,' quod the lark agane and leuch,
'Quhat have ye sene that causis yow to dreid?'
'Se ye yone churll,' quod scho, 'beyond yone pleuch
Fast sawand hemp and gude linget seid?
Yone lint will grow in lytill tyme indeid, 1745
And thairoff will yone churll his nettis mak,
Under the quhilk he thinkis us to tak.

'Thairfoir I reid we pas quhen he is gone
At evin, and with our naillis scharp and small
Out off the eirth scraip we yone seid anone 1750
And eit it up; for giff it growis, we sall
Have cause to weip heirefter ane and all:
Se we remeid thairfoir furth with instante—
Nam leuius laedit quicquid praeuidimus ante.

'For clerkis sayis it is nocht sufficient 1755
To considder that is befoir thyne ee;
Bot prudence is ane inwart argument
That garris ane man provyde and foirse
Quhat gude, quhat evill is liklie for to be,
Off everilk thing behald the fynall end 1760
And swa fra perrell the better him defend.'

The lark lauchand the swallow thus couth scorne,
And said scho fischit lang befoir the net—
The barne is eith to busk that is unborne—
All growis nocht that in the ground is set— 1765
The nek to stoup quhen it the straik sall get
Is sone aneuch—deith on the fayest fall:
Thus scornit thay the swallow ane and all.

Despysing thus hir helthsum document,
The foulis ferlie tuke thair flicht anone; 1770
Sum with ane bir thay braidit over the bent
And sum agane ar to the grene wod gone:
Upon the land quhair I wes left allone
I tuke my club and hamewart couth I carie,
Swa ferliand as I had sene ane farie. 1775

Thus passit furth quhill June, that jolie tyde,
And seidis that wer sawin off beforne
Wer growin hie, that hairis mycht thame hyde,
And als the quailye craikand in the corne;
I movit furth, betuix midday and morne,   1780
Unto the hedge under the hawthorne grene
Quhair I befoir the said birdis had sene.

And as I stude, be aventure and cace,
The samin birdis as I haif said yow air—
I hoip because it wes thair hanting-place,   1785
Mair off succour or yit mair solitair—
Thay lychtit doun: and quhen thay lychtit wair,
The swallow swyth put furth ane pietuous pyme,
Said: 'Wo is him can not bewar in tyme!

'O blind birdis and full off negligence,   1790
Unmyndfull of your awin prosperitie,
Lift up your sicht and tak gude advertence!
Luke to the lint that growis on yone le!
Yone is the thing I bad forsuith that we,
Quhill it wes seid, suld rute furth off the eird: 1795
Now is it lint; now is it hie on breird.

'Go yit quhill it is tender and small
And pull it up—let it na mair incres:
My flesche growis, my bodie quaikis all;
Thinkand on it I may not sleip in peis.'   1800
Thay cryit all and bad the swallow ceis,
And said: 'Yone lint heirefter will do gude,
For linget is to lytill birdis fude.

'We think, quhen that yone lint-bollis ar ryip,
To mak us feist and fill us off the seid   1805
Magre yone churll, and on it sing and pyip.'
'Weill,' quod the swallow, 'freindes, hardilie beid:
Do as ye will, bot certane sair I dreid;
Heirefter ye sall find als sour as sweit
Quhen ye ar speldit on yone carlis speit.   1810

'The awner off yone lint ane fouler is,
Richt cautelous and full off subteltie;
His pray full sendill-tymis will he mis
Bot giff we birdis all the warrer be;
Full mony off our kin he hes gart de,   1815
And thocht it bot ane sport to spill thair blude:
God keip me fra him, and the Halie Rude!'

Thir small birdis haveand bot lytill thocht
Off perrell that mycht fall be aventure,
The counsell off the swallow set at nocht,   1820
Bot tuke thair flicht and furth togidder fure;
Sum to the wode, sum markit to the mure.
I tuke my staff quhen this wes said and done,
And walkit hame, for it drew neir the none.

The lynt ryipit, the carll pullit the lyne,   1825
Rippillit the bollis and in beitis set,
It steipit in the burne and dryit syne,
And with ane bittill knokkit it and bet,
Syne swingillit it weill and hekkillit in the flet;
His wyfe it span and twynit it into threid,   1830
Off quhilk the fowlar nettis maid indeid.

The wynter come, the wickit wind can blaw;
The woddis grene wer wallowit with the weit;
Baith firth and fell with froistys wer maid faw,
Slonkis and slaik maid slidderie with the sleit: 1835
The foulis fair for falt thay fell off feit;
On bewis bair it wes na bute to byde,
Bot hyit unto housis thame to hyde.

Sum in the barn, sum in the stak off corne
Thair lugeing tuke and maid thair residence;   1840
The fowlar saw, and grit aithis hes sworne
Thay suld be tane trewlie for thair expence:
His nettis hes he set with diligence,
And in the snaw he schulit hes ane plane,
And heillit it all over with calf agane.   1845

55

Thir small birdis seand the calff wes glaid;
Trowand it had bene corne thay lychtit doun;
Bot of the nettis na presume thay had,
Nor of the fowlaris fals intentioun;
To scraip and seik thair meit thay maid thame boun: 1850
The swallow on ane lytill branche neir by,
Dreiddand for gyle, thus loud on thame couth cry:

'Into that calf scraip quhill your naillis bleid;
Thair is na corne—ye laubour all in vane;
Trow ye yone churll for pietie will yow feid?   1855
Na, na! He hes it heir layit for ane trane;
Remove I reid, or ellis ye will be slane;
His nettis he hes set full prively,
Reddie to draw; in tyme be war forthy.'

Grit fule is he that puttis in dangeir   1860
His lyfe, his honour, for ane thing off nocht;
Grit fule is he that will not glaidle heir
Counsall in tyme, quhill it availl him nocht;
Grit fule is he that hes na thing in thocht
Bot thing present—and efter quhat may fall   1865
Nor off the end hes na memoriall.

Thir small birdis for hunger famischit neir,
Full besie scraipand for to seik thair fude,
The counsall off the swallow wald not heir—
Suppois thair laubour dyd thame lytill gude.   1870
Quhen scho thair fulische hartis understude
Sa indurate, up in ane tre scho flew;
With that [this] churll over thame his nettis drew.

Allace, it wes grit hartsair for to se
That bludie bowcheour beit thay birdis doun,   1875
And for till heir, quhen thay wist weill to de,
Thair cairfull sang and lamentatioun!
Sum with ane staf he straik to eirth on swoun,
Off sum the heid he straik, off sum he brak the crag,
Sum half on lyfe he stoppit in his bag.   1880

56

And quhen the swallow saw that thay wer deid,
'Lo,' quod scho, 'thus it happinnis mony syis
On thame that will not tak counsall nor reid
Off prudent men or clerkis that ar wyis;
This grit perrell I tauld thame mair than thryis;   1885
Now ar thay deid and wo is me thairfoir!'
Scho tuke hir flicht, bot I hir saw no moir.

Moralitas

Lo, worthie folk, Esope that nobill clerk,
Ane poet worthie to be lawreate,
Quhen that he waikit from mair autentik werk,   1890
With uther ma this foirsaid fabill wrate,
Quhilk at this tyme may weill be applicate
To gude morall edificatioun,
Haifand ane sentence according to ressoun.

This carll and bond of gentrice spoliate,   1895
Sawand this calf thir small birdis to sla,
It is the feind, quhilk fra the angelike state
Exylit is as fals apostata;
Quhilk day and nycht weryis not for to ga
Sawand poysoun in mony wickit thocht   1900
In mannis saull, quhilk Christ full deir hes bocht.

And quhen the saull as seid into the eird
Gevis consent unto delectioun,
The wickit thocht beginnis for to breird
In deidlie sin—quhilk is dampnatioun;   1905
Ressoun is blindit with affectioun,
And carnall lust grouis full grene and gay,
Throw consuetude hantit from day to day.

Proceding furth be use and consuetude,
The sin ryipis, and schame is set onsyde;   1910
The feynd plettis his nettis scharp and rude,
And under plesance previlie dois hyde;
Syne on the feild he sawis calf full wyde—
Quhilk is bot tume and verray vanitie
Of fleschlie lust and vaine prosperitie.   1915

Thir hungrie birdis wretchis we may call,
Ay scraipand in this warldis vane plesance,
Greddie to gadder gudis temporall,
Quhilk as the calf ar tume without substance,
Lytill of availl and full of variance,   1920
Lyke to the mow befoir the face of wind
Quhiskis away and makis wretchis blind.

This swallow quhilk eschaipit is the snair
The halie preichour weill may signifie,
Exhortand folk to walk and ay be wair   1925
Fra nettis of our wickit enemie—
Quha sleipis not, bot ever is reddie,
Quhen wretchis in this warld calf dois scraip,
To draw his net than thay may not eschaip.

Allace, quhat cair, quhat weiping is and wo   1930
Quhen saull and bodie departit ar in twane!
The bodie to the wormis keitching go,
The saull to fyre, to everlestand pane.
Quhat helpis than this calf, thir gudis vane,
Quhen thow art put in Luceferis bag   1935
And brocht to hell and hangit be the crag?

Thir hid nettis for to persave and se,
This sarie calf wyislie to understand,
Best is bewar in maist prosperitie;
For in this warld thair is na thing lestand;   1940
Is na man wait how lang his stait will stand,
His lyfe will lest, nor how that he sall end
Efter his deith, nor quhidder he sall wend.

Pray we thairfoir quhill we ar in this lyfe
For four thingis: the first, fra sin remufe;   1945
The secund is fra all weir and stryfe;
The thrid is perfite cheritie and lufe;
The feird thing is—and maist for oure behufe—
That is in blis with angellis to be fallow.
And thus endis the preiching of the swallow.   1950

The Taill of the Wolf that gat the Nek-hering throw the wrinkis of the Foxe that begylit the Cadgear

Qwhylum thair wynnit in ane wildernes—
As myne authour expreslie can declair—
Ane revand wolff that levit upon purches
On bestiall, and maid him weill to fair:
Wes nane sa big about him he wald spair,   1955
And he war hungrie, outher for favour or feid;
Bot in his wraith he weryit thame to deid.

Swa happinnit him in watching as he went
To meit ane foxe in middis off the way;
He him foirsaw and fenyeit to be schent,   1960
And with ane bek he bad the wolff gude-day.
'Welcum to me,' quod he, 'thow Russell gray!'
Syne loutit doun and tuke him be the hand:
'Ryse up, Lowrence! I leif the for to stand.

'Quhair hes thow bene this sesoun fra my sicht?   1965
Thow sall beir office and my stewart be;
For thow can knap doun caponis on the nicht,
And lourand law thow can gar hennis de.'
'Schir,' said the foxe, 'that ganis not for me;
And I am rad, gif thay me se onfar,   1970
That at my figure beist and bird will skar.'

'Na!' quod the wolff. 'Thow can in covert creip
Upon thy wame and hint thame be the heid;
And mak ane suddand schow upon ane scheip,
Syne with thy wappinnis wirrie him to deid.'   1975
'Schir,' said the foxe, 'ye knaw my roib is reid;
And thairfoir thair will na beist abyde me
Thocht I wald be sa fals as for to hyde me.'

'Yis,' quod the wolff, 'throw buskis and throw brais
Law can thow lour to cum to thy intent.'   1980
'Schir,' said the foxe, 'ye wait weill how it gais;
Ane lang space fra thame thay will feill my sent;
Than will thay eschaip suppois I suld be schent;
And I am schamefull for to cum behind thame,
Into the feild thocht I suld sleipand find thame.'   1985

'Na,' quod the wolff, 'thow can cum on the wind;
For everie wrink forsuith thow hes ane wyle.'
'Schir,' said the foxe, 'that beist ye micht call blind
That micht not eschaip than fra me ane myle:
How micht I ane off thame that wyis begyle?   1990
My tippit twa eiris and my twa gray ene
Garris me be kend quhair I wes never sene.'

'Than,' said the wolff, 'Lowrence I heir the le,
And castys for perrellis thy ginnes to defend;
Bot all thy [sonyes] sall not availl the,   1995
About the busk with wayis thocht thow wend;
Falset will failye ay at the latter end:
To bow at bidding and byde not quhill thow brest,
Thairfoir I giff the counsall for the best.'

'Schir,' said the foxe, 'it is Lentring ye se;   2000
I can nocht fische, for weiting off my feit,
To tak ane banestikill; thocht we baith suld de
I have nane uther craft to win my meit;
Bot wer it Pasche, that men suld pultrie eit,
As kiddis, lambis or caponis into ply,   2005
To beir your office than wald I not set by.'

'Than,' said the wolff in wraith, 'wenis thou with wylis
And with thy mony mowis me to mat?
It is ane auld dog, doutles, that thow begylis:
Thow wenis to drau the stra befoir the cat!'   2010
'Schir,' said the foxe, 'God wait I mene not that;
For and I did, it wer weill worth that ye
In ane reid raip had tyit me till ane tre.

60

'Bot nou I se he is ane fule perfay
That with his maister fallis in ressoning;   2015
I did bot till assay quhat ye wald say;
God wait, my mynd wes on ane uther thing;
I sall fulfill in all thing your bidding,
Quhatever ye charge on nichtis or on dayis.'
'Weill,' quod the wolff, 'I heir weill quhat thou sayis.   2020

'Bot yit I will thow mak to me ane aith
For to be leill attour all levand leid.'
'Schir,' said the foxe, 'that ane word maks me wraith—
For nou I se ye have me at ane dreid:
Yit sall I sweir, suppois it be nocht neid,   2025
Be Juppiter and on pane off my heid,
I sall be treu to you quhill I be deid.'

With that ane cadgear with capill and with creillis
Come carpand furth; than Lawrence culd him spy:
The foxe the flewer off the fresche hering feillis,   2030
And to the wolff he roundis prively:
'Schir, yone ar hering the cadgear caryis by;
Thairfoir I reid that we se for sum wayis
To get sum fische aganis thir fasting dayis.

'Sen I am stewart I wald we had sum stuff;   2035
And ye ar silver-seik, I wait richt weill;
Thocht we wald thig, yone verray churlische chuff
He will not giff us ane hering off his creill—
Befoir yone churle on kneis thocht we wald kneill;
Bot yit I trou alsone that ye sall se   2040
Giff I can craft to bleir yone carlis ee.

'Schir, ane thing is, and we get off yone pelff,
Ye man tak travell and mak us sum supple;
For he that will not laubour and help himselff
Into thir dayis—he is not worth ane fle;   2045
I think to work als besie as ane be;
And ye sall follou ane lytill efterwart
And gadder hering, for that sall be your part.'

With that he kest ane cumpas far about
And straucht him doun in middis off the way—   2050
As he wer deid he fenyeit him but dout,
And than upon lenth unliklie lay;
The quhyte he turnit up off his ene tuay,
His toung out hang ane handbreid off his heid,
And still he lay, als straucht as he wer deid.   2055

The cadgear fand the foxe and he wes fane;
And till himself thus softlie can he say:
'At the nixt bait in faith ye sall be flane,
And off your skyn I sall mak mittenis tway.'
He lap full lichtlie about him quhair he lay,   2060
And all the trace he trippit on his tais;
As he had hard ane pyper play he gais.

'Heir lyis the devyll,' quod he, 'deid in ane dyke:
Sic ane selcouth sau I not this sevin yeir;
I trou ye have bene tussillit with sum tyke,   2065
That garris yeu ly sa still withoutin steir:
Schir Foxe, in faith ye ar deir welcum heir;
It is sum wyfis malisone, I trow,
For pultrie pyking, that lychtit hes on yow.

'Thair sall na pedder for purs nor yit for glufis,   2070
Nor yit for poyntis, pyke your pellet fra me;
I sall off it mak mittenis to my lufis,
Till hald my handis hait quhairever I be;
Till Flanderis sall it never saill the se.'
With that in hy he hint him be the heillis,   2075
And with ane swak he swang him on the creillis.

Syne be the heid the hors in hy hes hint;
The fraudfull foxe thairto gude tent hes tane,
And with his teith the stoppell, or he stint,
Pullit out, and syne the hering ane and ane   2080
Out off the creillis he swakkit doun gude wane:
The wolff wes war, and gadderit spedilie;
The cadgear sang 'Huntis up, up!' upon hie.

Yit at ane burne the cadgear lukit about;
With that the foxe lap quyte the creillis fray;   2085
The cadgear wald have raucht the foxe ane rout—
Bot all for nocht: he wan his hoill that day.
Than with ane schout thus can the cadgear say:
'Abyde! And thou ane nek-hering sall haif
Is worth my capill, creillis and all the laif.'   2090

'Now,' quod the foxe, 'I schreu me and we meit:
I hard quhat thou hecht to do with my skyn.
Thy handis sall never in thay mittinnis tak heit—
And thou wer hangit, carll, and all thy kyn!
Do furth thy mercat; at me thou sall nocht wyn;   2095
And sell thy hering thou hes thair till hie price—
Ellis thow sall wyn nocht on thy merchandice.'

The cadgear trimmillit for teyne quhair that he stude:
'It is weill worthie,' quod he, 'I want yone tyke,
That had nocht in my hand sa mekill gude   2100
As staff or sting yone truker for to stryke!'
With that lychtlie he lap out over ane dyke
And hakkit doun ane staff—for he wes tene—
That hevie wes and off the holyne grene.

With that the foxe unto the wolff could wend   2105
And fand him be the hering quhair he lyis:
'Schir,' said he than, 'maid I not fair defend?
Ane wicht man wantit never and he wer wyis;
Ane hardie hart is hard for to suppryis.'
Than said the wolff: 'Thow art ane berne full bald   2110
And wyse at will—in gude tyme be it tald.

'Bot quhat wes yone the carll cryit on hie,
And schuke his hand?' quod he. 'Hes thou no feill?'
'Schir,' said the foxe, 'that I can tell trewlie;
He said the nek-hering wes intill the creill.'   2115
'Kennis thou that hering?' 'Ye, schir, I ken it weill,
And at the creill-mouth I had it thryis but dout;
The wecht off it neir tit my tuskis out.

'Now suithlie schir, micht we that hering fang
It wald be fische to us thir fourtie dayis.'   2120
Than said the wolff: 'Nou God nor that I hang,
Bot to be thair I wald gif all my clays
To se gif that my wappinnis mycht it rais.'
'Schir,' said the foxe, 'God wait, I wischit you oft
Quhen that my pith micht not beir it onloft.   2125

'It is ane syde off salmond, as it wair,
And callour, pypand lyke ane pertrik ee;
It is worth all the hering ye have thair—
Ye, and we had it swa, is it worth sic thre.'
'Than,' said the wolff, 'quhat counsell gevis thou me?'   2130
'Schir,' said the foxe, 'wirk efter my devyis
And ye sall have it—and tak you na suppryis.

'First ye man cast ane cumpas far about;
Syne straucht you doun in middis off the way;
Baith heid and feit and taill ye man streik out;   2135
Hing furth your toung and clois weill your ene tway;
Syne se your heid on ane hard place ye lay;
And dout not for na perrell may appeir,
Bot hald you clois quhen that the carll cummis neir.

'And thocht ye se ane staf, have ye na dout,   2140
Bot hald you wonder still into that steid;
And luke your ene be clois as thay wer out,
And se that ye schrink nouther fute nor heid:
Than will the cadgear carll trou ye be deid
And intill haist will hint you be the heillis   2145
As he did me, and swak you on his creillis.'

'Now,' quod the wolff, 'I sweir the be my thrift
I trou yone cadgear carll he will me beir.'
'Schir,' said the foxe, 'onloft he will you lift
Upon his creillis—and do him lytill deir: 2150
Bot ane thing dar I suithlie to you sweir—
Get ye that hering sicker in sum place,
Ye sall not fair in fisching mair quhill Pasche.

'I sall say *In Principio* upon yow,
And crose your corps from the top to tay;   2155
Wend quhen ye will, I dar be warrand now
That ye sall de na suddand deith this day!'
With that the wolff gird up sone and to gay,
And caist ane cumpas about the cadgear far;
Syne raucht him in the gait or he come nar.   2160

He laid his halfheid sicker hard and sad,
Syne straucht his four feit fra him and his heid,
And hang his toung furth as the foxe him bad;
Als styll he lay as he wer verray deid,
Rakkand nathing off the carlis favour nor feid;   2165
Bot ever upon the nek-hering he thinkis,
And quyte forgettis the foxe and all his wrinkis.

With that the cadgear, wavering as the wind,
Come rydand on the laid, for it wes licht,
Thinkand ay on the foxe that wes behind—   2170
Upon quhat wyse revengit on him he micht;
And at the last of the wolff gat ane sicht
Quhair he in lenth lay streikit in the gait;
Bot giff he lichtit doun or nocht, God wait!

Softlie he said: 'I wes begylit anis—   2175
Be I be gylit twyis I schrew us baith,
That evill bot it sall licht upon thy banis
He suld have had that hes done me the skaith!'
On hicht he hovit the staf, for he wes wraith,
And hit him with sic will upon the heid   2180
Quhill neir he swonit and swelt into that steid.

Thre battis he bure or he his feit micht find;
Bot yit the wolff wes wicht and wan away;
He mycht not se—he wes sa verray blind—
Nor wit reddilie quhether it wes nicht or day.   2185
The foxe beheld that service quhair he lay
And leuch onloft quhen he the wolff sa seis,
Baith deif and dosinnit, fall swonand on his kneis.

He that of ressoun can not be content,
Bot covetis all, is abill all to tyne: 2190
The foxe quhen that he saw the wolff wes schent
Said to himself: 'Thir hering sall be myne.'
I le or ellis he wes efterwart [fyne]
That fand sic wayis his maister for to greif:
With all the fische thus Lowrence tuke his leif.   2195

The wolff wes neir weill dungin to the deid,
That uneith with his lyfe away he wan—
For with the bastoun weill brokin wes his heid.
The foxe into his den sone drew him than,
That had betraisit his maister and the man: 2200
The ane wantit the hering off his creillis,
The utheris blude wes rynnand over his heillis.

Moralitas

This taill is myngit with moralitie,
As I sall schaw sumquhat or that I ceis:
The foxe unto the warld may likkinnit be;   2205
The revand wolf unto ane man but leis;
The cadgear deith quhome under all man preis—
That ever tuke lyfe throw cours of kynd man dee,
As man and beist and fische into the see.

The warld, ye wait, is stewart to the man,   2210
Quhilk makis man to haif na mynd of deid,
Bot settis for winning all the craftis thay can;
The hering I likkin unto the gold sa reid,
Quhilk gart the wolf in perrell put his heid—
Richt swa the gold garris landis and cieteis   2215
With weir be waistit daylie as men seis.

And as the foxe with dissimulance and gyle
Gart the wolf wene to haif worschip for ever,
Richt swa this warld with vane-glore for ane quhyle

66

Flatteris with folk as thay suld failye never—   2220
Yit suddandlie men seis it oft dissever;
With thame that trowis oft to fill the sek,
Deith cummis behind and nippis thame be the nek.

The micht of gold makis mony men sa blind,
That settis on avarice thair felicitie,   2225
That thay foryet the cadgear cummis behind
To stryke thame—of quhat stait sa ever thay be:
Quhat is mair dirk than blind prosperitie?
Quhairfoir I counsell mychtie men to haif mynd
Of the nek-hering interpreit in this kynd.   2230

10

The Taill of the Foxe that begylit the Wolf in the schadow of the Mone

In elderis dayis, as Esope can declair,
Thair wes ane husband quhilk had ane plewch to steir.
His use wes ay in morning to ryse air:
Sa happinnit him in streiking-tyme off yeir
Airlie in the morning to follou furth his feir   2235
Unto the pleuch, bot his gadman and he;
His stottis he straucht with 'Benedicite!'

The caller cryit: 'How! Haik upon hicht!
Hald draucht my dowis!' Syne broddit thame full sair:
The oxin wes unwsit, young and licht,   2240
And for fersnes thay couth the fur forfair:
The husband than woxe angrie as ane hair,
Syne cryit and caist his patill and grit stanis;
'The wolff,' quod he, 'mot have you all at anis!'

Bot yit the wolff wes neirar nor he wend,   2245
For in ane busk he lay, and Lowrence baith,
In ane rouch rone wes at the furris end,

67

And hard the hecht: than Lowrence leuch full raith:
'To tak yone bud,' quod he, 'it wer na skaith!'
'Weill,' quod the wolff, 'I hecht the, be my hand,   2250
Yone carlis word as he wer king sall stand!'

The oxin waxit mair reulie at the last;
Syne efter thay lousit, fra that it worthit weill lait;
The husband hamewart with his cattell past.
Than sone the wolff come hirpilland in his gait   2255
Befoir the oxin, and schupe to mak debait.
The husband saw him and worthit sumdeill agast,
And bakwart with his beistis wald haif past.

The wolff said: 'Quhether dryvis thou this, pray?
I chalenge it, for nane off thame ar thyne!'   2260
The man thairoff wes in ane felloun fray
And soberlie to the wolff answerit syne:
'Schir, be my saull, thir oxin ar all myne;
Thairfoir I studdie quhy ye suld stop me,
Sen that I faltit never to you trewlie.'   2265

The wolff said: 'Carll, gaif thou not me this drift
Airlie, quhen thou wes eirrand on yone bank?
And is thair oucht, sayis thou, frear than gift?
This tarying wyll tyne the all thy thank;
Far better is frelie for to giff ane plank   2270
Nor be compellit on force to giff ane mart:
Fy on the fredome that cummis not with hart!'

'Schir,' quod the husband, 'ane man may say in greif,
And syne ganesay fra he avise and se:
I hecht to steill—am I thairfoir ane theif?'   2275
'God forbid, schir, all hechtis suld haldin be!'
'Gaif I my hand or oblissing?' quod he:
'Or have ye witnes or writ for to schau?
Schir, reif me not, but go and seik the lau!'

68

'Carll,' quod the wolff, 'ane lord, and he be leill,   2280
That schrinkis for schame or doutis to be repruvit—
His sau is ay als sikker as his seill:
Fy on the leid that is not leill and lufit!
Thy argument is fals and eik contrufit,
For it is said in proverb: "But lawte   2285
All uther vertewis ar nocht worth ane fle." '

'Schir,' said the husband, 'remember of this thing:
Ane leill man is not tane at halff ane taill:
I may say and ganesay—I am na king.
Quhair is your witnes that hard I hecht thame haill?'   2290
Than said the wolff: 'Thairfoir it sall nocht faill;
Lowrence,' quod he, 'cum hidder of that schaw,
And say na thing bot as thow hard and saw!'

Lowrence come lourand—for he lufit never licht—
And sone appeirit befoir thame in that place;   2295
The man leuch nathing quhen he saw that sicht;
'Lowrence,' quod the wolff, 'thow man declair this cace,
Quhairof we sall schaw the suith in schort space;
I callit on the leill witnes for to beir:
Quhat hard thou that this man hecht me lang eir?'   2300

'Schir,' said the tod, 'I can not hastelie
Swa sone as now gif sentence finall;
Bot wald ye baith submit yow heir to me,
To stand at my decreit perpetuall,
To pleis baith I suld preif gif it may fall.'   2305
'Weill,' quod the wolff, 'I am content for me.'
The man said: 'Swa am I how ever it be.'

Than schew thay furth thair allegeance but fabill,
And baith proponit thair pley to him compleit:
Quod Lowrence: 'Now I am ane juge amycabill: 2310
Ye sall be sworne to stand at my decreit,
Quhether heirefter ye think it soure or sweit.'
The wolff braid furth his fute, the man his hand,
And on the toddis taill sworne thay ar to stand.

Than tuke the tod the man furth till ane syde   2315
And said him: 'Freind, thou art in blunder brocht;
The wolff will not forgif the ane oxe-hyde—
Yit wald myself fane help the and I mocht;
Bot I am laith to hurt my conscience ocht:
Tyne nocht thy querrell in thy awin defence—   2320
This will not throu but grit coist and expence.

'Seis thou not buddis beiris bernis throw,
And giftis garris crukit materis hald full evin?
Sumtymis ane hen haldis ane man in ane kow;
All ar not halie that heifis thair handis to hevin.'   2325
'Schir,' said the man, 'ye sall have sex or sevin
Richt off the fattest hennis off all the floik:
I compt not all the laif, leif me the coik.'

'I am ane juge!' quod Lowrence than and leuch:
'Thair is na buddis suld beir me by the rycht;   2330
I may tak hennis and caponis weill aneuch,
For God is gane to sleip; as for this nycht,
Sic small thingis ar not sene into His sicht.
Thir hennis,' quod he, 'sall mak thy querrell sure:
With emptie hand na man suld halkis lure.'   2335

Concordit thus, than Lowrence tuke his leiff
And to the wolff he went into ane ling;
Syne prevelie he plukkit him be the sleiff:
'Is this in ernist,' quod he, 'ye ask sic thing?
Na be my saull, I trow it be in heithing!'   2340
Than said the wolff: 'Lowrence, quhy sayis thou sa?
Thow hard the hecht thyselff that he couth ma.'

'The hecht,' quod he, 'yone man maid at the pleuch—
Is that the cause quhy ye the cattell craif?'
Halff into heithing said Lowrence than and leuch: 2345
'Schir, be the Rude, unroikit now ye raif:
The devill ane stirk taill thairfoir sall ye haif!
Wald I tak it upon my conscience
To do sa pure ane man as yone offence?

'Yit haif I commonnit with the carll,' quod he;   2350
'We ar concordit upon this cunnand:
Quyte off all clamis, swa ye will mak him fre,
Ye sall ane cabok have into your hand
That sic ane sall not be in all this land;
For it is somer cheis, baith fresche and fair;   2355
He sayis it weyis ane stane and sumdeill mair.'

'Is that thy counsell,' quod the wolff, 'I do—
That yone carll for ane cabok suld be fre?'
'Ye be my saull, and I wer sworne yow to,
Ye suld nane uther counsell have for me;   2360
For gang ye to the maist extremitie,
It will not wyn yow worth ane widderit neip;
Schir, trow ye not I have ane saull to keip?'

'Weill,' quod the wolff, 'it is aganis my will
That yone carll for ane cabok suld ga quyte.'   2365
'Schir,' quod the tod, 'ye tak it in nane evill,
For be my saull, yourself had all the wyte.'
'Than,' said the wolff, 'I bid na mair to flyte—
Bot I wald se yone cabok off sic pryis.'
'Schir,' said the tod, 'he tauld me quhair it lyis.'   2370

Than hand in hand thay held unto ane hill;
The husband till his [hous] hes tane the way,
For he wes fane; he schaippit from thair ill
And on his feit woke the dure quhill day.
Now will we turne unto the uther tway: 2375
Throw woddis waist thir freikis on fute can fair
Fra busk to busk quhill neir midnycht and mair.

Lowrence wes ever remembring upon wrinkis
And subtelteis the wolff for to begyle;
That he had hecht ane caboik he forthinkis;   2380
Yit at the last he findis furth ane wyle,
Than at himselff softlie couth he smyle.
The wolff sayis: 'Lowrence, thow playis bellie-blind;
We seik all nycht bot nathing can we find.'

71

'Schir,' said the tod, 'we ar at it almaist;   2385
Soft yow ane lytill, and ye sall se it sone.'
Than to ane manure-place thay hyit in haist.
The nycht wes lycht and pennyfull the mone:
Than till ane draw-well thir senyeours past but hone,
Quhair that twa bukkettis severall suithlie hang;   2390
As ane come up ane uther doun wald gang.

The schadow off the mone schone in the well:
'Schir,' said Lowrence, 'anis ye sall find me leill;
Now se ye not the caboik weill yoursell,
Quhyte as ane neip and round als as ane seill?   2395
He hang it yonder that na man suld it steill;
Schir, traist ye weill, yone caboik ye se hing
Micht be ane present to ony lord or king!'

'Na,' quod the wolff, 'mycht I yone caboik haif
On the dry land as I it yonder se,   2400
I wald quitclame the carll off all the laif—
His dart-oxin I compt thame not ane fle—
Yone wer mair meit for sic ane man as me.
Lowrence,' quod he, 'leip in the bukket sone,
And I sall hald the ane quhill thow have done.'   2405

Lowrence gird doun baith sone and subtellie;
The uther baid abufe and held the flaill:
'It is sa mekill,' quod Lowrence, 'it maisteris me—
On all my tais it hes not left ane naill;
Ye man mak help upwart and it haill: 2410
Leip in the uther bukket haistelie,
And cum sone doun and mak me sum supple!'

Than lychtlie in the bukket lap the loun—
His wecht but weir the uther end gart ryis;
The tod come hailland up, the wolff yeid doun: 2415
Than angerlie the wolff upon him cryis:
'I cummand thus dounwart, quhy thow upwart hyis?'
'Schir,' quod the foxe, 'thus fairis it off Fortoun—
As ane cummis up scho quheillis ane uther doun!'

Than to the ground sone yeid the wolff in haist;   2420
The tod lap on land als blyith as ony bell
And left the wolff in watter to the waist:
Quha haillit him out, I wait not, off the well.
Heir endis the text—thair is na mair to tell.
Yit men may find ane gude moralitie   2425
In this sentence, thocht it ane fabill be.

Moralitas

This wolf I likkin to ane wickit man
Quhilk dois the pure oppres in everie place,
And pykis at thame all querrellis that he can,
Be rigour, reif and uther wickitnes: 2430
The foxe the feind I call into this cais,
Actand ilk man to ryn unrychteous rinkis,
Thinkand thairthrow to lok him in his linkis.

The husband may be callit ane godlie man
With quhome the feynd falt findes, as clerkis reids,   2435
Besie to tempt him with all wayis that he can;
The hennis ar warkis that fra ferme faith proceidis—
Quhair sic sproutis spreidis, the evill spreit thair not speidis,
Bot wendis unto the wickit man agane;
That he hes tint his travell is full unfane.   2440

The wodds waist quhairin wes the wolf wyld
Ar wickit riches quhilk all men gaipis to get;
Quha traistis in sic trusterie ar oft begyld;
For Mammon may be callit the devillis net,
Quhilk Sathanas for all sinfull hes set: 2445
With proud plesour quha settis his traist thairin,
But speciall grace lychtlie can not outwin.

The cabok may be callit covetyce,
Quhilk blomis braid in mony mannis ee—
Wa worth the well of that wickit vyce,   2450
For it is all bot fraud and fantasie,

73

Dryvand ilk man to leip in the buttrie
That dounwart drawis unto the pane of hell!
Christ keip all Christianis from that wickit well!

II

The Taill of the Wolf and the Wedder

Qwhylum thair wes, as Esope can report,   2455
Ane scheipheird duelland be ane forrest neir,
Quhilk had ane hound that did him grit comfort;
Full war he wes to walk his fauld but weir,
That nouther wolff, nor wild cat durst appeir,
Nor foxe on feild nor yit no uther beist—   2460
Bot he thame slew or chaissit at the leist.

Sa happinnit it—as everilk beist man de—
This hound off suddand seiknes to be deid;
Bot than, God wait, the keipar off the fe
For verray wo woxe wanner nor the weid: 2465
'Allace,' quod he, 'now se I na remeid
To saif the selie beistis that I keip,
For [with] the wolff weryit beis all my scheip!'

It wald have maid ane mannis hart sair to se
The selie scheiphirdis lamentatioun: 2470
'Now is my darling deid, allace!' quod he;
'For now to beg my breid I may be boun,
With pyikstaff and with scrip to fair off toun;
For all the beistis befoir bandonit bene
Will schute upon my beistis with ire and tene!'   2475

With that ane wedder [wichtlie] wan on fute:
'Maister', quod he, 'mak merie and be blyith:
To brek your hart for baill it is na bute;
For ane deid dogge ye na cair on yow kyith:
Ga fetche him hither and fla his skyn off swyth;   2480
Syne sew it on me—and luke that it be meit,
Baith heid and crag, bodie, taill and feit.

'Than will the wolff trow that I am he,
For I sall follow him fast quharever he fair.
All haill the cure I tak it upon me   2485
Your scheip to keip at midday, lait and air.
And he persew, be God, I sall not spair
To follow him as fast as did your doig,
Swa that I warrand ye sall not want ane hoig.'

Than said the scheipheird: 'This come of ane gude wit; 2490
Thy counsall is baith sicker, leill and trew;
Quha sayis ane scheip is daft, thay lieit of it.'
With that in hy the doggis skyn off he flew
And on the scheip rycht softlie couth it sew.
Than worth the wedder wantoun off his weid: 2495
'Now off the wolff,' quod he, 'I have na dreid.'

In all thingis he counterfait the dog,
For all the nycht he stude and tuke na sleip—
Swa that weill lang thair wantit not ane hog:
Swa war he wes and walkryfe thame to keip,   2500
That Lowrence durst not luke upon ane scheip—
For and he did, he followit him sa fast
That off his lyfe he maid him all agast.

Was nowther wolff, wild cat nor yit tod
Durst cum within thay boundis all about,   2505
Bot he wald chase thame baith throw rouch and snod;
Thay bailfull beistis had of their lyvis sic dout,
For he wes mekill and semit to be stout,
That everilk beist thay dreid him as the deid
Within that woid, that nane durst hald thair heid.   2510

Yit happinnit thair ane hungrie wolff to slyde
Out throw his scheip quhair thay lay on ane le;
'I sall have ane,' quod he, 'quhatever betyde—
Thocht I be werryit, for hunger or I de!'
With that ane lamb intill his cluke hint he.   2515
The laif start up for thay wer all agast:
Bot God wait gif the wedder followit fast!

Went never hound mair haistelie fra the hand
Quhen he wes rynnand maist raklie at the ra
Nor went this wedder baith over mois and strand,   2520
And stoppit nouther at bank, busk nor bra,
Bot followit ay sa ferslie on his fa,
With sic ane drift, quhill dust and dirt over-draif him,
And maid ane vow to God that he suld have him.

With that the wolff let out his taill on lenth,   2525
For he wes hungrie and it drew neir the ene,
And schupe him for to ryn with all his strenth,
Fra he the wedder sa neir cummand had sene:
He dred his lyfe and he overtane had bene;
Thairfoir he spairit nowther busk nor boig,   2530
For weill he kennit the kenenes off the doig.

To mak him lycht he kest the lamb him fra,
Syne lap over leis and draif throw dub and myre.
'Na,' quod the wedder, 'in faith, we part not swa:
It is not the lamb bot the that I desyre;   2535
I sall cum neir, for now I se the tyre.'
The wolff ran still quhill ane strand stude behind him—
Bot ay the neirar the wedder he couth bind him.

Sone efter that he followit him sa neir
Quhill that the wolff for fleidnes fylit the feild;   2540
Syne left the gait and ran throw busk and breir,
And schupe him fra the schawis for to scheild.
He ran restles, for he wist off na beild;
The wedder followit him baith out and in,
Quhill that ane breir-busk raif rudelie off the skyn.   2545

The wolff wes wer and blenkit him behind
And saw the wedder come thrawand throw the breir,
[Syne] saw the doggis skyn hingand on his lind:
'Na,' quod he, 'is this ye that is sa neir?
Richt now ane hound and now quhyte as ane freir;   2550
I fled over-fer and I had kennit the cais:
To God I vow that ye sall rew this rais!

'Quhat wes the cause ye gaif me sic ane katche?'
With that in hy he hint him be the horne:
'For all your mowis ye met anis with your matche,   2555
Suppois ye leuch me all this yeir to scorne.
For quhat enchessoun this doggis skyn have ye borne?'
'Maister,' quod he, 'bot to have playit with yow;
I yow requyre that ye nane uther trow.'

'Is this your bourding in ernist than?' quod he: 2560
'For I am verray effeirit and on flocht;
Cum bak agane and I sall let yow se.'
Than quhar the gait wes grimmit he him brocht:
'Quhether call ye this fair play or nocht—
To set your maister in sa fell effray   2565
Quhill he for feiritnes hes fylit up the way?

'Thryis, be my saull, ye gart me schute behind—
Upon my hoichis the senyeis may be sene;
For feiritnes full oft I fylit the wind:
Now is this ye? Na, bot ane hound I wene!   2570
Me think your teith over-schort to be sa kene.
Blissit be the busk that reft yow your array,
Ellis fleand, bursin had I bene this day!'

'Schir,' quod the wedder, 'suppois I ran in hy,
My mynd wes never to do your persoun ill;   2575
Ane flear gettis ane follower commounly,
In play or ernist—preif quhasaever will:
Sen I bot playit, be gracious me till,
And I sall gar my freindis blis your banis:
Ane full gude servand will crab his maister anis.'   2580

'I have bene oftymis set in grit effray;
Bot be the Rude, sa rad yit wes I never
As thow hes maid me with thy prettie play.
I schot behind quhen thow overtuke me ever;
Bot sikkerlie now sall we not dissever!'   2585
Than be the crag-bane smertlie he him tuke
Or ever he ceissit, and it in-schunder schuke.

77

Esope that poete, first father of this fabill,
Wrait this parabole—quhilk is convenient
Because the sentence wes fructuous and agreabill,   2590
In moralitie exemplative prudent—
Quhais problemes bene verray excellent;
Throw similitude of figuris, to this day,
Gevis doctrine to the redaris of it ay.

Heir may thow se that riches of array   2595
Will cause pure men presumpteous for to be;
Thay think thay hald of nane, be thay als gay,
Bot counterfute ane lord in all degre.
Out of thair cais in pryde thay clym sa hie
That thay forbeir thair better in na steid—   2600
Quhill sum man tit thair heillis over thair heid.

Richt swa in service uther sum exceidis,
And thay haif withgang, welth and cherising,
That thay will lychtlie lordis in thair deidis,
And lukis not to thair blude nor thair offspring: 2605
Bot yit nane wait how lang that reull will ring;
Bot he wes wyse that bad his sone considder:
'Bewar in welth, for hall-benkis ar rycht slidder!'

Thairfoir I counsell men of everilk stait
To knaw thameself and quhome thay suld forbeir,   2610
And fall not with thair better in debait,
Suppois thay be als galland in thair geir:
It settis na servand for to uphald weir,
Nor clym sa hie quhill he fall of the ledder;
Bot think upon the wolf and on the wedder.   2615

12

The Taill of the Wolf and the Lamb

Ane cruell wolff richt ravenous and fell
Upon ane tyme past to ane reveir
Descending from ane rotche unto ane well;

To slaik his thrist drank of the watter cleir.
Swa upon cace ane selie lamb come neir;   2620
Bot of his fa the wolff nathing he wist,
And in the streme laipit to cule his thrist.

Thus drank thay baith—bot not of ane intent:
The wolfis thocht wes all on wickitnes,
The selie lamb wes meik and innocent: 2625
Upon the rever in ane uther place
Beneth the wolff he drank ane lytill space
Quhill he thocht gude, belevand thair nane ill:
The wolff him saw and rampand come him till.

With girnand teith and awfull angrie luke   2630
Said to the lamb: 'Thow cative wretchit thing!
How durst thow be sa bald to fyle and bruke,
Quhar I suld drink, with thy foull slavering?
It wer almous the for to draw and hing
That suld presume, with thy foull lippis vyle,   2635
To glar my drink and this fair watter fyle!'

The selie lamb, quaikand for verray dreid,
On kneis fell and said: 'Schir, with yuor leif,
Suppois I dar not say thairoff ye leid,
Bot be my saull, I wait ye can nocht preif   2640
That I did ony thing that suld yow greif;
Ye wait alswa that your accusatioun
Failyeis fra treuth and contrair is to ressoun.

'Thocht I can nocht, nature will me defend,
And off the deid perfyte experience: 2645
All hevie thing man off the selff discend—
Bot giff sum thing on force mak resistence—
Than may the streme on na way mak ascence
Nor ryn bakwart: I drank beneth yow far:
Ergo, for me your bruke wes never the war.   2650

79

Alswa my lippis, sen that I wes ane lam,
Tuitchit na thing that wes contagious;
Bot sowkit milk from pappis off my dam,
Richt naturall, sweit and als delitious.'
'Weill,' quod the wolff, 'thy language rigorous   2655
Cummis the off kynd; swa thy father before
Held me at bait baith with boist and schore.

'He wraithit me—and than I culd him warne
Within ane yeir, and I brukit my heid,
I suld be wrokkin on him or on his barne   2660
For his exorbetant and frawart pleid:
Thow sall doutles for his deidis be deid!'
'Schir, it is wrang that for the fatheris gilt
The saikles sone suld punist be or spilt!

'Haif ye not hard quhat Halie Scripture sayis,   2665
Endytit with the mouth off God Almycht?
Off his awin deidis ilk man sall beir the prais—
As pane for sin, reward for werkis rycht:
For my trespas quhy suld my sone have plycht?
Quha did the mis lat him sustene the pane!'   2670
'Yaa!' quod the wolff. 'Yit pleyis thow agane?

'I let the wit quhen that the father offendis,
I will refuse nane off his successioun;
And off his barnis I may weill tak amendis
Unto the twentie degre descending doun.   2675
Thy father thocht to mak ane strang poysoun,
And with his mouth in my watter did spew.'
'Schir,' quod the lamb, 'thay twa ar nouther trew!

'The law sayis, and ye will understand,
Thair suld na man for wrang nor violence   2680
His adversar punis at his awin hand,
Without proces off law and evidence;
Quhilk suld have leif to mak lawfull defence,
And thairupon summond peremtourly
For to propone, contrairie or reply.   2685

80

'Set me ane lauchfull court, I sall compeir
Befoir the lyoun, lord and leill justice;
And be my hand, I oblis me rycht heir,
That I sall byde ane unsuspect assyis:
This is the law, this is the instant gyis;   2690
Ye suld pretend thairfoir; ane summondis mak
Aganis that day to gif ressoun and tak.'

'Na!' quod the wolff. 'Thou wald intruse ressoun
Quhair wrang and reif suld duell in propertie:
That is ane poynt and part of fals tressoun,   2695
For to gar reuth remane with crueltie.
Be His woundis, fals tratour thow sall de
For thy trespas and for thy fatheris als!'
With that anone he hint him be the hals.

The selie lamb culd do na thing bot bleit: 2700
Sone wes he deid—the wolff wald do na grace;
Syne drank his blude and off his flesche can eit
Quhill he wes full, and went his way onpace.
Of his murther quhat sall we say, allace?
Wes not this reuth—wes not this grit pietie   2705
To gar this selie lamb but gilt thus de?

Moralitas

The pure pepill this lamb may signifie—
As maill-men, merchandis and all lauboureris,
Of quhome the lyfe is half ane purgatorie
To wyn with lautie leving as efferis;   2710
The wolf betakinnis fals extortioneris
And oppressouris of pure men—as we se—
Be violence or craft in facultie.

Thre kynd of wolfis in this warld now rings:
The first ar fals perverteris of the lawis,   2715
Quhilk under [poleit] termis falset mingis,

Lettand that all wer gospell that he schawis;
Bot for ane bud the pure man he overthrawis,
Smoirand the richt, garrand the wrang proceid:
Of sic wolfis hellis fyre sall be thair meid.   2720

O man of law, let be thy subteltie,
With nice gimpis and fraudis intricait!
And think that God, in His Divinitie,
The wrang, the richt, of all thy werkis wait.
For prayer, price, for hie nor law estait   2725
Of fals querrellis se thow mak na defence!
Hald with the richt, hurt not thy conscience!

Ane-uther kynd of wolfis ravenous
Ar mychtie men haifand full grit plentie,
Quhilk ar sa gredie and sa covetous   2730
Thay will not thoill the pure in pece to be;
Suppois he and his houshald baith suld de
For falt of fude, thairof thay gif na rak,
Bot over his heid his mailling will thay tak.

O man, but mercie quhat is in thy thocht?   2735
War than ane wolf and thow culd understand!
Thow hes aneuch—the pure husband richt nocht
Bot croip and caff upon ane clout of land.
For Goddis aw, how durst thow tak on hand—
And thow in barn and byre sa bene and big—   2740
To put him fra his tak and gar him thig?

The thrid wolf ar men of heritage—
As lordis that hes land be Goddis lane,
And settis to the mailleris ane village,
And for ane tyme gressome payit and tane;   2745
Syne vexis him or half his terme be gane,
With pykit querrellis for to mak him fane
To flit or pay his gressome new agane.

82

His hors, his meir, he man len to the laird,
To drug and draw in court or in cariage; 2750
His servand or his self may not be spaird
To swing and sweit withoutin meit or wage:
Thus how he standis in labour and bondage,
That scantlie may he purches by his maill
To leve upon dry breid and watter-caill. 2755

Hes thow not reuth to gar thy tennentis sweit
Into thy laubour with faynt and hungrie wame,
And syne hes lytill gude to drink or eit
With his menye at evin quhen he cummis hame?
Thow suld dreid for richteous Goddis blame; 2760
For it cryis ane vengeance unto the hevinnis hie
To gar ane pure man wirk but meit or fe.

O thow grit lord that riches hes and rent,
Be nocht ane wolf thus to devoir the pure!
Think that nathing cruell nor violent 2765
May in this warld perpetuallie indure:
This sall thow trow and sikkerlie assure—
For till oppres thow sall haif als grit pane,
As thow the pure had with thy awin hand [slane].

God keip the lamb, quhilk is the innocent, 2770
From wolfis byit and fell exortioneris;
God grant that wrangous men of fals intent
Be manifestit and punischit as effeiris;
And God, as Thow all rychteous prayer heiris,
Mot saif our king and gif him hart and hand 2775
All sic wolfis to banes out of the land.

13

The Taill of the Paddok and the Mous

Upon ane tyme, as Esope culd report,
Ane lytill mous come till ane rever-syde;
Scho micht not waid—hir schankis were sa schort;

Scho culd not swym; scho had na hors to ryde: 2780
Of verray force behovit hir to byde,
And to and fra besyde that revir deip
Scho ran, cryand with mony pietuous peip.

'Help over! Help over!' this silie mous can cry,
'For Goddis lufe, sumbodie over the brym!'   2785
With that ane paddok, in the watter by,
Put up hir heid and on the bank can clym,
Quhilk be nature culd douk and gaylie swym;
With voce full [rauk] scho said on this maneir:
'Gude morne, Schir Mous! Quhat is your erand heir?' 2790

'Seis thow,' quod scho, 'off corne yone jolie flat,
Off ryip aitis, off barlie, peis and quheit?
I am hungrie and fane wald be thairat;
Bot I am stoppit be this watter greit;
And on this syde I get na thing till eit   2795
Bot hard nuttis quhilkis with my teith I bore:
Wer I beyond, my feist wer fer the more.

'I have no boit; heir is no maryner;
And thocht thair war, I have no fraucht to pay.'
Quod scho: 'Sister lat be thy hevie cheir!   2800
Do my counsall and I sall find the way,
Without hors, brig, boit or yit galay,
To bring the over saiflie—be not afeird—
And not wetand the campis off thy beird!'

'I haif grit wounder,' quod the lytill mous,   2805
'How can thow fleit without fedder or fin:
This rever is sa deip and dangerous,
Me think that thow suld drounit be thairin:
Tell me thairfoir quhat facultie or gin
Thow hes to bring the over this watter wan.'   2810
That to declair the paddok thus began:

84

'With my twa feit,' quod scho, 'lukkin and braid,
Insteid off airis I row the streme full styll;
And thocht the brym be perrillous to waid,
Baith to and fra I row at my awin will.   2815
I may not droun forquhy my oppin gill
Devoidis ay the watter I resaiff:
Thairfoir to droun forsuith na dreid I haif.'

The mous beheld unto hir fronsit face,
Hir runkillit cheikis and hir lippis syde,   2820
Hir hingand browis and hir voce sa hace,
Hir loggerand leggis and hir harsky hyde.
Scho ran abak and on the paddok cryde:
'Giff I can ony skill off phisnomy,
Thow hes sum part off falset and invy.   2825

'For clerkis sayis the inclinatioun
Of mannis thocht proceidis commounly
Efter the corporall complexioun
To gude or evill as nature will apply:
Ane thrawart will, ane thrawin phisnomy: 2830
The auld proverb is witnes off this lorum—
Distortum vultum sequitur distortio morum.'

'Na,' quod the taid, 'that proverb is not trew;
For fair thingis oftymis ar fundin faikin:
The blaberyis, thocht thay be sad off hew,   2835
Ar gadderit up quhen primeros is forsakin;
The face may faill to be the hartis takin:
Thairfoir I find this scripture in all place—
Thow suld not juge ane man efter his face.

'Thocht I unhailsum be to luke upon   2840
I have na cause quhy I suld lakkit be;
Wer I als fair as jolie Absolon,
I am no causer off that grit beutie:
This difference in forme and qualitie
Almychtie God hes causit Dame Nature   2845
To prent and set in everilk creature.

'Off sum the face may be full flurischand,
Off silkin toung and cheir rycht amorous,
With mynd inconstant, fals and wariand,
Full off desait and menis cautelous.'   2850
'Let be thy preiching!' quod the hungrie mous.
'And be quhat craft thow gar me understand
That thow wald gyde me to yone yonder land?'

'Thow wait,' quod scho, 'ane bodie that hes neid
To help thameself suld mony wayis cast;   2855
Thairfoir ga tak ane doubill twynit threid
And bind thy leg to myne with knottis fast:
I sall the leir to swym—be not agast—
Als weill as I.' 'As thow?' than quod the mous.
'To preif that play it war rycht perrillous!   2860

'Suld I be bund and fast quhar I am fre,
In hoip off help? Na! Than I schrew us baith!
For I mycht lois baith lyfe and libertie.
Gif it wer swa, quha suld amend the skaith—
Bot gif thow sweir to me the murthour-aith,   2865
But fraud or gyle to bring me over this flude
But hurt or harme?' 'In faith,' quod scho, 'I dude!'

Scho goikit up and to the hevin can cry:
'O Juppiter, off nature god and king,
I mak ane aith trewlie to the that I   2870
This lytill mous sall over this watter bring!'
This aith wes maid; the mous, but persaving
The fals ingyne of this foull-carpand pad,
Tuke threid and band hir leg as scho hir bad.

Than fute for fute thay lap baith in the brym—   2875
Bot in thair myndis thay wer rycht different:
The mous thocht off na thing bot for to swym;
The paddok for to droun set hir intent:
Quhen thay in midwart off the streme wer went,
With all hir force the paddok preissit doun   2880
And thocht the mous without mercie to droun.

86

Persavand this, the mous on hir can cry:
"Tratour to God and manesworne unto me!
Thow swore the murthour-aith richt now that I
But hurt or harme suld ferryit be and fre!'   2885
And quhen scho saw thair wes bot do or de,
With all hir mycht scho forsit hir to swym,
And preissit upon the taiddis bak to clym.

The dreid of deith hir strenthis gart incres,
And forcit hir defend with mycht and mane.   2890
The mous upwart, the paddok doun can pres—
Quhyle to, quhyle fra, quhyle doukit up agane.
This selie mous, plungit into grit pane,
Gan fecht als lang als breith wes in hir breist;
Till at the last scho cryit for ane preist.   2895

Fechtand thus-gait, the gled sat on ane twist,
And to this wretchit battell tuke gude heid;
And with ane wisk, or ony off thame wist,
He claucht his cluke betuix thame in the threid;
Syne to the land he flew with thame gude speid,   2900
Fane off that fang, pyipand with mony pew;
Syne lowsit thame and baith but pietie slew.

Syne bowellit thame that boucheour with his bill,
And belliflaucht full fettillie thame fled;
Bot all thair flesche wald scant be half ane fill—   2905
And guttis als—unto that gredie gled.
Off thair debait thus quhen I hard out-red,
He tuke his flicht and over the feildis flaw:
Giff this be trew speir ye at thame that saw.

Moralitas

My brother, gif thow will tak advertence   2910
Be this fabill, thow may persave and se
It passis far all kynd of pestilence
Ane wickit mynd with wordis fair and sle,

Be war thairfore with quhome thow fallowis the;
To the wer better beir the stane barrow—   2915
For all thy dayis to delf quhill thow may dre—
Than to be machit with ane wickit marrow.

Ane fals intent under ane fair pretence
Hes causit mony innocent for to de.
Grit folie is to gif over-sone credence   2920
To all that speiks fairlie unto the.
Ane silkin toung, ane hart of crueltie,
Smytis more sore than ony schot of arrow.
Brother, gif thow be wyse, I reid the fle
To matche the with ane thrawart fenyeit marrow.   2925

I warne the als, it is grit nekligence
To bind the fast quhair thow wes frank and fre;
Fra thow be bund thow may mak na defence
To saif thy lyfe nor yit thy libertie.
This simpill counsall, brother, tak of me—   2930
And it to cun perqueir se thow not tarrow:
Better but stryfe to leif allane in le
Than to be matchit with ane wickit marrow.

This hald in mynde: rycht more I sall the tell
Quhairby thir beistis may be figurate: 2935
The paddok usand in the flude to duell,
Is mannis bodie, swymmand air and lait
Into this warld with cairis implicate—
Now hie, now law, quhylis plungit up, quhylis doun,
Ay in perrell and reddie for to droun.   2940

Now dolorus, now blyth as bird on breir;
Now in fredome, now wrappit in distres;
Now haill and sound, now deid and brocht on beir;
Now pure as Job, now rowand in riches;
Now gouins gay, now brats laid in pres;   2945
Now full as fitche, now hungrie as ane hound;
Now on the quheill, now wrappit to the ground.

This lytill mous heir knit thus be the schyn
The saull of man betakin may indeid,
Bundin, and fra the bodie may not wyn   2950
Quhill cruell deith cum brek of lyfe the threid;
The quhilk to droun suld ever stand in dreid
Of carnall lust be the suggestioun
Quhilk drawis ay the saull and druggis doun.

The watter is the warld, ay welterand   2955
With mony wall of tribulatioun,
In quhilk the saull and bodie wer steirrand,
Standand rycht different in thair opinioun;
The saull upwart, the body precis doun;
The saull rycht fane wald be brocht over, iwis,   2960
Out of this warld into the hevinnis blis.

The gled is deith, that cummis suddandlie
As dois ane theif, and cuttis sone the battall:
Be vigilant thairfoir and ay reddie,
For mannis lyfe is brukill and ay mortall: 2965
My freind, thairfoir mak the ane strang castell
Of faith in Christ; for deith will the assay
Thow wait not quhen—evin, morrow or midday.

Adew my freind! And gif that ony speiris
Of this fabill sa schortlie I conclude,   2970
Say thow I left the laif unto the freiris
To mak exempill and ane similitude.
Now Christ for us that deit on the Rude,
Of saull and lyfe as Thow art Salviour,
Grant us till pas intill ane blissit hour!   2975

THE TESTAMENT OF CRESSEID

ANE doolie sessoun to ane cairfull dyte
Suld correspond and be equivalent:
Richt sa it wes quhen I began to wryte
This tragedie—the wedder richt fervent,
Quhen Aries, in middis of the Lent,   5
Schouris of haill can fra the north discend,
That scantlie fra the cauld I micht defend.

Yit nevertheles within myne oratur
I stude quhen Titan had his bemis bricht
Withdrawin doun and sylit under cure;   10
And fair Venus, the bewtie of the nicht,
Uprais, and set unto the west full richt
Hir goldin face, in oppositioun
Of God Phebus, direct discending doun.

Throwout the glas hir bemis brast sa fair   15
That I micht se on everie syde me by
The northin wind had purifyit the air,
And sched the mistie cloudis fra the sky;
The froist freisit, the blastis bitterly
Fra Pole Artick come quhisling loud and schill,   20
And causit me remufe aganis my will.

For I traistit that Venus, luifis quene,
To quhome sum tyme I hecht obedience,
My faidit hart of lufe scho wald mak grene;
And therupon with humbill reverence   25
I thocht to pray hir hie magnificence;
Bot for greit cald as than I lattit was,
And in my chalmer to the fyre can pas.

Thocht lufe be hait, yit in ane man of age
It kendillis nocht sa sone as in youtheid,   30
Of quhome the blude is flowing in ane rage,

And in the auld the curage doif and deid—
Of quhilk the fyre outward is best remeid;
To help be phisike quhair that nature faillit
I am expert, for baith I have assaillit.   35

I mend the fyre and beikit me about,
Than tuik ane drink my spreitis to comfort,
And armit me weill fra the cauld thairout;
To cut the winter nicht and mak it schort,
I tuik ane quair—and left all uther sport—   40
Writtin be worthie Chaucer glorious,
Of fair Creisseid and worthie Troylus.

And thair I fand, efter that Diomeid
Ressavit had that lady bricht of hew,
How Troilus neir out of wit abraid,   45
And weipit soir, with visage paill of hew;
For quhilk wanhope his teiris can renew,
Quhill Esperus rejoisit him agane:
Thus quhyle in joy he levit, quyle in pane.

Of hir behest he had greit comforting,   50
Traisting to Troy that scho suld mak retour,
Quhilk he desyrit maist of eirdly thing
Forquhy scho was his only paramour;
Bot quhen he saw passit baith day and hour
Of hir gane-come, than sorrow can oppres   55
His wofull hart in cair and hevines.

Of his distres me neidis nocht reheirs,
For worthie Chauceir, in the samin buik,
In gudelie termis and in joly veirs,
Compylit hes his cairis—quha will luik.   60
To brek my sleip aneuther quair I tuik,
In quhilk I fand the fatall destenie
Of fair Cresseid, that endit wretchitlie.

91

Quha wait gif all that Chauceir wrait was trew?
Nor I wait nocht gif this narratioun   65
Be authoreist, or fenyeit of the new
Be sum poeit, throw his inventioun
Maid to report the lamentatioun
And wofull end of this lustie Creisseid,
And quhat distres scho thoillit, and quhat deid.   70

Quhen Diomeid had all his appetyte,
And mair, fulfillit of this fair ladie,
Upon ane-uther he set his haill delyte,
And send to hir ane lybell of repudie,
And hir excludit fra his companie.   75
Than desolait scho walkit up and doun,
And sum men sayis into the court commoun.

O fair Creisseid, the flour and *A per se*
Of Troy and Grece, how was thow fortunait!
To change in filth all thy feminitie,   80
And be with fleschelie lust sa maculait,
And go amang the Greikis air and lait
Sa giglotlike, takand thy foull plesance!
I have pietie thow suld fall sic mischance!

Yit nevertheles, quhatever men deme or say   85
In scornefull langage of thy brukkilnes,
I sall excuse, als far furth as I may,
Thy womanheid, thy wisedome and fairnes—
The [quhilk] Fortoun hes put to sic distres
As hir pleisit, and nathing throw the gilt   90
Of the, throw wickit langage to be spilt.

This fair lady, in this wyse destitute
Of all comfort and consolatioun,
Richt privelie but fellowschip, on fute
Disagysit passit far out of the toun   95
Ane myle or twa unto ane mansioun
Beildit full gay, quhair hir father Calchas
Quhilk than amang the Greikis dwelland was.

Quhen he hir saw, the caus he can inquyre
Of hir cumming; scho said, siching full soir: 100
'Fra Diomeid had gottin his desyre
He wox werie and wald of me no moir.'
Quod Calchas: 'Douchter, weip thow not thairfoir;
Peraventure all cummis for the best:
Welcum to me! Thow art full deir ane gest.'   105

This auld Calchas, efter the law was tho,
Wes keiper of the tempill as ane priest,
In quhilk Venus and hir sone Cupido
War honourit, and his chalmer was thame neist;
To quhilk Cresseid, with baill aneuch in breist,   110
Usit to pas, hir prayeris for to say;
Quhill at the last, upon ane solempne day,

As custome was, the pepill far and neir,
Befoir the none, unto the tempill went
With sacrifice devoit in thair maneir;   115
Bot still Cresseid, hevie in hir intent,
Into the kirk wald not hirself present,
For giving of the pepill ony deming
Of hir expuls fra Diomeid the king;

Bot past into ane secreit orature   120
Quhair scho micht weip hir wofull desteny;
Behind hir bak scho cloisit fast the dure
And on hir kneis bair fell doun in hy:
Upon Venus and Cupide angerly
Scho cryit out and said on this same wyse: 125
'Allace that ever I maid you sacrifice!

'Ye gave me anis ane devine responsaill
That I suld be the flour of luif in Troy;
Now am I maid ane unworthie outwaill,
And all in cair translatit is my joy.   130
Quha sall me gyde? Quha sall me now convoy,
Sen I fra Diomeid and nobill Troylus
Am clene excludit as abject odious?

93

'O fals Cupide, is nane to wyte bot thow,
And thy mother, of lufe the blind goddes!   135
Ye causit me alwayis understand and trow
The seid of lufe was sawin in my face,
And ay grew grene throw your supplie and grace:
Bot now, allace, that seid with froist is slane,
And I fra luifferis left and all forlane!'   140

Quhen this was said, doun in ane extasie,
Ravischit in spreit, intill ane dreame scho fell,
And be apperance hard quhair scho did ly
Cupide the King ringand ane silver bell,
Quhilk men micht heir fra hevin unto hell—   145
At quhais sound befoir Cupide appeiris
The sevin planetis discending fra thair spheiris—

Quhilk hes power of all thing generabill
To reull and steir be thair greit influence,
Wedder and wind and coursis variabill: 150
And first of all Saturne gave his sentence,
Quhilk gave to Cupide litill reverence—
Bot as ane busteous churle on his maneir,
Come crabitlie with auster luik and cheir.

His face [fronsit], his lyre was lyke the leid,   155
His teith chatterit and cheverit with the chin,
His ene drowpit, how sonkin in his heid,
Out of his nois the meldrop fast can rin,
With lippis bla and cheikis leine and thin;
The ice-schoklis that fra his hair doun hang   160
Was wonder greit and as ane speir als lang.

Atouir his belt his lyart lokkis lay
Felterit unfair, ovirfret with froistis hoir;
His garmound and his gyis full gay of gray;
His widderit weid fra him the wind out woir;   165
Ane busteous bow within his hand he boir,
Under his girdill ane flasche of felloun flanis,
Fedderit with ice and heidit with hailstanis.

Than Juppiter richt fair and amiabill,
God of the starnis in the firmament   170
And nureis to all thing generabill;
Fra his father Saturne far different,
With burelie face and browis bricht and brent;
Upon his heid ane garland wonder gay,
Of flouris fair, as it had bene in May.   175

His voice was cleir, as cristall wer his ene,
As goldin wyre sa glitterand was his hair,
His garmound and his gyis full [gay] of grene,
With goldin listis gilt on everie gair;
Ane burelie brand about his middill bair;   180
In his richt hand he had ane groundin speir,
Of his father the wraith fra us to weir.

Nixt efter him come Mars the god of ire,
Of strife, debait and all dissensioun,
To chide and fecht, als feirs as ony fyre;   185
In hard harnes, hewmound and habirgeoun,
And on his hanche ane roustie fell fachioun;
And in his hand he had ane roustie sword;
Wrything his face with mony angrie word.

Schaikand his sword, befoir Cupide he come,   190
With reid visage and grislie glowrand ene;
And at his mouth ane bullar stude of fome,
Lyke to ane bair quhetting his tuskis kene—
Richt tuilyeour-lyke, but temperance in tene;
Ane horne he blew with mony bosteous brag,   195
Quhilk all this warld with weir hes maid to wag.

Than fair Phebus, lanterne and lamp of licht
Of man and beist, baith frute and flourisching,
Tender nureis and banischer of nicht,
And of the warld causing, be his moving   200
And influence, lyfe in all eirdlie thing,
Without comfort of quhome, of force to nocht
Must all ga die that in this warld is wrocht.

As king royall he raid upon his chair
The quhilk Phaeton gydit sum tyme upricht;   205
The brichtnes of his face, quhen it was bair,
Nane micht behald for peirsing of his sicht:
This goldin cart with fyrie bemis bricht
Four yokkit steidis, full different of hew,
But bait or tyring throw the spheiris drew.   210

The first was soyr, with mane als reid as rois,
Callit Eoye into the orient;
The secund steid to name hecht Ethios,
Quhitlie and paill and sumdeill ascendent;
The thrid Peros, richt hait and richt fervent;   215
The feird was blak—[and callit Philogey]—
Quhilk rollis Phebus doun into the sey.

Venus was thair present, that goddes [gay],
Hir sonnis querrell for to defend and mak
Hir awin complaint, cled in ane nyce array—   220
The ane half grene, the uther half sabill blak;
Quhyte hair as gold kemmit and sched abak;
Bot in hir face semit greit variance—
Quhyles perfyte treuth and quhyles inconstance.

Under smyling scho was dissimulait,   225
Provocative with blenkis amorous,
And suddanely changit and alterait,
Angrie as ony serpent vennemous,
Richt pungitive with wordis odious:
Thus variant scho was, quha list tak keip,   230
With ane eye lauch, and with the uther weip,

In taikning that all fleschelie paramour
Quhilk Venus hes in reull and governance,
Is sumtyme sweit, sumtyme bitter and sour,
Richt unstabill and full of variance,   235
Mingit with cairfull joy and fals plesance,
Now hait, now cauld, now blyith, now full of wo,
Now grene as leif, now [widderit] and ago.

With buik in hand than come Mercurius,
Richt eloquent and full of rethorie,   240
With polite termis and delicious,
With pen and ink to report all reddie,
Setting sangis and singand merilie;
His hude was reid, heklit atouir his croun,
Lyke to ane poeit of the auld fassoun.   245

Boxis he bair with fine electuairis,
And sugerit syropis for digestioun,
Spycis belangand to the pothecairis,
With mony hailsum sweit confectioun;
Doctour in Phisick cled in ane skarlot goun,   250
And furrit weill—as sic ane aucht to be—
Honest and gude, and not ane word culd lie.

Nixt efter him come Lady Cynthia,
The last of all, and swiftest in hir spheir,
Of colour blak, buskit with hornis twa,   255
And in the nicht scho listis best appeir;
Haw as the leid, of colour nathing cleir—
For all hir licht scho borrowis at hir brother
Titan, for of hirself scho hes nane uther.

Hir gyse was gray and ful of spottis blak,   260
And on hir breist ane churle paintit full evin,
Beirand ane bunche of thornis on his bak,
Quhilk for his thift micht clim na nar the hevin.
Thus quhen thay gadderit war thir goddes sevin,
Mercurius thay cheisit with ane assent   265
To be foirspeikar in the parliament.

Quha had bene thair and liken for to heir
His facound toung and termis exquisite,
Of rethorick the prettick he micht leir,
In breif sermone ane pregnant sentence wryte;   270
Befoir Cupide veiling his cap a lyte,
Speiris the caus of that vocatioun,
And he anone schew his intentioun.

'Lo!' quod Cupide, 'quha will blaspheme the name
Of his awin god, outher in word [or] deid,   275
To all goddis he dois baith lak and schame,
And suld have bitter panis to his meid:
I say this by yone wretchit Cresseid,
The quhilk throw me was sum tyme flour of lufe,
Me and my mother starklie can reprufe,   280

'Saying of hir greit infelicitie
I was the caus and my mother Venus,
Ane blind goddes hir cald that micht not se,
With sclander and defame injurious:
Thus hir leving unclene and lecherous   285
Scho wald returne on me and my mother,
To quhome I schew my grace abone all uther.

'And sen ye ar all sevin deificait,
Participant of devyne sapience,
This greit [injure] done to our hie estait   290
Me think with pane we suld mak recompence;
Was never to goddes done sic violence.
As weill for yow as for myself I say;
Thairfoir ga help to revenge I yow pray.'

Mercurius to Cupide gave answeir   295
And said: 'Schir King, my counsall is that ye
Refer yow to the hiest planeit heir,
And tak to him the lawest of degre
The pane of Cresseid for to modifie—
As god Saturne, with him tak Cynthia.'   300
'I am content,' quod he, 'to tak thay twa.'

Than thus proceidit Saturne and the Mone
Quhen thay the mater rypelie had degest:
For the dispyte to Cupide scho had done,
And to Venus oppin and manifest,   305
In all hir lyfe with pane to be opprest,
And torment sair with seiknes incurabill,
And to all lovers be abhominabill.

98

This duleful sentence Saturne tuik on hand
And passit doun quhair cairfull Cresseid lay,   310
And on hir heid he laid ane frostie wand;
Than lawfullie on this wyse can he say:
'Thy greit fairnes and all thy bewtie gay,
Thy wantoun blude, and eik thy goldin hair,
Heir I exclude fra the for evermair.   315

'I change thy mirth into melancholy
Quhilk is the mother of all pensivenes;
Thy moisture and thy heit in cald and dry;
Thyne insolence, thy play and wantones
To greit diseis; thy pomp and thy riches   320
In mortall neid; and greit penuritie
Thow suffer sall, and as ane beggar die.'

O cruell Saturne, fraward and angrie,
Hard is thy dome and to malitious!
On fair Cresseid quhy hes thow na mercie,   325
Quhilk was sa sweit, gentill and amorous?
Withdraw thy sentence and be gracious—
As thow was never; sa schawis thow thy deid
Ane wraikfull sentence gevin on fair Cresseid.

Than Cynthia, quhen Saturne past away,   330
Out of hir sait discendit doun belyve,
And red ane bill on Cresseid quhair scho lay,
Contening this sentence diffinityve:
'Fra heit of bodie I the now depryve,
And to thy seiknes sall be na recure,   335
Bot in dolour thy dayis to indure.

'Thy cristall ene minglit with blude I mak;
Thy voice sa cleir, unplesand, hoir and hace;
Thy lustie lyre ouirspred with spottis blak,
And lumpis haw appeirand in thy face;   340
Quhair thow cummis ilk man sall fle the place:
This sall thow go begging fra hous to hous
With cop and clapper lyke ane lazarous.'

99

This doolie dreame, this uglye visioun
Brocht to ane end, Cresseid fra it awoik,   345
And all that court and convocatioun
Vanischit away: than rais scho up and tuik
Ane poleist glas and hir schaddow culd luik;
And quhen scho saw hir face sa deformait,
Gif scho in hart was wa aneuch, God wait!   350

Weiping full sair, 'Lo, quhat it is,' quod sche,
'With fraward langage for to mufe and steir
Our craibit goddis! And sa is sene on me!
My blaspheming now have I bocht full deir;
All eirdlie joy and mirth I set areir.   355
Allace this day! Allace this wofull tyde
Quhen I began with my goddis for to chyde!'

Be this was said ane chyld come fra the hall
To warne Cresseid the supper was reddy,
First knokkit at the dure and syne culd call: 360
'Madame, your father biddis yow cum in hy:
He hes mervell sa lang on grouf ye ly,
And sayis your prayers bene to lang sumdeill;
The goddis wait all your intent full weill.'

Quod scho: 'Fair chylde, ga to my father deir,   365
And pray him cum to speik with me anone.'
And sa he did, and said: 'Douchter, quhat cheir?'
'Allace!' quod scho. 'Father, my mirth is gone!'
'How sa?' quod he; and scho can all expone,
As I have tauld, the vengeance and the wraik   370
For hir trespas Cupide on hir culd tak.

He luikit on hir uglye lipper face
The quhylk befor was quhite as lillie-flour;
Wringand his hands oftymes he said: allace
That he had levit to se that wofull hour!   375
For he knew weill that thair was na succour
To hir seiknes, and that dowblit his pane.
Thus was thair cair aneuch betuix thame twane.

100

Quhen thay togidder murnit had full lang,
Quod Cresseid: 'Father, I wald not be kend;   380
Thairfoir in secreit wyse ye let me gang
Unto yone hospitall at the tounis end;
And thidder sum meit for cheritie me send
To leif upon; for all mirth in this eird
Is fra me gane—sic is my wickit weird!'   385

Than in ane mantill and ane bawer hat,
With cop and clapper, wonder prively,
He opnit ane secreit yet and out thairat
Convoyit hir, that na man suld espy,
Unto ane village half ane myle thairby;   390
Delyverit hir in at the spittaill-hous
And daylie sent hir part of his almous.

Sum knew hir weill, and sum had na knawledge
Of hir becaus scho was sa deformait
With bylis blak ouirspred in hir visage,   395
And hir fair colour faidit and alterait.
Yit thay presumit, for hir hie regrait
And still murning, scho was of nobill kin:
With better will thairfoir thay tuik hir in.

The day passit and Phebus went to rest,   400
The cloudis blak ovirquhelmit all the sky.
God wait gif Cresseid was ane sorrowfull gest,
Seing that uncouth fair and harbery!
But meit or drink scho dressit hir to ly
In ane dark corner of the hous allone,   405
And on this wyse, weiping, scho maid hir mone:

The Complaint of Cresseid

'O sop of sorrow, sonkin into cair!
O cative Creisseid! For now and evermair
Gane is thy joy and all thy mirth in eird;
Of all blyithnes now art thou blaiknit bair;   410

Thair is na salve may saif the of thy sair:
Fell is thy fortoun, wickit is thy weird;
Thy blys is baneist, and thy baill on breird:
Under the eirth God gif I gravin wer,
Quhair nane of Grece nor yit of Troy micht heird! 415

'Quhair is thy chalmer wantounlie besene,
With burely bed and bankouris browderit bene?
Spycis and wyne to thy collatioun,
The cowpis all of gold and silver schene;
The sweit meitis, servit in plaittis clene, 420
With saipheron sals of ane gud sessoun?
Thy gay garmentis with mony gudely goun;
Thy plesand lawn pinnit with goldin prene?
All is areir, thy greit royall renoun!

'Quhair is thy garding with thir greissis gay 425
And fresche flowris quhilk the Quene Floray
Had paintit plesandly in everie pane,
Quhair thou was wont full merilye in May
To walk and tak the dew be it was day,
And heir the merle and mawis mony ane; 430
With ladyis fair in carrolling to gane,
And se the royall rinkis in thair array,
In garmentis gay garnischit on everie grane?

'Thy greit triumphand fame and hie honour,
Quhair thou was callit of eirdlye wichtis flour, 435
All is decayit—thy weird is welterit so.
Thy hie estait is turnit in darknes dour.
This lipper-ludge tak for thy burelie bour,
And for thy bed tak now ane bunche of stro;
For waillit wyne and meitis thou had tho 440
Tak mowlit breid, peirrie and ceder sour:
Bot cop and [clapper] now is all ago.

'My cleir voice and courtlie carrolling,
Quhair I was wont with ladyis for to sing,
Is rawk as ruik, full hiddeous, hoir and hace;   445
My plesand port all utheris precelling,
Of lustines I was hald maist conding;
Now is deformit the figour of my face—
To luik on it na leid now lyking hes.
Sowpit in syte, I say with sair siching,   450
Ludgeit amang the lipper leid: "Allace!"

'O ladyis fair of Troy and Grece attend
My miserie quhilk nane may comprehend,
My frivoll fortoun, my infelicitie,
My greit mischeif quhilk na man can amend: 455
Be war in tyme—approchis neir the end—
And in your mynd ane mirrour mak of me
As I am now; peradventure that ye
For all your micht may cum to that same end—
Or ellis war, gif ony war may be.   460

'Nocht is your fairnes bot ane faiding flour;
Nocht is your famous laud and hie honour
Bot wind inflat in uther mennis eiris;
Your roising reid to rotting sall retour.
Exempill mak of me in your memour,   465
Quhilk of sic thingis wofull witnes beiris.
All welth in eird away as wind it weiris:
Be war thairfoir—approchis neir the hour—
Fortoun is fikkill quhen scho beginnis and steiris.'

Thus chydand with hir drerie destenye,   470
Weiping scho woik the nicht fra end to end;
Bot all in vane—hir dule, hir cairfull cry,
Micht not remeid nor yit hir murning mend.
Ane lipper-lady rais and till hir wend
And said: 'Quhy spurnis thow aganis the wall   475
To sla thyself and mend nathing at all?

103

'Sen thy weiping dowbillis bot thy wo,
I counsall the mak vertew of ane neid—
To leir to clap thy clapper to and fro,
And [leve] efter the law of lipper leid.'   480
Thair was na buit, bot furth with thame scho yeid
Fra place to place, quhill cauld and hounger sair
Compellit hir to be ane rank beggair.

That samin tyme of Troy the garnisoun,
Quhilk had to chiftane worthie Troylus,   485
Throw jeopardie of weir had strikken doun
Knichtis of Grece in number [mervellous;]
With greit tryumphe and laude victorious
Agane to Troy [richt] royallie thay raid
The way quhair Cresseid with the lipper baid.   490

Seing that companie, thai come all with ane stevin;
Thay gaif ane cry and schuik coppis gude speid;
Said: 'Worthie lordis, for Goddis lufe of hevin,
To us lipper part of your almous-deid!'
Than to thair cry nobill Troylus tuik heid;   495
Having pietie, neir by the place can pas
Quhair Cresseid sat, not witting quhat scho was.

Than upon him scho kest up baith hir ene—
And with ane blenk it come into his thocht
That he sumtime hir face befoir had sene.   500
Bot scho was in sic plye he knew hir nocht;
Yit than hir luik into his mynd it brocht
The sweit visage and amorous blenking
Of fair Cresseid, sumtyme his awin darling.

Na wonder was suppois in mynd that he   505
Tuik hir figure sa sone—and lo now quhy:
The idole of ane thing in cace may be
Sa deip imprentit in the fantasy
That it deludis the wittis outwardly,
And sa appeiris in forme and lyke estait   510
Within the mynd as it was figurait.

Ane spark of lufe than till his hart culd spring
And kendlit all his bodie in ane fyre:
With hait fevir ane sweit and trimbling
Him tuik quhill he was reddie to expyre;   515
To beir his scheild his breist began to tyre;
Within ane quhyle he changit mony hew,
And nevertheles not ane ane-uther knew.

For knichtlie pietie and memoriall
Of fair Cresseid, ane gyrdill can he tak,   520
[Ane purs of gold, and mony gay jowall,]
And in the skirt of Cresseid doun can swak;
Than raid away and not ane word [he] spak,
Pensive in hart, quhill he come to the toun,
And for greit cair oftsyis almaist fell doun.   525

The lipper folk to Cresseid than can draw
To se the equall distributioun
Of the almous; bot quhen the gold thay saw,
Ilk ane to uther prevelie can roun,
And said: 'Yone lord hes mair affectioun,   530
How ever it be, unto yone lazarous
Than to us all: we knaw be his almous.'

'Quhat lord is yone,' quod scho,'—have ye na feill—
Hes done to us so greit humanitie?'
'Yes,' quod a lipper man, 'I knaw him weill;   535
Schir Troylus it is, gentill and fre.'
Quhen Cresseid understude that it was he,
Stiffer than steill thair stert ane bitter stound
Throwout hir hart, and fell doun to the ground,

Quhen scho ovircome, with siching sair and sad,   540
With mony cairfull cry and cald: 'Ochane!
Now is my breist with stormie stoundis stad;
Wrappit in wo, ane wretch full will of wane!'
Than swounit scho oft or scho culd refrane,
And ever in hir swouning cryit scho thus: 545
'O fals Cresseid and trew knicht Troylus!

'Thy lufe, thy lawtie and thy gentilnes
I countit small in my prosperitie,
Sa elevait I was in wantones
And clam upon the fickill quheill sa hie.   550
All faith and lufe I promissit to the
Was in the self fickill and frivolous:
O fals Cresseid and trew knicht Troilus!

'For lufe of me thow keipt gude continence,
Honest and chaist in conversatioun.   555
Of all wemen protectour and defence
Thou was, and helpit thair opinioun.
My mynd in fleschelie foull affectioun
Was inclynit to lustis lecherous:
Fy, fals Cresseid! O trew knicht Troylus!   560

'Lovers be war and tak gude heid about
Quhome that ye lufe, for quhome ye suffer paine:
I lat yow wit thair is richt few thairout
Quhome ye may traist to have trew lufe agane—
Preif quhen ye will, your labour is in vaine.   565
Thairfoir I reid ye tak thame as ye find,
For thay ar sad as widdercock in wind.

'Becaus I knaw the greit unstabilnes,
Brukkill as glas, into myself, I say,
Traisting in uther als greit unfaithfulnes—   570
Als unconstant and als untrew of fay—
Thocht sum be trew, I wait richt few ar thay:
Quha findis treuth lat him his lady ruse!
Nane but myself as now I will accuse.'

Quhen this was said, with paper scho sat doun,   575
And on this maneir maid hir testament:
'Heir I beteiche my corps and carioun
With wormis and with taidis to be rent:
My cop and clapper and myne ornament,
And all my gold, the lipper folk sall have   580
Quhen I am deid, to burie me in grave.

'This royall ring set with this rubie reid
Quhilk Troylus in drowrie to me send,
To him agane I leif it quhen I am deid
To mak my cairfull deid unto him kend: 585
Thus I conclude schortlie, and mak ane end:
My spreit I leif to Diane quhair scho dwellis,
To walk with hir in waist woddis and wellis.

'O Diomeid, thou hes baith broche and belt
Quhilk Troylus gave me in takning   590
Of his trew lufe!' And with that word scho swelt.
And sone ane lipper man tuik of the ring,
Syne buryit hir withouttin tarying.
To Troylus furthwith the ring he bair
And of Cresseid the deith he can declair.   595

Quhen he had hard hir greit infirmitie,
Hir legacie and lamentatioun,
And how scho endit in sic povertie,
He swelt for wo and fell doun in ane swoun;
For greit sorrow his hart to brist was boun: 600
Siching full sadlie said: 'I can no moir—
Scho was untrew and wo is me thairfoir.'

Sum said he maid ane tomb of merbell gray,
And wrait hir name and superscriptioun,
And laid it on hir grave quhair that scho lay,   605
In goldin letteris, conteining this ressoun:
'Lo, fair ladyis! Cresseid of Troyis toun,
Sumtyme countit the flour of womanheid,
Under this stane, lait lipper, lyis deid.'

Now, worthie wemen, in this ballet schort,   610
Maid for your worschip and instructioun,
Of cheritie, I monische and exhort:
Ming not your lufe with fals deceptioun.
Beir in your mynd this schort conclusioun
Of fair Cresseid—as I have said befoir;   615
Sen scho is deid, I speik of hir no moir.

THE TALE OF ORPHEUS AND ERUDICES
HIS QUENE

THE nobilness and gret magnificence
Off prince or lord quha list to magnify,
His gret ancestry and lyneall discence
Suld first extoll, and his genology,
So that his hart he mycht inclyne thairby   5
The mor to vertewe and to worthyness,
Herand rehers his eldaris gentilness.

It is contrar the lawis of nature
A gentill man to be degenerate,
Nocht following of his progenitour   10
The worthy reule and the lordly estate;
A ryall reulre for to be rusticat
Is bot a monstour in comparisoun,
Had in dispyte and foule derisioun.

I saye this be the gret lordis of Grewe,   15
Quhilkis set thar hart and all thair hale corage
Thar faderis steppis justlie to persewe,
Ekyng the worschipe of thair hie lynnage;
The ancient and sad wysmen of age
War tendouris to the young and insolent,   20
To mak thaim in all vertewe excellent.

Lyke as a strand of watter or a spring
Haldis the sapoure of his fontale well,
So did in Grece ilk lord and worthy king—
Of forbearis thai tuke carage and smell;   25
Amangis the [quhilkis] of ane I think to tell:
Bot first his gentill generacioun
I sall rehers, with your correctioun.

Apon the montane of Eliconee,
The most famous of all Arabia,   30

A goddes duelt, excellent of bewte,
Gentill of blude, callit Memoria,
Quhilk Jubiter that god to wyf can ta
And carnaly hir knewe, quhilk efter syne,
Apon a day, baire him fair douchteris nyne.   35

The first in Grewe was callit Euterpe—
In our langage gud delictacioun;
The secound maide named Melpomane,
As hony sweit in modelacioun;
Tersitor, quhilk is gud instructioun   40
Of every thing, the thrid sister, iwis,
Thus out of Grewe in Latyne translat is.

Caliope, that madyn mervalous,
The ferd sister, of all musik mastress,
And moder to the king Schir Orpheus,   45
Quhilk throw his wyf was efter king of Trace;
Cleo the fyft, that now is a goddass—
In Latyne callit Meditacioun
Of every thing that has creacioun.

The sext lady was callit Herato,   50
Quhilk drawis lyke to lyke in every thing;
The sevynt lady was callit fair Pollymyo,
Quhilk coude a thousand sangis swetly syng;
Thelya syne, quhilk can our sawlis bring
To profound wit and gret agilite,   55
To understand and have capacite.

Uranya, the nynt and last of all,
In oure langage, quha coude it wele expound,
Is callit armony celestiall,
Rejosing men with melody and sound.   60
Amang thire nyne Caliope was crownd
And maid a quene be mychti god Phebus,
Of quhom he gat this prince Schir Orpheus.

No wounder is thocht he was faire and wise,
Gentill and full of liberalite—   65
His fader god, and his progenitryss
A goddess, fyndar of all ermonye.
Quhen he was borne scho set him on hir kne,
And gart him sowke of hir twa palpis quhyte
The sweit licour of all musike perfyte.   70

Quhen he was auld, sone to manhed he drewe,
Of statur large and farly faire of face;
His noble fame so far it sprang and grewe
Till, at the last, the mychti quene of Trace,
Excellent fair, haboundand in riches,   75
Ane message send unto this prince so ying,
Requyrand him to wed hir and be king.

Erudices that lady had to name;
Quhen that scho saw this prince so glorius,
Hir erand to propone scho thocht no schame—   80
With wordis sweit and blenkis amorus
Said: 'Welcome lord and luf Schir Orpheus!
In this province ye sall be king and lord.'
Thai kissit syne, and thus ware at accord.

Betwene Orpheus and faire Erudices,   85
Fra thai war weddit, on fra day to day
The lowe of luf couth kendill and encres,
With myrth, blythness, gret plesans and gret play.
Off wardlie joye, allace, quhat sall we say?
Lyke till a floure that plesandly will spring,   90
Quhilk fadis sone and endis with murnyng!

I say this be Erudices the quene,
Quhilk walkit furth intill a maii mornyng,
And with a madin, in a medowe grene,
To tak the dewe and se the flouris spring,   95
Quhar in a schawe nere by this lady ying,
A bustuos herd callit Arystyus,
Kepand his bestis lay under a bus.

And quhen he saw this lady solitare,
Barfute, with schankis quhytar than the snawe,   100
Prikkit with lust, he thocht withoutin mare
Hir till oppress, and till hir can he drawe.
Dredand for scaith, sche fled quhen scho him saw,
And as scho ran, all bairfut in ane bus
Scho trampit on a serpent vennomus.   105

This cruell vennome was so penitryf,
As natur is of all mortall poisoun,
In pecis small this quenis hart couth ryf,
And scho anone fell in a dedly swoun:
Seand this cais, Proserpyne maid hir boune,   110
Quhilk clepit is the goddes infernall,
And till hire court this gentill quene couth call.

And quhen scho vanyst was and invisible,
Hir madin wepit with a wofull cheire,
Cryand with mony schout and voce terrible,   115
Till at the last Schir Orpheus couth heire,
And of hir cry the caus than can he speire;
Scho said: 'Allace, Erudices your quene
Is with fary tane befor myne ene!'

This noble king inflammit all in ire,   120
And rampand as ane lyoun ravenus,
With awfull luke and eyne glowand as fyre,
Speris the maner, and the maid said thus:
'Scho trampit on a serpent vennomus,
And fell in swoun; with that the quene of fary   125
Claucht hir up sone and furth with hire can cary.'

Quhen scho had said, the king sichit full sore—
His hert nere birst for verray dule and wo;
Half out of mynd, he maid na tary more,
Bot tuke his harpe and to the wod can go,   130
Wryngand his handis, walkand to and fro
Quhill he mycht stand, syne sat doun on a stone,
And to his harpe thus-gate he maid his mone:

'O dulfull harpe with mony dolly stryng,
Turne all thi mirth and musik in murnyng,   135
And ces of all thi subtell sangis sweit!
Now wepe with me, thi lord and carefull kyng,
Quhilk losit has in erd all his lyking;
And all thi game thow change in gule and greit,
Thy goldin pynnis with thi teris weit,   140
And all my pane for to report thow press,
Cryand with me in every steid and streit:
"Quhar art thou gane, my luf Erudices?" '

Him to rejos yit playit he a spryng,
Quhill all the foulis of the wod can syng,   145
And treis dansit with thair leves grene,
Him to devoid of his gret womenting:
Bot all in vane—thai comfort him nothing—
His hart was sa apon his lusty quene;
The bludy teres sprang out of his eyne,   150
Thar was na solace mycht his sobbing ces,
Bot cryit ay with caris cald and kene:
'Quhar art thow gane, my luf Erudices?

'Faire-weill my place, fair-weile plesance and play,
And welcome woddis wyld and wilsome way,   155
My wikit werd in wilderness to waire;
My rob ryall and all my riche array
Changit sall be in rude russat of gray,
My diademe intill ane hat of haire;
My bed sall be with bever, broke and baire   160
In buskis bene with mony bustuos bes,
Withoutin sang, saying with siching saire:
"Quhar art thow gane, my luf Erudices?"

'I the beseike, my faire fader Phebus,
Have pete of thi awne sone Orpheus;   165
Wait thow nocht wele I am thi barne and child?
Now heire my plant, panefull and petuous;
Direct me fra this deid sa dolorus,

Quhilk gois thus withoutin gilt begild;
Lat nocht thi face with clowdis be oursyld;   170
Len me thi licht, and lat me nocht ga less
To fynd the faire in fame that never was fyld,
My lady, quene and luf, Erudices.

'O Jupiter, thow god celestiall,
And grantschir to myself, on the I call   175
To mend my murnyng and my drery mone!
Thow gif me fors that I nocht fant nor fall
Quhill I hire fynd—for seike hire suth I sall,
And nother stynt nor stand for stok nor stone:
Throwe thi godhed gyde me quhar scho is gone,   180
Gar hir appeire and put myne hert in pes!'
Thus King Orpheus with his harpe allone
Sore wepit for his wyf Erudices.

Quhen endit was the sangis lamentable,
He tuke his harpe and on his brest can hyng;   185
Syne passit to the hevin, as sayis the fable,
To seike his wyf—bot that avalit nathing;
By Wadlyng Streit he went but tarying,
Syne come downe throw the speir of Saturn ald,
Quhilk fader is of all thire sternis cald.   190

Quhen scho was soucht out-throw that cald regioun,
To Jubiter his grantschir can he wend,
Quhilk rewit saire his lamentacioun,
And gart his speire be soucht fra end to end:
Scho was nocht thar—than doun he can descend   195
To Mars the god of batall and of stryf,
And socht his speir—yit gat he nocht his wyf.

Syne went he downe to his fader [Phebus],
God of the son, with bemes bricht and cleire;
Quhen that he saw his son Orpheus   200
In sic a plyte, it changit all his cheire;
He gart anone go seike throw all his speire,

Bot all in vane—that lady come nocht thare:
Than tuke he leif and to Venus can faire.

Quhen he hir saw, he knelit and said thus: 205
'Wait ye nocht weile I am your awne trew knycht—
In luf nane lelar than Schir Orpheus?
And ye of luf goddess and most of mycht,
Of my lady helpe me to get a sicht!'
'Forsuth,' quod scho, 'ye mon seike nethir-mare.'   210
Than fra Venus he tuke his lef but maire.

To Marcury but tary is he gone,
Quhilk callit is the god of eloquens;
Bot of his wyf thare knawlege gat he none.
With wofull hart than passit he doune fro thens—   215
Unto the mone he maid no residens.
Thus fra the hevin he went doun to the erd,
Yit be the way sum melody he lerd.

In his passage amang the planetis all,
He herd ane hevinlie melody and sound   220
Passing all instrumentis musicall,
Causit be rolling of the speris round;
Quhilk ermony throw all this mapamound,
[Quhill] moving ces, unite perpetuall,
Quhilk of this warld [Plato] the saull can call.   225

Thar leryt he tonys proporcionate,
As duplere, triplere and emetricus,
Enoleus and eike the quadruplat,
Epodyus richt hard and curious;
And of thir sex, swet and delicious,   230
Richt consonant five hevinly [symphonis]
Componit ar, as clerkis can devys.

First diatasseron full sweit iwis,
And diapason, symple and duplate,
And diapente, componit with a dis: 235

114

This makis five of thre multiplicat.
This mery musik and mellifluate,
Complete and full with noumeris od and evyn,
Is causit be the moving of the hevin.

Off sic musik to wryte I do bot dote;   240
Tharfor at this matter a stra I lay,
For in my lyf I couth never syng a note.
Bot I will tell how Orpheus tuke the way
To seike his wyf attour the gravis gray,
Hungry and cald, our mony wilsome wane,   245
Withoutin gyde, he and his harpe allane.

He passit furth the space of twenty days,
Far and full ferthere than I can tell,
And ay he fand stretis and redy wayis;
Till at the last unto the yet of hell   250
He come, and thar he fand a portar fell,
With thre hedis, wes callit Cerberus—
A hound of hell, a monstour mervalous.

Than Orpheus began to be agast
Quhen he beheld that ugly hellis hound;   255
He tuke his harpe and on it plait fast,
Till at the last, throu swetness of the sound,
The dog slepit and fell unto the ground:
And Orpheus attour his wame in stall,
And nethir-mare he went, as ye heir sall.   260

Than come he till a ryver wounder depe,
Our it a brig and on it sisteris thre,
Quhilk had the entre of the brig to kepe—
Alecto, Megera and [Thesiphonee],
Tornand, a quheile was uglie for to se   265
And on it spred a man hecht Ixioun,
Rollit about, richt wounder wo begone.

Than Orpheus playit a joly spring—
The thre sisteris full fast thai fell on slepe,

115

The uglye quheile cessit of hire quhirling: 270
Thus left was nane the entre for to kepe—
Than Ixioun out of the quhele can crepe,
And stall away; than Orpheus anone,
Without stopping, attour the brig is gone.

Syne come he till a wounder grysly flude,   275
Drowbly and depe, that rathly doun can ryn,
Quhar Tantalus nakit full thristy stude,
And yit the watter stud abone his chyn;
Thocht he gapit thair wald na drop cum in—
Quhen he dulkit, the watter wald discend;   280
Thus gat he nocht his thrist to slaike nor mend.

Befor his face ane apill hang also,
Fast at his mouth apon a tolter threid;
Quhen he gapit it rokkit to and fro,
And fled as it refusit him to feid.   285
Than Orpheus had reuth of his gret neid,
Tuke owt his harpe and fast on it can clynke:
The watter stude, and Tantalus gat a drink.

Syne oure a mure, with thornis thik and scharpe,
Weping allone, a wilsome way he went,   290
And had nocht bene throw suffrage of his harpe,
With scharpe pykis he had bene schorne and schent:
And as he blent, besyde him on the bent
He sawe speldit a wounder wofull wicht,
Nalit full fast, and [Titius] he hicht.   295

And on his brest thair sat ane grysly grype,
Quhilk with his bill his baly throu can bore—
Baith mawe, mydred, hart, levere and tripe
He ruggit owt—his panys wer the more;
Quhen Orpheus saw him thus suffer sore,   300
Has tane his harpe and maide sweit melody—
The grype is fled and [Titius] left his cry.

Beyonde this mure he fande a ferefull strete,
Myrk as the nycht, to pass richt dangerous—
For slidderness scant mycht he hald his feit—   305
In quhilk thair was ane stynk richt odious
[That] gydit him to hidowis hellis hous
Quhar Rodomantus and Proserpina
War king and qwene: Orpheus in can ga.

O dolly place, and groundless depe dungeoun,   310
Furnes of fyre with stynk intollerable,
Pite of dispaire without remissioun!
Thy meit vennome, thi drink is poysonable,
Thy gret panis to compt innomerable;
Quhat creatur cummis to duell in the   315
Is aye deand and never more may de.

Thar fand he mony cairefull kyng and qwene,
With crowne on hed, of brass full hate birnand,
Quhilk in thar lyf richt masterfull had bene,
Conquerour of gold, riches and of land.   320
Hector of Troye and Pryame thar he fand,
And Alexander for his wrang conquest;
Antiochus thar for his fowle incest.

Thar fand he Julius Cesar for his cruelte;
And Herod with his brotheris wyf he saw,   325
And Nero for his gret iniquite,
And Pylat for his breking of the law.
Syne efter that he lukit and couth knawe
Cresus the king, non mychtiar on mold
For covatus, yet full of birnand gold.   330

Thar fand he Pharo, for oppressioun
Of Godis folk on quhilk the plagis fell,
And Saull eke, for the gret abusioun
Of justice to the folk of Israell;
Thar fand Acab and the quene Jesabell,   335
Quhilk sely Nabot, that was a prophet trewe,
For his wyne-yard withoutin pete slew.

Thar fand he mony pape and cardinale
In haly kirk quhilk dois abusioun,
And bischopis in thar pontificall,   340
Be symony for wrang ministracioun;
Abbotis and men of all religioun,
For evill disponyng of thar placis rent,
In flam of fyre war bitterly torment.

Syne nethir-mar he went quhar Pluto was,   345
And Proserpyne, and thidder-wart he drewe,
Aye playand on his harpe as he couth pass;
Till at the last Erudices he knewe,
Lene and ded-lyke, petuos and pale of hewe,
Richt warsche and wan and wallowit as a weid—   350
Hir lely lyre was lyke unto the leid.

Quod he: 'My lady leile and my delyte,
Full wa is me till se yow changit thus:
Quhar is thi rude as ros with cheikis quhyte,
Thy cristall eyne with blenkis amorus,   355
Thy lippis red to kiss delicious?'
Quod scho: 'As now I dar nocht tell, perfaye;
Bot ye sall wit the caus aneothir day.'

Quod Pluto: 'Schir, thocht sche be lyke ane elf,
Thar is na caus to plenye, and forquhy: 360
Scho fure alswele daly as dois my self
Or King Herod for all his chevalry:
It is langour that putis hire in sic ply;
War scho at hame in hir cuntre of Trace,
Scho wald refet full sone in fax and face.'   365

Than Orpheus befor Pluto sat doune,
And in his handis quhyte his harp can ta,
And playit mony sweit proporcioun,
With base tonys in Ypodorica,
With gemynyng in Ypolerica;   370
Till at the last for reuth and gret pete
Thai wepit sore that couth him heire or se.

Than Proserpyne and Pluto bad him as
His warisoun, and he wald ask richt nocht
Bot licence with his wyf away to pass   375
Till his countre, that he so fer had socht.
Quod Proserpyne: 'Sen I hir hiddire brocht,
We sall nocht part bot with condicioun.'
Quod he: 'Thairto I mak promissioun.'

'Erudices than be the hand thow tak,   380
And pass thi way—bot underneth this pane:
Gif thow tornes or blenkis behynd thi bak,
We sall hir have for ever till hell agane.'
Thocht this was hard, yit Orpheus was fane,
And on thai went, talkand of play and sport,   385
Quhill thai allmast come to the utter port.

Thus Orpheus, with inwart luf replet,
So blyndit was in gret effectioun,
Pensyf apon his wyf and lady sweit,
Rememberit nocht his hard condicioun: 390
Quhat will ye more? In schort conclusioun,
He blent bakwart, and Pluto come anone
And unto hell agane with hir is gone.

Allace, it was rycht gret hart-sair to heire
Off Orpheus the weping and the wo   395
Quhen that his wyf, quhilk he had bocht so deire,
Bot for a luke so sone was hynt him fro!
Flatlyngis he fell and mycht no forther go,
And lay a quhyle in swown and extasy:
Quhen he ourcome, thus owt of luf can cry: 400

'Quhat art thow, luf? How sall I the diffyne?
Bitter and sweit, cruell and merciable,
Plesand to sum, till uthir playnt and pyne,
Till sum constant, till uther variable!
Hard is thi law, thi bandis unbrekable;   405
Quha servis the, thocht he be never so trewe,
Perchance sum tyme he sall have caus to rewe.

119

'Now fynd I weile this proverbe trewe,' quod he,
' "Hart is on the hurd and hand is on the sore;
Quhar luf gois, on fors tornes the e."   410
I am expert, and wo is me thairfor—
Bot for a luke my lady is forlore!'
Thus chydand on with luf, our burn and bent,
A wofull wedowe hamwart is he went.

Moralitas

Lo, worthy folke, Boece that senature,   415
To wryte this faynit fable tuke in cure
In his gay Buke of Consolacioun
For our doctryne and gud instructioun,
Quhilk in the self suppos it fenyeit be
And hid under the cloke of poecye,   420
Yit Master Trewit, Doctor Nycholas,
Quhilk in his tyme a noble theologe was,
Applyis it to gud moralite,
Richt full of frut and serusite.
Fair Phebus is the god of sapiens;   425
Calliope his wyf is eloquens:
Thir twa mariit gat Orpheus belyf,
Quhilk callit is the part intellectif
Of mannis saull, in understanding fre,
And separate fra sensualite.   430
Erudices is our effectioun,
Be fantasye oft movit up and doun—
Quhilis to resoun it castis the delyte,
Quhilis to the flesche settis the appetit.
Aristyus, this herd that couth persewe   435
Erudices, is nocht bot gud vertewe,
Quhilk besy is aye to kepe our myndis clene;
Bot quhen we fle out throu the medowe grene
Fra vertewe to this warldis vane plesans,
Mengit with caire and full of varians,   440
The serpent stangis—that is dedly syn
That poysonis the saule bath without and in;
And than is it deid and eike oppressit doun

To warldly lust—all our effectioun.
Than perfyte resoun wepis wounder saire,   445
Seand our appetit thus-gate misfaire,
And passis up to the hevin belyf,
Schawand till us the lyf contemplatif,
The parfyt will and als the fervent luf
We suld have allway to the hevin abuf;   450
Bot seldyn thare our appetit is fund—
It is so fast into the body bund;
Tharfore downwart we cast our myndis e,
Blyndit with lust, and may nocht upwart fle;
Suld our desyre be soucht up in the speris,   455
Quhen it is tedderit on this warldis breris,
Quhile on the flesche, quhile on this warldis wrak,
And to the hevin small entent we tak.
Schir Orpheus, thow seikis all in vane
Thy wyf so hie; thairfor cum doune agane   460
And pass unto yone monstour mervalus
With thre hedis, that we call Cerberus,
Quhilk feynit is to haf sa mony heidis
For to betakin thre maner of deidis:
The first is in the tender young barnage;   465
The secound deid is in the myddle age;
The thrid is in gret eld quhen men ar tane.
Thus Cerberus to swelly sparis nane.
Bot quhen that ressoun and intelligens
Playis apon the harpe of eloquens,   470
That is to saye, makis perswasioun
To draw our will and our affectioun,
In every eild, fra syn and foule delyte,
This dog our saull has na powere to byte.
The secound mounstouris ar the sisteris thre;   475
Alecto, Megera and Thesiphonee
Ar nocht ellis, in bukis as we reid,
Bot wikit thocht, evill word and frawerd deid.
Alecto is the bolnyng of the hert;
Megera is the wikit word outwart;   480
Thesiphonee is operacioun,

121

That makis fynale executioun
Off dedly syn; and thir thre tornes aye
Ane uglye quheile—is nocht ellis to say
That warldie men sumtyme ar cassyn hie   485
Apon the quhele in gret prosperite,
And with a quhirll unwarly, or thai wait,
Ar thrawin doune to pure and law estaite.
Of Ixioun that in the quhele was spred,
I sall the tell sum part, as I have red.   490
He was on lyf broukle and lichorus,
And in that craft hardy and coragious,
That he wald nocht luf in na lawar place
Bot Juno, quene of natur and goddass;
And on a day, he went up in the sky,   495
Sekand Juno, thinkand with hir to ly;
Scho saw him cum and knewe his full entent—
A rany clud doune fro the firmament
Scho gart discend and kest betwene thaim two,
And in that clud his natur yeid him fro,   500
Of quhilk was generit the Centauris,
Half man, half hors, apon a ferly wys.
Than for the inwart crabbing and offence
That Juno tuke for his gret violence,
Scho send him doune unto the sisteris thre,   505
Apon thair quhele ay torned for to be.
Bot quhen that ressoun and intelligens
Plays apon the harpe of consciens,
[And persuadis our fleschly appetyte
To leif the thocht of this warldly delyte,   510
Than [seissis] of our hert the wicket will,
Fra frawart language than the tong is still,
Our synfull deids fallis doun on sleip,
Thane Exione out of the quheill gan creip.]
That is to say, the gret sollicitud,   515
Quhile up, quhile doun, to wyn this warldis gud,
Cessis furth-with, and our complexioun
Waxis quyet in contemplacioun.
This Tantalus of quhom I spak of aire,

Quhill he levit he was a gay hostillare;   520
And on a nycht, come travelland thairby
The god of riches, and tuke herbery
With Tantalus; and he at the supare
Slewe his awne sone that was to him leif and deire—
Intill a sewe with spycis soddyn wele,   525
And gart the god eite up his flesche ilk dele.
For this despyte, quhen he was deid, anone
Was dampnit in the flude of Acheron
To suffer hunger, thrist, nakit and cald,
Richt wo-begone, as I to-fore have tald.   530
This hungry man and thristy Tantalus
Betakinnis men gredy and covatus,
The god of riches that [ar] ay redy
For to resaif and call in herbery;
And to thaim seith thair sone in pecis small,   535
That is thair flesche and blud, with gret travall,
To fill the bag and nevir fynd in thair hert
Apon thaim self to spend nor tak thair part.
Allace! In erd quhar is thair mare foly
Than for to want and have haboundantly,   540
To have distress on bed, bak and burd,
And spaire till uther men of gold a hurde?
And in the nycht slepe soundly may thai nocht,
To gadder geir sa gredy is thair thocht.
Bot quhen that ressoun and intelligens   545
Playis apon the harpe of eloquens,
[Schawand to us quhat perrell on ilk syd
That thai incur quhay will trest or confyd
Into this warlds vaine prosperitie,
Quhilk hes thir sory properteis thre—]   550
That is to say, gottin with gret laubour,
Kepit with dreid, and tynt is with dolour.
This avarice, be grace quha understud,
I trow suld leve thair gret sollicitud
And ythand thochtis and thair besyness   555
To gadder gold, syne leif in distress;
Bot he suld drink yneuch quhen-ever him list

Of covatus, and slaike the birnand thrist.
This [Titius] lay nalit on the bent,
And with the grype his bowallis revyn and rent;   560
Quhill he levit, set his entencioun
To fynd the craft of divinacoun,
And lerit it unto the spamen all,
To fele befor sic thingis as wald fall,
Quhat lyf, quhat deid, quhat destany and werd   565
Prevydit war to every man in erd.
Appollo than for his abusioun,
Quhilk is the god of divinacoun,
For he usurpit in his faculte,
Put him till hell, and thar remanis he.   570
Bot Orpheus has wone Erudices
Quhen our desyre with resoun makis pes,
And sekis up to contemplacoun,
Of syn detestand the abusioun.
Bot ilk man suld be war, and wysly se   575
That he bakwart cast nocht his myndis e,
Gevand consent and dilectacoun
Off wardlie lust for the effectioun;
For than gois bakwart to the syn agane
Our appetit, as it befor was slane,   580
In wardlie lust and sensualite,
And makis resoun wedowe for to be.
Now pray we God, sen our affectioun
Is allway prompe and redy to fall doun,
That He wald helpe us with His haly hand   585
Of manteinans, and gif us grace to stand
In parfyte luf, as He is glorius.
And thus endis the tale of Orpheus.

[THE GARMONT OF GUD LADEIS]

WALD my gud lady lufe me best
And wirk efter my will,
I suld ane garmond gudliest
Gar mak hir body till.

Off he honour suld be hir hud   5
Upon hir heid to weir,
Garneist with governance so gud,
Na demyng suld hir deir.

Hir sark suld be hir body nixt,
Of chestetie so quhyt;   10
With schame and dreid togidder mixt,
The same suld be perfyt.

Hir kirtill suld be of clene constance,
Lasit with lesum lufe,
The mailyeis of continwance   15
For nevir to remufe.

Hir gown suld be of gudliness,
Weill ribband with renowne,
Purfillit with plesour in ilk place,
Furrit with fyne fassoun.   20

Hir belt suld be of benignitie
Abowt hir middill meit;
Hir mantill of humilitie
To tholl bayth wind and weit.

Hir hat suld be of fair having   25
And hir tepat of trewth;
Hir patelet of gud pansing,
Hir hals-ribbane of rewth.

Hir slevis suld be of esperance
To keip hir fra dispair;   30
Hir gluvis of gud govirnance
To gyd hir fyngearis fair.

Hir schone suld be of sickernes,
In syne that scho nocht slyd;
Hir hois of honestie, I ges,   35
I suld for hir provyd.

Wald scho put on this garmond gay,
I durst sweir by my seill
That scho woir nevir grene nor gray
That set hir half so weill.   40

[THE ANNUNCIATION]

FORCY as deith is likand lufe,
Throuch quhome al bittir [suet is];
Nothing is hard, as Writ can pruf,
Till him in lufe that letis;
Luf us fra barret betis;   5
Quhen fra the hevinly sete abufe
In message Gabriell couth muf,
And with myld Mary metis,
And said: 'God wele the gretis;
In the He will tak rest and rufe,   10
But hurt of syne or yit reprufe:
In Him sett thi decretis.'

This message mervale gart that myld,
And silence held but soundis,
As weill aferit a maid infild: 15
The angell it expoundis,
How that hir wame but woundis
Consave it suld, fra syne exild.
And quhen this carpin wes compilit
Brichtnes fra bufe aboundis: 20
Thane fell that gay to groundis,
Of Goddis grace nathing begild;
Wox in hir chaumer chaist with child,
With Crist our Kyng that [cround is].

Thir tithingis tauld, the messinger   25
Till hevin agane he glidis:
That princes pure, withoutyn peir,
Full plesandly [applid is]
And blith with barne abidis.
O worthy wirschip singuler,   30
To be moder and madyn meir,
As Cristin faith confidis!

127

That borne was of hir sidis,
Our Maker Goddis Sone so deir,
Quhilk erd, wattir and hevinnis cleir   35
Throw grace and virtu gidis.

The miraclis ar mekle and meit,
Fra luffis ryver rynnis:
The low of luf haldand the hete,
Unbrynt full blithlie birnis,   40
Quhen Gabriell beginnis
With mouth that gudely may to grete.
The wand of Aarone, dry but wete,
To burioun nocht blynnis;
The flesch all donk within is,   45
Upone the erd na drop couth fleit;
Sa was that may maid moder suete,
And sakeless of all synnis.

Hir mervalus haill madinhede
God in hir bosum bracis,   50
And hir divinite fra dreid
Hir kepit in all casis.
The hie God of His gracis
Himself dispisit us to speid,
And dowtit nocht to dee one-deid: 55
He panit for our peacis
And with His blude us bacis;
Bot quhen He ras up, as we rede,
The cherite of His Godhede
Was plane in every placis.   60

O lady lele and lusumest,
Thy face moist fair and schene is!
O blosum blithe and bowsumest,
Fra carnale cryme that clene is,
This prayer fra my splene is—   65
That all my werkis wikkitest

Thow put away, and mak me chaist
Fra Termigant that teyne is,
And fra his cluke that kene is;
And syne till hevin my saule thou haist,   70
Quhar thi Makar of michtis mast
Is Kyng, and thow thair quene is!

L

THE BLUDY SERK

THIS hindir yeir I hard [betald]
Thair was a worthy king;
Dukis, erlis and barronis bald
He had at his bidding.
The lord was anceane and ald,
And sexty yeiris cowth ring;
He had a dochter fair to fald,
A lusty lady ying.

Off all fairheid scho bur the flour,
And eik hir faderis air,   10
Off lusty laitis and he honour,
Meik bot and debonair;
Scho wynnit in a bigly bour,
On fold wes none so fair;
Princis luvit hir paramour   15
In cuntreis our allquhair.

Thair dwelt a lyt besyde the king
A fowll gyane of ane;
Stollin he hes the lady ying,
Away with hir is gane,   20
And kest hir in his dungering,
Quhair licht scho micht se nane;
Hungir and cauld and grit thristing
Scho fand into hir wame.

He wes the laithliest on to luk   25
That on the ground mycht gang;
His nailis wes lyk ane hellis cruk,
Thairwith fyve quarteris lang;
Thair wes nane that he ourtuk,
In rycht or yit in wrang,   30
Bot all in-schondir he thame schuke—
The gyane wes so strang.

He held the lady day and nycht
Within his deip dungeoun;
He wald nocht gif of hir a sicht,   35
For gold nor yit ransoun,
Bot gife the king mycht get a knycht
To fecht with his persoun—
To fecht with him both day and nycht
Quhill ane wer dungin doun.   40

The king gart seik baith fer and neir,
Beth be se and land,
Off ony knycht gife he micht heir
Wald fecht with that gyand;
A worthy prince that had no peir   45
Hes tane the deid on hand,
For the luve of the lady cleir,
And held full trew cunnand.

That prince come prowdly to the toun
Of that gyane to heir,   50
And fawcht with him his awin persoun,
And tuke him presoneir;
And kest him in his awin dungeoun,
Allane withouttin feir,
With hungir, cauld and confusioun,   55
As full weill worthy weir.

Syne brak the bour, had hame the bricht
Unto hir fadir deir;
Sa evill wondit was the knycht
That he behuvit to de;   60
Unlusum was his likame dicht,
His sark was all bludy;
In all the warld was thair a wicht
So peteous for to sy?

The lady murnyt and maid grit mone   65
With all hir mekle micht:
'I luvit nevir lufe bot one
That dulfully now is dicht:
God sen my lyfe wer fra me tone
Or I had sene yone sicht,   70
Or ellis in begging evir to gone
Furth with yone curtas knycht!'

He said: 'Fair lady, now mone I
De, trestly ye me trow;
Tak ye my sark that is bludy   75
And hing it forrow yow;
First think on it and syne on me
Quhen men cumis yow to wow.'
The lady said: 'Be Mary fre,
Thairto I mak a vow!'   80

Quhen that scho lukit to the serk
Scho thocht on the persoun,
And prayit for him with all hir harte,
That lowsd hir of bandoun,
Quhair scho was wont to sit full merk   85
In that deip dungeoun;
And evir quhill scho wes in quert,
That was hir a lessoun.

Sa weill the lady luvit the knycht
That no man wald scho tak.   90
Sa suld we do our God of micht
That did all for us mak;
Quhilk fullely to deid wes dicht
For sinfull manis saik;
Sa suld we do both day and nycht   95
With prayaris to Him mak.

This king is lyk the Trinitie,
Baith in hevin and heir;
The manis saule to the lady,
The gyane to Lucefeir,   100
The knycht to Chryst that deit on tre
And coft our synnis deir,
The pit to hell with panis fell,
The syn to the woweir.

The lady was wowd, bot scho said nay   105
With men that wald hir wed;
Sa suld we wryth all syn away
That in our breistis bred.
I pray to Jesu Chryst verrey,
For us His blud that bled,   110
To be our help on Domysday,
Quhair lawis are straitly led.

The saule is Godis dochtir deir,
And eik His handewerk,
That was betrasit with Lucifeir   115
Quha sittis in hell full merk.
Borrowit with Chrystis angell cleir,
Hend men, will ye nocht herk?
For His lufe that bocht us deir,
Think on the bludy serk.   120

THE THRE DEID-POLLIS

O SINFULL man into this mortall se
Quhilk is the vaill of murnyng and of cair,
With gaistly sicht behold our heidis thre,
Oure holkit ene, oure peilit pollis bair!
As ye ar now into this warld we wair,   5
Als fresche, als fair, als lusty to behald;
Quhan thow lukis on this suth examplair
Off thyself, man, thow may be richt unbald.

For suth it is that every man mortall
Mon suffer deid, and de that lyfe hes tane;   10
Na erdly stait aganis deid ma prevaill;
The hour of deth and place is uncertane,
Quhilk is referrit to the hie God allane;
[Heirfoir haif mynd of deth, that thow mon dy:]
This fair exampill to se quotidiane   15
Sowld caus all men fra wicket vycis fle.

O wantone yowth als fresche as lusty May,
Farest of flowris renewit quhyt and reid,
Behald our heidis! O lusty gallands gay,
Full laichly thus sall ly thy lusty heid,   20
Holkit and how and wallowit as the weid;
Thy crampand hair and eik thy cristall ene
Full cairfully conclud sall dulefull deid;
Thy example heir be us it may be sene.

O ladeis quhyt, in claithis corruscant   25
Poleist with perle and mony pretius stane;
With palpis quhyt, and hals [so] elegant,
Sirculit with gold and sapheris mony ane;
Your fingearis small, quhyt as quhailis bane,
Arrayit with ringis and mony rubeis reid—   30
As we ly thus, so sall ye ly ilk ane
With peilit pollis, and holkit thus your heid.

O wofull pryd, the rute of all distres,
With humill hairt upon our pollis pens!
Man, for thy miss ask mercy with meikness;   35
Aganis deid na man may mak defens:
The empriour for all his excellens,
King and quene, and eik all erdly stait,
Peure and riche, sal'be but differens
Turnit in as and thus in erd translatit.   40

This questioun quha can obsolve lat see—
Quhat phisnamour or perfyt palmester:
Quha was farest or fowlest of us thre?
Or quhilk of us of kin was gentillar?
Or maist excellent in science or in lare,   45
In art, musik, or in astronomye?
Heir sowld be your study and repair;
And think as thus all your heidis mon be.

O febill aige, [ay] drawand neir the dait
Of dully deid, and hes thy dayis compleit,   50
Behald our heidis with murning and regrait!
Fall on thy kneis! Ask grace at God greit
With oritionis and haly salmes sweit,
Beseikand Him on the to haif mercy,
Now of our sawlis bydand the decreit   55
Of His Godheid, quhen He sall call and cry.

Als we exhort that every man mortall,
For His saik that maid of nocht all thing,
For our sawlis to pray in general
To Jesus Chryst, of hevin and erd the King,   60
That throwch His blude we may ay leif and ring
With the hie Fader be eternitie,
The Sone alswa, the Haly Gaist conding,
Thre knit in ane be perfyt unitie.

[NERAR HEVYNNIS BLYSS]

INTYL ane garth undir ane reid roseir,
[Ane] ald man and decrepit hard I syng;
Gay wes the noit, suet wes the voce and cleyr;
It wes grit joy to heir of sic ane thing;
And, to my dowme, he said in his dittyng: 5
'For to be yowng I wald nocht, for my wys
Of al this warld to mak me lord and kyng:
The moyr of age the nerar hevynnis blyss.

'Fals is this warld and ful of varyance,
Ourset with syt and other synnys mo;   10
Now trewtht is tynt, gyl his the governance,
And wrachitness his turnyt al fra weil to wo;
Fredowme is flemyt al the lordis fro,
And covatyce is al the caus of this;
I am content that yowthed is ago: 15
The moyr of age the nerar hevynnys blyss.

'The stait of yowutht I repit for na gud,
For in that stait grit perel now I se;
Can naine ganestand the ragyne of his blud,
Na yit be stabil one-til he agit be;   20
Than in the thing that mast rajoisit he
Nathing ramanys for to be callit his,
Forquhy it wes bot veray vanite:
The moyr of age the nerar hevynnys blyss.

'This wrachit warld may na man trow, forquhy   25
Of erdly joy ay sorow is the end;
The gloyr of it can na man certify—
The day a kyng, the morne na thing to spend.
Quhat hef we heyr bot grace us to defend?
The quhilk God grant us til amend our myss,   30
That til His joy He may our saullis send:
The moyr of age the nerar hevynnys blyss.'

ANE PRAYER FOR THE PEST

O ETERNE God of power infinyt,
To quhois hie knawlege nathing is obscure—
That is, or was, [or sal be, is perfyt]
Into Thy sicht quhill that this warld indure—
Haif mercy of us, indigent and peure!   5
Thow dois na wrang to puneis our offens;
O Lord, that is to mankynd haill succure,
Preserve us fra this perrelus pestilens!

We The beseik, O Lord of lordis all,
Thy eiris inclyne and heir our grit regrait!   10
We ask remeid of The in generall,
That is of help and confort desolait;
Bot Thow with rewth our hairtis recreat,
We are bot deid but only Thy clemens:
We The exhort on kneis law prostrait,   15
Preserf us fra this perrellus pestilens!

We ar richt glaid Thow puneis our trespass
Be ony kynd of uthir tribulatioun,
Wer it Thy will, O Lord of hevin! Allais
That we sowld thus be haistely put doun,   20
And dye as beistis without confessioun,
That nane dar mak with uthir residence!
O blissit Jesu that woir the thorny croun,
Preserve us frome this perrellus pestilens!

Use derth, O Lord, or seiknes and hungir soir,   25
And slaik Thy plaig that is so penetryve!
Thy pepill ar perreist: quha ma remeid thairfoir,
Bot Thow, O Lord, that for thame lost Thy lyve?
Suppois our syn be to The pungityve,
Oure deid ma nathing our synnys recompens.   30
Haif mercy Lord: we ma not with The stryve:
Preserve us, etc.

137

Haif mercy Lord! Haif mercy hevynis King!
Haif mercy of Thy pepill penetent!
Haif mercy of our petous punissing!   35
Retreit the sentence of Thy just jugement
Aganis us synnaris that servis to be schent!
Without mercy we ma mak no defens:
Thow that but rewth upoun the Rude was rent
Preserve us frome this perrellus pestilens!   40

Remmember Lord, how deir Thow hes us bocht,
That for us synnaris sched Thy pretius blude,
Now to redeme that Thow hes maid of nocht,
That is of vertew barrane and denude;
Haif rewth Lord, of Thyne awin symilitude!   45
Puneis with pety and nocht with violens!
We knaw it is for our ingratitude
That we ar puneist with this pestilens.

Thow grant us grace for till amend our miss
And till evaid this crewall suddane deid;   50
We knaw our syn is all the cause of this;
For oppin syn thair is set no remeid;
The justice of God mon puneis than bot dreid,
For by the law He will with non dispens;
Quhair justice laikis, thair is eternall feid   55
Of God that sowld preserf fra pestilens.

Bot wald the heiddismen that sowld keip the law
Pueneis the peple for thair transgressioun,
Thair wald na deid the peple than overthraw;
Bot thay ar gevin so planely till oppressioun   60
That God will nocht heir thair intercessioun;
Bot all ar puneist for thair inobediens
Be sword or deid, withowttin remissioun,
And hes just cause to send us pestilens.

Superne Lucerne, guberne this pestilens;   65
Preserve and serve that we not sterve thairin!
Declyne that pyne be Thy devyne prudens!
O Trewth, haif rewth—lat not our slewth us twin!
Our syt full tyt, wer we contryt, wald blin.
Dissiver did never quha-evir The besocht.   70
Send grace with space, and us imbrace fra syn!
Latt nocht be tynt that Thow so deir hes bocht!

O Prince preclair, this cair cotidiane,
We The exhort, distort it in exyle!
Bot Thow remeid, this deid is bot ane trane   75
For to dissaif the laif, and thame begyle;
Bot Thow sa wyis devyis to mend this byle,
Of this mischeif quha ma releif us ocht—
For wrangus win bot Thow our syn oursyll?
Lat nocht be tynt, etc.   80

Sen for our vyce that justyce mon correct,
O King most hie now pacifie Thy feid!
Our syn is huge; refuge we not suspect;
As Thow art juge, deluge us of this dreid:
In tyme assent or we be schent with deid;   85
We us repent and tyme mispent forthocht:
Thairfoir evirmoir be gloir to Thy Godheid:
Lat nocht be tynt that Thow sa deir hes bocht!

[ROBENE AND MAKYNE]

Robene sat on gud grene hill
Kepand a flok of fe;
Mirry Makyne said him till:
'Robene, thow rew on me!
I haif the luvit lowd and still   5
Thir yeiris two or thre;
My dule in dern bot gif thow dill,
Dowtless but dreid I de.'

Robene ansuerit: 'Be the Rude,
Nathing of lufe I knaw,   10
Bot keipis my scheip under yone [wude]—
Lo quhair thay raik on raw!
Quhat hes marrit the in thy mude,
Makyne, to me thow schaw:
Or quhat is lufe, or to be lude?   15
Fane wald I leir that law.'

'At luvis lair gife thow will leir,
Tak thair ane ABC:
Be heynd, courtas and fair of feir,
Wyse, hardy and fre;   20
So that no denger do the deir,
Quhat dule in dern thow dre,
Preiss the with pane at all poweir—
Be patient and previe.'

Robene anserit hir agane: 25
'I wait nocht quhat is luve,
Bot I haif mervell in certane
Quhat makis the this wanrufe;
The weddir is fair and I am fane,
My scheip gois haill aboif;   30
And we wald play us in this plane
Thay wald us bayth reproif.'

140

'Robene, tak tent unto my taill,
And wirk all as I reid,
And thow sall haif my hairt all haill,   35
Eik and my madinheid:
Sen God sendis bute for baill
And for murnyng remeid,
I dern with the bot gif I daill,
Dowtles I am bot deid.'   40

'Makyne, tomorne this ilka tyde,
And ye will meit meit me heir,
Peraventure my scheip ma gang besyd
Quhill we haif liggit full neir—
Bot mawgre haif I and I byd,   45
Fra thay begin to steir;
Quhat lyis on hairt I will nocht hyd;
Makyn, than mak gud cheir.'

'Robene, thow reivis me roif and rest—
I luve bot the allone.'   50
'Makyne, adew; the sone gois west,
The day is neir-hand gone.'
'Robene, in dule I am so drest
That lufe wil be my bone.'
'Ga lufe, Makyne, quhairever thow list,   55
For lemman I lue none.'

'Robene, I stand in sic a styll;
I sicht—and that full sair.'
'Makyne, I haif bene heir this quhyle;
At hame God gif I wair!'   60
'My huny Robene, talk ane quhill,
Gif thow will do na mair.'
'Makyne, sum uthir man begyle,
For hamewart I will fair.'

Robene on his wayis went   65
Als licht as leif of tre;
Mawkin murnit in hir intent
And trowd him nevir to se.
Robene brayd attour the bent;
Than Mawkyne cryit on hie: 70
'Now ma thow sing, for I am schent!
Quhat alis lufe at me?'

Mawkyne went hame withowttin faill;
Full wery eftir cowth weip:
Than Robene in a ful fair daill   75
Assemblit all his scheip.
Be that, sum pairte of Mawkynis aill
Outthrow his hairt cowd creip;
He fallowit fast thair till assaill,
And till hir tuke gude keip.   80

'Abyd, abyd, thow fair Makyne!
A word for ony thing!
For all my luve it sal be thyne,
Withowttin depairting.
All haill thy harte for till haif myne   85
Is all my cuvating;
My scheip tomorne quhill houris nyne
Will neid of no keiping.'

'Robene, thow hes hard soung and say
In gestis and storeis auld,   90
The man that will nocht quhen he may
Sall haif nocht quhen he wald.
I pray to Jesu every day
Mot eik thair cairis cauld
That first preiss with the to play   95
Be firth, forrest or fawld.'

'Makyne, the nicht is soft and dry,
The wedder is warme and fair,
And the grene woid rycht neir us by
To walk attour allquhair;   100
Thair ma na janglour us espy,
That is to lufe contrair;
Thairin, Makyne, bath ye and I
Unsene we ma repair.'

'Robene, that warld is all away   105
And quyt brocht till ane end,
And nevir agane thairto perfay,
Sall it be as thow wend:
For of my pane thow maid it play,
And all in vane I spend: 110
As thow hes done, sa sall I say:
Murne on! I think to mend.'

'Mawkyne, the howp of all my heill,
My hairt on the is sett,
And evirmair to the be leill,   115
Quhill I may leif but lett;
Nevir to faill—as utheris feill—
Quhat grace that evir I gett.'
'Robene, with the I will nocht deill;
Adew! For thus we mett.'   120

Malkyne went hame blyth annewche
Attour the holttis hair:
Robene murnit, and Malkyne lewche,
Scho sang, he sichit sair—
And so left him bayth wo and wrewche,   125
In dolour and in cair,
Kepand his hird under a huche,
Amangis the holtis hair.

NOTES

ABBREVIATIONS

(i) *Textual sources* (for details see Textual Note, pp. xxv–xxvii)

A Asloan;	H Harleian;
?AN Anderson;	HT Hart;
B Bannatyne;	K Kinaston;
B★ Bannatyne 'first draft';	M Makculloch;
BS Bassandyne;	MT Maitland Folio;
C Charteris (*Fabillis*);	S Smith;
C★ Charteris (*Cresseid*);	SJ St. John;
CM Chepman and Myllar;	T Thynne.
G Gray;	

(ii) *Illustrative texts*

References to Chaucer follow the system of abbreviation and locating used in *The Poetical Works of Chaucer*, F. N. Robinson, ed., 1933, 1957.

MF Morall Fabillis;

TC The Testament of Cresseid.

(iii) *Dictionaries*

DOST W. A. Craigie and A. J. Aitken, *Dictionary of the Older Scottish Tongue*, Chicago, 1931–;

EDD J. Wright, *English Dialect Dictionary*, 6 vols., 1898–1905;

OED Oxford English Dictionary, 13 vols., Oxford, 1933.

The Morall Fabillis

Text: BS. 'The Morall Fabillis of Esope the Phrygian, Compylit in Eloquent, & Ornate Scottis Meter, be M. Robert Henrisone, Scolmaister of Dunfermling.' See H. H. Wood, p. 219, for its textual superiority. No apology is needed for using BS. The over-riding fact, of great editorial significance, is that it provides the most complete version. H. H. Wood (p. 219) notes its superiority over C and H in terms of non-anglicisation of spellings and forms, and of fewer cases of mis-reading, misunderstanding. J. MacQueen (pp. 189–99) defends the virtues of B's ten-only Fables; but his arguments, sometimes irrational, occasionally prejudiced, hardly convince.

Of Henryson's thirteen Fables seven (first, second, sixth, seventh, eighth, twelfth, and thirteenth) belong generally to the Æsopian tradition as first found in the *Fabulæ Æsopiæ* (in Latin verse) of the 1st-cent. Phaedrus. Romulus's prose *Æsop* (9th cent.) and Gualterus Anglicus's verse-rendering of Romulus (12th cent.) further popularize the tradition. In the 14th cent. French *Ysopets* appear, embodying Anglicus's text with a vernacular and metrical translation; in the next century Steinhöwel's *Æsop* includes texts of both Romulus and Anglicus, and gives a German prose version of the former. And from Steinhöwel, by way of a French translation, Caxton's prose Fables are derived.

The other six of Henryson's Fables can be related to the *Fabulæ Extravagantes*, best typified by the cycle of *Reynard the Fox*. This kind of animal tale is possibly of Indian origin, and it comes to be regarded loosely as Æsopian. Thus Marie de France includes the type in her 13th-cent. *Ysopis Fabulæ*, and Steinhöwel finds room for such under the title *Extravagantes*. In 1481 Caxton printed his translation of a Dutch version of the Reynard cycle.

The question of Caxton's influence on Henryson's Fables is matter for debate. MacQueen (pp. 208–21) argues in favour of influence, but D. Fox's findings (*JEGP* lxvii. 586–93) are much more tentative and open.

John Lydgate's 'Isopes Fabules' include a Prologue (the emphases in which correspond largely with those of Henryson's Prologue) and seven Aesopian fables deriving chiefly from Marie de France (and four of these tales are similar in content and *sentence* to four of Henryson's: his first, sixth, twelfth, and thirteenth). For Henryson's probable acquaintance with Lydgate's Fables, see G. Gregory Smith's edn. (hereafter cited as G. G. S.) i. xxxv–xxxix.

I. A. Jamieson (*N & Q*, Nov. 1967, 403–5) sees some influence from Odo of Cheriton in Henryson's second and fifth Fables.

The Prolog

15–16. For similar analogies in such contexts cp. the translated quot. from *Livres des Rois, The Works of Sir Thomas Malory*, ed. E. Vinaver (1947), i. lxii; Chaucer, *NPT*, l. 3443; ll. 22–28 of Lydgate's Fables-prologue. More particularly apt is the last couplet in the prologue to Gualterus's text (printed first at Rome, 1473, and often thereafter):

> Verborum leuitas morum fert pondus honestum,
> Ut nucleum celat arida testa bonum.

For Henryson's apparent echoings of Gualterus see G. G. S. i. xxx–xxxv. In l. 16 *Haldis* lacks its first letter in the original.

19–21. A probable reference to *Disticha Catonis*, iii. 7:

> Interpone tuis interdum gaudia curis,
> Ut possis animo quemvis sufferre laborem.

The work, a collection of Latin maxims in four books, was perhaps written in the third or fourth century and supposedly by Dionysius

Cato. It was a favourite school-book of the Middle Ages. See Chaucer, *MillT*, 3227 and *Piers Plowman* (B Text, ?*c*. 1377), xii. 20–25.

22–23. The bow '. . . is one of the central images by which the Middle Ages understood the human psyche' (V. Kolve, *The Play called Corpus Christi*, 1965, p. 129). See entries under B 561 in *The Oxford Dictionary of English Proverbs*, 3rd edn., 1970. The missing head-syllable in l. 22 is given in B: 'For as we see þe bow', &c.

27–28. The Latin is from Gualterus's opening lines:

> Ut iuuet, ut prosit, conatur pagina praesens:
> Dulcius arrident seria picta iocis.

Henryson occasionally thus uses verbal detail deriving from Gualterus; but his general treatment of the fable-material is 'personally' expansive and imaginative. And so the mention of *Esope*, *author*, and *clerk* in his Prologue, and the declaration of translating *of Latyng* (l. 31), are best taken as illustrating the medieval liking for quoting 'authority'.

31–32. 'I want to try to make a kind of translation from the Latin into our vernacular.'

34–35. A. Lawson (ed.), *The Kingis Quair* (1910) suggests on pp. xlvii–xlviii that the 'lord' is Henry, Lord Sinclair, Gavin Douglas's patron. Yet Henryson's allusion could hardly be more vague. More probably, he is here attempting to establish an initial attitude of objectivity. Cp. *TC*, 11. 61 ff., where something similar is more subtly achieved.

36–38. Expression of shortcomings in 'rhetoric' is a medieval literary commonplace. Cp. Chaucer, *FrT*, ll. 716 ff., Lydgate's Fables-prologue, ll. 29–35, and ll. 119 below. For a general note on the modesty-formula, see E. P. Hammond, *English Verse between Chaucer and Surrey* (Durham, N.C., 1927), p. 392, and E. R. Curtius, *European Literature and the Latin Middle Ages* (trans. W. R. Trask, 1953), pp. 411–12.

39–42. The request for 'correction' is again conventional. Again cp. Lydgate's prologue (ll. 43–49); and see Hammond, pp. 527–8, for further references.

43–49. *dispute*, *argow*, *propone*, and *conclude* are best taken as infins. depending on *understude*, 'knew how to'. *Put* and *tellis* having the same subj. show the not uncommon medieval breaking of tense-sequence. Thus: 'In his fables the author I am following relates how irrational animals had power of speech, and knew how to dispute and debate profitably, to broach an argument and take it to its conclusion: ⟨he⟩ gave examples and parallels ⟨showing⟩ how many men in their dispositions resemble the animal state.'

53. *takis*: either 'it (shamefastness) is encumbered by' or 'he (man) accepts'. For the first sense see *OED*, s.v. 'Take' *v*. 44 b.

60. *Lak the disdane off*: 'Show insufficient respect towards'. For this chiefly Sc. use of the verb see *OED*, s.v. 'Lack' *v.* 6.

I

64 ff. This sequence, in which cock-fable succeeds Prologue, is distinctive of those versions following Romulus. *Jasp*, used by Henryson in title, tale, and *Moralitas*, is apparently peculiar to him in this part of the English *Æsop*. Cp. suggestion in G. G. S. that it is directly formed from the last word in the heading given by Gualterus to this fable—'De Gallo et Jaspide': *iaspide* also occurs in ll. 2, 9.

70. Suppression of the relative is common in MSc.; see ll. 95, 529, 678, 1050, &c.

86. *vertew*: 'innate power'. On the medieval belief in the special potency residing in precious stones, see L. Thorndike, *A History of Magic and Experimental Science* (New York, 1923–41), ch. xxxix. Cp. *Tr*, iii. 891–2, and *William of Palerne* (c. 1350), ll. 4425–8. Lydgate, in that part of his cock-fable corresponding to this in Henryson's (ll. 148–9), particularizes the powers of the *iacynte* (the Scot's *jasp*).

92. *haif*: from C to replace the unfitting *ga* of BS.

102. 'For it is an old wives' saying that an onlooker's work is easily done.'

120. The *Moralitas* materially commences at this point; but B alone indicates this; all other texts begin it at l. 127. *sevin* connotes perfection; for this sense, and that of 'a large number' (ll. 533, 2064), see *OED*, s.v. 'Seven' A. *adj.* 1 d.

129. 'Possessed of the power to accomplish many virtuous deeds.' Whereas for Henryson the stone symbolizes distinct ethical qualities, for Lydgate it signifies 'rychesse', to attain which the 'worldly man laboreth'. Lydgate preaches on the text 'Suche as God sent, eche man take at gre'.

138–40. Reminiscence of Matthew vi. 19, 20. *screit*: M, C, and S show the straightforward 'fre(i)t'; B has 'ket' (? cut). G. G. S. discusses *screit* (in H also) as a possible scribal error from 'fret'; yet cp. the dialectal 'screit' (pare) in *EDD*.

141–7. As often, the analogy is somewhat forced: strictly, for the moral to be valid, the cock should live without corn. Likewise with the sow and her food. Throughout Lydgate's fable the cock is a 'moral' figure (whose triple crowing is praise of the Trinity, &c.), and his bestirring and his rejection of the stone decorously point the 'vertuos man' avoiding 'all ydelnesse', content 'with suffisaunce'.

159. 'To take the matter further would be a waste of time.'

164. *borous-toun*: a town possessing the rights of a borough. Such privileges were chiefly commercial; see T. Pagan, *The Convention of the Royal Burghs of Scotland* (Glasgow, 1926), pp. 2–4.

167–8. *and uther mennis skaith*: 'and to the harm of others'. The tale has not yet here reached that point at which animal–human approximations have real piquancy. *owtlawis* carries the fig. sense of 'wild or hunted beasts'. *OED* provides two quotations, both dated later than Henryson's period, wherein the word has this force; see s.v. 'Outlaw' *sb*. 1. d.

172–5. Here the juxtaposing of the animal and human worlds as a deliberate device begins. Cp. Chaucer's similar practice in *HF*, l. 868 and *NPT*, l. 2967.

173. *but custum mair or les*: allusion to the *magna custuma* (a levy on imports and exports) and to the *parva custuma* (that on market-goods). See G. G. S.

190–1. 'Would to God that you had witnessed the heart-felt joy manifested when these two sisters met.' Lit. *Beis kith* = 'Is shown'.

203. Cp. 'He that dois evill haits the licht', No. 706 in *The James Carmichaell Collection of Proverbs in Scots*, ed. M. L. Anderson (Edinburgh, 1957). For further parallels with Henryson's frequent gnomic statements, see pp. 117–37 of this same work; also *Fergusson's Scottish Proverbs*, ed. E. Beveridge (S.T.S., 1923–4). Also B. J. Whiting, 'Proverbs and Proverbial Sayings from Scottish Writings before 1600', *Mediaeval Studies*, xi (1949), 123–205, xii (1951), 87–164.

207. 'Whether this was welcome fare is a question I leave them to answer.'

235. *than seith to him ane kow*: 'than if a whole ox were to be cooked for him'.

236–8. 'Provided goodwill dispenses it, a moderate portion is to be more commended than an abundance of highly-seasoned dishes served up with an ill-tempered countenance.' Cp. Proverbs xv. 17, the obvious source of the thoughts of this whole stanza.

248. *Gude Friday* implies fasting, and *Pace* (Easter Day) a feast.

253. *In stubbill array*: B has 'In skugry ay' (All the time concealed); A reads 'In stowthry ay' (Always stealthily). The reading of BS, also found in C and H, is not necessarily corrupt; it is acceptable as meaning 'In awkward fashion', 'With difficulty'. For *stubble* signifying 'difficult', &c., cp. *Cursor Mundi*, ll. 23910–12:

> For-sak þu noht this stubil werk
> For þoh it royd and stubil be.
> It [es] in worsip wroht to þe.

For *array* with force of 'condition', 'plight', see Chaucer, *WBT*, ll. 902–3.

262. *Withowt 'God speid!'*: 'Without any ceremony', 'Straightway'; cp. l. 268.

283. *Thraf-caikkis*: for the now dialectal 'tharf-, thar-cakes'; explained by John Ray as being 'cakes made of oat meal, as it comes from the mill, and fair water, without yeast or leaven, and so baked'. See s.v. 'Bannock' in his *A Collection of English Words not generally used* (2nd edn., 1691).

285. *mane full fyne*: C's reading in place of BS's *manfully fyne* which appears corrupt. The phrase signifies 'fine white bread of exceptional quality', with *mane* aphet. for *demaine*. The usual expression is the fuller one 'pain-demaine', from med. L. *panis dominicus*, 'the master's bread', i.e. bread of special quality and whiteness. See R. F. Patterson, *MLR* vii. 376.

326. *Gib Hunter*: the tom-cat. *Gib* is the familiar abbrev. of 'Gilbert' (see l. 338) once commonly used for a cat. In l. 6204 of the Chaucerian *Rom* 'Gibbe' renders the Fr. 'Tiberz'; cp. 'Tibert' in Caxton's *Reynard*.

336. *burde*: probably 'board', i.e. the wainscoting between which and the stone wall the mouse finds a space. B reads 'dressour' (dresser) and A 'dosor' (dosser or wall-hanging).

337. *parraling*: for 'parpalling', a partition-wall made of parpens or stones passing through the wall from side to side. Cp. *perpall* in l. 348, appearing as 'parpane' in B.

347. *na fall*: lit. 'no downcome', suggesting inevitability.

360. *but and ben*: 'outer and inner parts'; from OE *butan*, *binnan*. The expression is often applied to the old and chiefly Sc. type of dwelling-house in which the room adjoining the external door is called the 'but' and the next one the 'ben'.

374. *quietie*: a rare form of 'quiet', useful for rhyme; it is used so in Lindsay, *Dreme* (c. 1528), l. 283.

383. *Luke*: for original *Lieke*. Cp. 'Luik' in H and 'Luke' in B and A.

391–6. Such commonplace encomiums of lowly contentment are probably echoes of Biblical utterances, as in Proverbs xvi. 8, xvii. 1, &c. (ascribed to Solomon as the repository of wisdom).

3

406–7. 'Demonstrating such great diversity in their natures ⟨that⟩ my little skill cannot be called upon to write of them.'

426. *toun*: the farm with its house; still used in this sense in Sc. dialects.

429. *Lowrence*: a familiar name for the fox. The origin suggested in G. G. S. (*lour*, 'skulk') ignores the vowel-difference.

449. *Dirigie*: a popular designation of Matins in the Office for the Dead, it being the first word of the antiphon *Dirige, Domine, Deus meus, in conspectu tuo viam meam* (Psalms v. 8).

469. *sa mot I the*: a common medieval tag, lit. 'so may I prosper'; but best taken as an intensifying expression 'I do declare', &c.

477. *wawland*: 'rolling his eyes'. B reads 'walkit', which is as logical and gives better tense-sequence.

483. Probably these hen-names show the common diminutive-forming suffix *-ock*. Cp. 'Jamock', 'Kittock', 'lassock', 'pinnock', 'ruddock', 'wyfock', &c. *Pertok*: either a reminiscence of the Chaucerian 'Pertelote' or a formation of 'Pert' (comely). *Sprutok*, the 'speciall' of Cok Coby in *The Tale of Colkebie's Sow* (iii. 117), is probably connected with 'sprutil' (a speckle), or from 'Sprotinus', found in the Latin *Reynard. Toppok*: possibly to be linked with 'top', 'tap' (the crest or tufting of a bird).

496. Either *fell* = 'falling' or *With* = 'While'. For the latter sense cp. variant readings in *Bruce*, xvii. 454–5; the St. John MS. (1487) has

> And saw it wes nocht eyth till ta
> The toune, with sic defens wes maid.

In the Edinburgh MS. (1489) 'with' is replaced by 'quhill'.

511. The tag-like *Sanct Johne to borrow* is best given expletive force, 'by St. John', 'indeed', &c.

523 ff. As they stand the lines have a measure of sense in them. Previously Pertok has spoken with 'feinyeit faith' only; now will come her true and meditated opinion: the cock found all his pleasure in a love purely sensual—but the hens themselves outdid him in sensuality. Pertok has first spoken of Chantecleir as the chivalric lover; Sprutok has found him 'cauld and dry' in love-matters (thereby demonstrating her own 'animalness'); Pertok then underlines his and their lustfulness and Toppok further stresses his lecherousness. The interchanges thus make up a brief meditation on deception: Pertok begins with praise of Chantecleir's 'courtly' yet 'external' qualities (*paramouris* designates something not wholly sensual); Sprutok pierces this chivalric façade; Pertok, thereby drawn to realistic appraisal, takes the disabusing further, so as to embrace themselves and him; Toppok discriminates and gives the final emphasis—the cock was at greater fault and so disaster has overtaken him. In B ll. 523–4 appear as

> Thus sprowtok, þat feynȝeit fayth befoir,
> In luste but luif þat sett all hir delyte.

They obviously permit a less involved interpretation of the whole passage.

527–9. 'Since he is gone, I'll undertake—if modesty will let me mention it—to get within a week a mate better able to satisfy my desires.' Evidently false modesty.

533. *ma than sevin*: 'in great plenty'; see note on l. 120.

546–7. *Berrie*: 'Shaggy'; see *OED*, s.v. 'Burry'. *Bawsie Broun*: probably 'Tawny', 'Brindly'; cp. 'Bausond' (*OED*). *Rype Schaw*: 'Covert Searcher'. *Rin Weil*: 'Swifty'. *Curtes*: formed on 'Cortois', the Reynardian dog-name. *Nuttie Clyde*: 'Browny Clyde'.[1]

563. *for ane yeir*: 'for some time to come' = 'assured', 'trusted'. In l. 575 something pseudo-technical is implied (term of hire, &c.).

570. *out off the bewch*: 'out from the shoulder' = 'out and away from the fox's mouth'. B's reading, 'vnto a buche' (up to a bough), is more straightforward and prepares for the tree-reference in the following stanza.

581. *still*: inactive in the sense of being unthinking, unperceiving. Cp. *The Pricke of Conscience* (*c.* 1340), ll. 3448–9, where one of the 'veniel sins' is expressed as:

> When þou may vaile thurgh wytte and skille
> And wille noght help bot haldes þe stylle.

4

621–2. *Thetes*: supplied from B. Thetis was a sea-deity. The sense is that the sun had sunk beneath the waves.

631. *spheir*: in the older astrology the spheres were imagined as hollow, transparent, concentric globes revolving around the earth and respectively carrying the heavenly bodies.

632. *retrograde*: apparently moving backwards and contrary to the succession of the signs of the Zodiac.

635–41. This astronomical catalogue is not entirely gratuitous: it demonstrates Lowrence's *lair* (l. 648) and identifies the warm season in which the action takes place (Phebus would be in the sign of the Lion from mid-July to mid-August); see ll. 756–7. In l. 639, *wes in* refers to Venus as well as Moon.

651. *men*: a difficult reading, also in H, signifying either 'mien' (in an unusual sense of 'way of life'; cp. the same spelling in Douglas, *Eneados*, VIII. xi. 20) or 'mean' (in the now obsolete sg. form denoting 'means',

[1] In a letter dated 16 May 1957, J. S. Ritchie of the National Library of Scotland informs me that 'The Keeper of Manuscripts has heard, indirectly, from the manager of the sheep auction market at Lanark . . . that in his experience the dog-name "Clyde" is to be found in use locally, i.e., in the Clyde valley.'

'methods'). C has 'Ene'. B has 'fait' (fate), answering to 'watt' (know) in l. 649.

661–2. 'Then too are we called "Withy-throat" and "Crack-rope", and for our reward get strung up by the neck.' Nicknames for the gallows-bird, a person destined for hanging with a halter of willow-twigs (wid-dies, withies) or likely to break the stringing-up rope.

667. *Waitskaith*: lit. 'one lying in wait to do harm'. In Caxton's *Rey-nard* 'wayte scathe' is an ally of Martin the ape; see D. B. Sands (ed.), *The History of Reynard the Fox* (Cambridge, Mass., 1960), pp. 126, 212.

693. *Benedicitie!* 'God's blessing on you!'; semi-technically used here to preface Confession. In l. 2237 it carries (but with a touch of dramatic irony) the common connotation of a means whereby evil is averted.

713. *perfyte Confessioun*: the full sacrament of Penance embraces (i) *contritio*, 'sorrow of heart and detestation of sin committed with the resolve to sin no more', (ii) *confessio*, 'the external manifestation of con-science to a priest in order to obtain pardon', (iii) *satisfactio*, 'the payment of the temporal punishment due on account of the offence committed against God by sin'. Henryson's fox confesses (ll. 691–7), cannot attain to full contrition (ll. 698–711), and accepts an ironic punishment (ll. 712–32).

741. *net nor bait*: emending of original word-order *nor net bait*.

751. Fish is penitential fare (cp. l. 723). H. M. Murray refers to the French *Ysopet*: 'Quant Ysangrin vit le mouton si le salua. . . . Et li dit: "Sawmon, Dieu te gart!".' Cp. the much later anecdotes referred to in *TLS* (1953), pp. 317, 333, 629.

760. 'My full belly is just the right target for an arrow now.'

780. *greit*: probably a rhyme-form of 'greitis' (weeps) balancing *repentis*.

786. 'Custom has such power to dominate the natures. . . .'

5

See M. E. Rowlands for interesting discussion of the legal background of this fable and of nos. 6, 10, and 12.

803–4. 'By reference to sound reasoning, and as is shown by all the steps of a sensible analogy, it clearly follows that. . . .'

824. *pietie*: probably 'pity', a quality more 'natural' than 'piety'.

843. *buste*: from B to replace *breist* in BS.

852. *bust*: emending *bus* in BS (also in H) to accord with *t*-forms in B and C.

869. 'With the grass growing apace, tall and luxuriant.'

870. *thay*: presumably the beams of the sun, which cause a fragrance to issue from every flowering branch, &c.

874. 'Carrying it so that it was taken to the hill-top.'

885 ff. Recourse to enumeration is a frequent device in medieval poetry. Cp. the Chaucerian *Rom*, ll. 1355 ff.; Chaucer, *PF*, ll. 330–64; *The Kingis Quair* (? 1424), ll. 1077 ff., beginning 'And also, as it comes unto my mynd, / Of bestis sawe I mony diverse kynd'. Also Montgomerie, *The Cherrie and the Slae* (*c.* 1585), st. 2. See E. P. Hammond (p. 435 n.) for the common listings of personages, especially in Lydgate.

887. The minotaur is *mervelous* since it is the offspring of Pasiphae and a bull, and shows its strange begetting in its bodily make-up.

888. Presumably Bellerophont is the Chimæra, slain by Bellerophon by the devising of Iobates, King of Lydia, acting on the request of Proteus, King of Ephyra, whose queen Anteia had played Potiphar's wife to Bellerophon. It is a beast of *bastardrie* because it is of 'mixed' form, with heads of lion, goat, and dragon.

889–90. Pegasus was *perillous* to the Chimæra, being instrumental in its slaying. The *assent of sorcerie* probably refers to the effects of the golden bit, given by Minerva to Bellerophon, whereby the steed assumed a tractable nature for the enterprise of killing the three-headed beast.

895. For discussion of this line, with suggested reading of 'The antelope ⟨indeed⟩ found its horns of use' or 'The antelope, that axe-wielding beast, sped onwards', see C. Elliott, *N & Q*, Mar. 1962, 86–87. Also for the readings for ll. 910, 914.

896. *peyntit pantheir*: 'All four-footed beasts have liking to behold the divers colours of the panther' (quoted from Bartholomew Anglicus in R. R. Steele, *Mediæval Lore*, 1905, p. 166).

910. *glebard*: appositional use of 'globard' (one extremely voracious) may be meant.

914. In the first half-line BS shows *Bowranbane*, which may be a mere running-together of 'bow', 'ran', and 'bane', with the first word used with a hint of humour in its sense of 'herd ⟨of cattle⟩', and the third as an adv. meaning 'promptly'. *lerion*: probably corruptly from Fr. *liron*, 'dormouse'.

918. *musk*: *OED* for this instance suggests the sense 'musk-deer', hardly apt to a context of smaller animals. See G. G. S. for the opinion that civet-cat may be intended; also quot. from Florio: 'Lattitio': 'a kind of Musk or Ziuet-cat'.

929 ff. The remarks on merciful mastery are conventional for the beast-fable lion. Cp. Dunbar, 'Quhen Merche wes with variand windis past', l. 118.

948, 951. 'to fence' is the Sc. legal term signifying the opening of court proceedings by uttering a formula forbidding interruption and obstruction.

975–7. 'Brought to the light, your features—your very looks—appear evil and deformed, ⟨and⟩ as a means of aiding you by any good-will they might engender, they are timorous, ineffectual and powerless.'

1008. *tak ye the flyrdome and the fon*: 'the joke is on you'. See *EDD*, s.v. 'fleer' *v.*¹ and *sb.*, 'fun' *v.* and *sb.*¹

1023. *hattrell*: 'crown'; from B (also in C) to replace *hattell* of BS.

1026. *wes worth sum coist!*: 'was of fine use to him!'

1033. Erasmus (*Adagia*, Venice, 1508) has this line. That another's perils can teach one caution is the gist of common Sc. proverbs.

1060. *hir*: from the other versions for *his* in BS.

1064. See comment in G. G. S., following A. R. Diebler, on the 'verbal identity' between this line and the corresponding passage in Caxton's *Reynard*: '. . . the beste clerkes ben not the wysest men'. But there is closer verbal approximation to Chaucer's 'The gretteste clerkes been noght wisest men' (*RvT*, l. 4054) which is given its fable-context by the succeeding line: 'As whilom to the wolf thus spak the mare.' The thought is provbl., and is found in the chief Eng. and Sc. collections.

1083. *be practik*: either 'the result of cunning' or 'by regular legal argument'.

1087. *assyis*: the local jury of presentment, whose function it was to pronounce the verdict. See also l. 1267.

1100. *fyne*: from B for original *syne*.

1102–3. 'Who through the medium of poetry can demonstrate their meaning and show its full and direct relevance to our way of life.'

1113. 'Commending service to God as the course of true religion.'

1131. Solomonian rather than Solomon's precise words. Cp. Proverbs xxviii. 5, 14.

6

1148. *consistorie*: an ecclesiastical court, the procedure of which is indicated by Henryson in some detail and with some irony. In the corresponding fable in Lydgate the action is more vaguely located 'afore a iuge'.

1153. 'And following accepted practice and procedure, and employing the customary expressions.'

1156–7. *Hie Suspensioun*: *suspensio totalis*, whereby a cleric is deprived of the exercise of every function and ecclesiastical right. *Grit Cursing*: *excommunicatio major*, involving exclusion from the Sacraments, the public services and prayers of the Church, ecclesiastical burial, jurisdiction, benefices, canonical rights, and social intercourse. *Interdictioun*: *interdictio,* embracing censure along with exclusion from the liturgy, Sacraments and ecclesiastical burial.

1166. *perrie doig*: 'the shaggy dog'; var. of 'burry' showing in B. Cp. note on ll. 546–7.

1170. 'The poor sheep dared not stop even for food.'

1172–3. 'The time of day set apart by the judge for trying the case being sundown.' See reference in G. G. S. to Lord Hailes's note (*Ancient Scottish Poems*, Edinburgh, 1770) for a suggestion that this is a 'lawless hour'. *oure off cause*: a set legal phrase.

1188. 'Such, in brief, are the essentials of my case.'

1199. 'This spot is off the beaten track, ⟨and as well⟩ no court can properly sit at this time of year.' *feriate* = 'legal vacation'. The location of the assembly prevents justice being seen to be done; the time of the convening is out of term and therefore invalid.

1218. *Contra and pro*, *strait*: suggested by B's 'prowe and contra, strait' to replace the obvious misreading *Contrait, Prostrait* of BS.

1229. 'I leave it to our learned friends whether this decision was a fair one.'

1234–5. 'Moreover he produced evidence that the sheep had wrongfully kept back the piece of bread.' The *borrow* was a written charge of a crime, signed by one or more persons, witnessing to the truth of the charge.

1251. *mair the executioun*: 'further execution' = 'that all the other potentialities of the judgement would be enforced against him'.

1260. *settis all thair cure*: 'give all their energies'. The social comments begun in this stanza contrast with Lydgate's rather diffuse moralizing on the text 'Periury is enemy to al rightwisnesse'.

1266. 'Who buys up the right to collect royal fines.'

1269–71. 'Though he (one of the *pure men*) is as innocent as ever St. John was, when he comes under the authority of the coroner he is as good as ruined (lit. 'slain'), unless he makes terms with the judge.'

1273. *portioun*: either 'section', 'part' or, more probably, an idiosyncratic form (as in Lindsay, *Satyre of the Thrie Estaitis*, c. 1535, l. 769) of 'porteous' (the reading in B), signifying in Sc. law the roll of the names of the offenders, retained by the coroner until the arrival of the king's justices.

1276–8. M. E. Rowlands, p. 225, refers to a Sc. Act of Parliament forbidding the practice of altering names on the roll. *tat* is probably 'entangled', 'involved', showing particip. use of 'tat', a verb of Sc. and north. provenance. See *OED*, s.v. 'Tat' *v*. 4. C shows assonance in the use of 'tak', while B has the unequivocal verb 'skat' (exact).

1295. 'The Sleep of God' was an image often used to denote a period of lawlessness and suffering, regarded exultingly by the evil and sorrowfully by the good. The figure derives from the traditional interpretation of Matthew viii. 24 ff. &c. Cp. l. 2332, and see note in Bennett and Smithers (edd.), *Early Middle English Verse and Prose* (Oxford, 1966), pp. 383–4.

7

1325. Between night-time and midday, i.e. in early morning.

1337. *ane poynt off Paradice*: 'to experience some of the joys of Paradise itself'.

1398. *Yit*: from B (also in H) for *Yis* in BS.

1399. *Not to displeis your fatherheid*: 'At the same time with no wish to appear disrespectful'; *fatherheid*: a term of address to those meriting respect.

1404. After this line the original has *The end of the Prolog, & Beginis the Taill*.

1405. *verray*: from C to replace *war* in BS which is deficient metrically and syntactically.

1410. *in ane gyis*: 'a round'; lit. a dance performed in disguises or masks.

1477. *conqueist*, from the rest of the stanza, seems to mean 'conquered one'.

1488. *Bot askand*: 'But one that craves'.

1501. *Keipit that*: '⟨And⟩ has saved him who . . .'.

1519. 'Then a band of hunters spread themselves out in a row within the wood.'

1558. *brother*: 'comrade'; cp. Job xxx. 29 in the 1611 Bible: 'I am a brother to dragons, and a companion to owls.'

1583. 'A place of hollow delight mingled with a pervading sorrow, as it were.'

1592. *forquhy thay stand nane aw*: 'because they stand in no awe ⟨of their superiors⟩'.

1599–1600. 'Who has paid fines both just and unjust, whereas a lord may have acted harshly sooner than in kindness towards him.' *kinbute*: lit. 'kin-boot', the compensation paid by a slayer to the slain person's kin.

1611. Cp. the entry in *OED*, s.v. 'Marble' *sb*. I. d.: 'In marble harde our harmes wee alwayes graue.'

8

1625. *far all mannis jugement*: 'to a degree far beyond any man's power of assessing'.

1636. In *Metaph.* I. M. i. 3.

1659. *spheir*: see note on l. 631.

1660. The ancient belief that the orderly motions of the planetary spheres produced ineffable music; cp. *PF*, ll. 60–63 and Robinson's note, and see note to *Orpheus and Erudices*, ll. 223–5.

1661. The four elements of medieval science; see Steele, *Med. Lore*, pp. 14, 23.

1675. *difference off tyme*: 'varying lengths of day'.

1676. 'To the accommodating of our needs.'

1685, 1706. *harvest, ver*: the old names for autumn and spring. See *Secreta Secretorum* (*c.* 1400): 'hervest . . . durith . . . from the xiij day of septembre vnto the xiij day of Novembre' (p. 28) and 'Ver . . . dewrith from the xiij day of marche vnto the xiij day of Iune' (p. 27).

1690. *Copia Temporis*: an obvious personif. to indicate the season of plenty.

1718–19. 'Glancing down at the soil, that was ⟨indeed⟩ in natural good state, fertile and ready to nurture all the seeds.'

1754. The provbl. idea that to be forewarned is to be forearmed; cp. l. 10 of Gualterus's fable 'De Yrundine et Lino':

Nam prouisa minus ledere tela solent.

1757. 'But ⟨true⟩ prudence consists of a ⟨more⟩ perceptive reasoning.'

1783. *be aventure and cace*: best reduced to 'it did so happen'.

1785–6. 'I suppose it was because they made it their haunt, being a spot which gave them both safety and seclusion.'

1807. *freindes, hardilie beid*: 'my friends, have it precisely your own way'. *hardilie*: 'certainly', 'assuredly'. *beid* = 'be it'.

1825–31. A concise yet clear and accurate account of flax-preparation. It is shown in G. G. S. that linen-manufacture was well established in Dunfermline by Henryson's day, though not confined to that area.

1836. *fair*: either the straightforward epithet or signifying 'fairly', 'right', &c. *fell off feit*: 'lost their footing'.

1842. *for thair expence*: 'for their pains'.

1873. *this*: correction of original *thus*.

1894. 'Possessing as it does a valid signification.'

1903. *delectioun*: probably var. of 'dilectioun', meaning '(sensual) love'.

9

This fable is summarized in Lydgate, *Pilgrimage of the Life of Man*, E.E.T.S., E.S., 83 (1901), 14605–20.

1954. *maid him weill to fair*: 'did well for himself thereby'.

1962. *Russell*: a conventional name for the fox in the Reynard cycle, from OFr. *russel*, 'reddish'; see l. 1976.

1986. *on the wind*: 'upwind', so as to avoid the carrying of the stalker's scent.

1987. 'For every trick they know you certainly have one of your own.'

1992. *quhair I wes never sene*: 'even in a place where I am seen for the very first time'.

1994. 'And you are fishing up talk of difficulties in order to hide your tricks for your own advantage.'

1995. *sonyes*: 'excuses'; from C to replace *senzes* in BS.

1996. 'For all your beating about the bush.'

1998. 'Better to bend than break.'

2013. *reid raip*: 'hanging-rope', reddened with the victim's blood.

2023. *ane word*: i.e. *leill*, implying present lack of such quality in the fox.

2036. *silver-seik*: 'silver-sick' = 'avaricious'; a connotation of 'hungry' is suggested in G. G. S.

2041. 'Whether I have cunning enough to trick that fellow there.'

2049. 'And then he made a lengthy detour.' See ll. 2133, 2159.

2052. 'And then he lay down full length—⟨indeed⟩ no pleasing sight.'

2061. 'And he jigged on his toes right across the track.'

2064. *this sevin yeir*: 'in many a year'; see note on l. 120.

2074. For selling to the skin-merchants of the Low Countries.

2083. See G. G. S. for references to this popular old song.

2094. *And thou wer*: 'Would that you were'.

2095. *Do furth thy mercat*: 'Carry on with your chaffering'. Ironic, since the fox has stolen all that the man had to sell.

2099–2100. '"I fully deserve," he exclaimed, "to have that rascal escape me for not having in my hand so much . . .".'

2120. *thir fourtie dayis*: 'for this present time of Lent'.

2127. 'And fresh (*callour*), moist and glossy (*pypand*) like a partridge's eye.'

2132. *tak you na suppryis*: 'and come to no harm'; here *suppryis* carries its former chiefly Sc. shade of meaning.

2147. *be my thrift*: either a rhyme-useful tag ('indeed', &c.) or 'by my good fortune' = 'if I have the luck'.

2150. *do him lytill deir*: 'it will give him little trouble'; the wolf is to act the part of a dead creature and so will offer no resistance to being handled by the man.

2154. *In principio*: the opening of St. John's Gospel and also the popular abbreviated name for its first fourteen verses. In the later Middle Ages such verses came to be thought of as having special powers, and as such formed part of friar-jargon (cp. Robinson's note on Chaucer, *Gen Prol*, l. 254). A similar pejorative force is intended here.

2158. *gird up sone and to gay*: 'quickly got ready to set off'.

2160. 'Afterwards he stretched himself out on the road before the carrier approached.'

2168. *wavering as the wind*: either 'in two minds', 'excercised' over the fox, &c., or 'trembling' (with anger and with anticipation of his revenge; cp. 'als wraith as ony wind' in C).

2170. *that wes behind*: better taken as a straight-forward reference to the fox left further back along the road by the *cadgear* than as assumed inverted word-order for the sense 'what the motives of the fox were'.

2177–8. 'Unless *you* will feel the punishment due more properly to him who has done me wrong!'

2190. *abill*: 'is fit', 'deserves'. Cp. J. Rolland, *The Sevin Seages* (Edinburgh, 1560), l. 1308: 'Зour present Sone war abill for to die.'

2193–4. 'The plain truth is that he showed himself artful in so discomfiting his master.' *fyne*: for original *syne*.

2207–8. 'The carter can be likened to death beneath the shadow of whose inevitable coming all men must live out their contentious existences—⟨for⟩ all that ever came into life must by way of nature die.' *preis*: 'contend', 'strive'.

2213. *reid*: the customary epithet for gold in the medieval period, when gold was often alloyed with copper, which gave it a reddish tinge.

10

2234. *in streiking-tyme off yeir*: 'in the early spring'. *streiking* is the ploughing of the first furrow.

2235. *feir*: either 'mate' (the *gadman*) or an otherwise unattested noun from 'feer' (to mark off the width of a strip of land for ploughing by drawing a furrow on each side of it). See *OED*, s.v. 'Feer' *v*.

2238–9. 'The driver shouted: "Ho there! Up and away now! Pull straight my hearties!" '

2241. 'And in their friskiness they began to spoil the furrow.'

2244. ' "Let the wolf take the whole pack of you!" he cried.'

2251. *as he wer king*: 'as if he had uttered them with royal potency'. See l. 2289.

2268. *frear than gift?*: 'more bespeaking of generosity than the act of giving itself?'.

2269. 'These efforts to obstruct will merely lose you my gratitude.'

2270, 2271. *plank*, also in C and H, is considered in G. G. S. as possible rhyme-variant of 'plack' (a small copper coin worth four pennies Scots; cp. 'mark', the coin valued at 13*s*. 4*d*. Scots, found in C for *mart*). Harvey Wood defends *plank* as a non-arbitrary form and refers to Gaelic *plang*. The collocation *plank-mart* (coin of little value—valuable ox fattened for market) is cogent enough as a juxtaposing of ideas of 'smallness' and 'greatness'. The first element occurs frequently in Sc. gnomic sayings to express something of very small worth. See, for example, No. 1587 in Carmichaell: 'They are tyred of their life wald gie a plak to stick them.'

2280–2. 'The wolf declared: "That lord's word is as good as his bond who out of regard for truth shuns what brings shame and is anxious to avoid reproach." '

2288. 'A man who sets store by truth is not likely to be convinced by a mere one-sided declaration.'

2304. *decreit perpetuall*: 'decision against which there shall be no appeal'.

2320. 'Do not ruin the force of your plea by attempting yourself to justify it.'

2321. 'This business will not be settled without a great deal of money.' For the ellipsis, cp. *The Kingis Quair*, l. 438: 'Bot hert, quhere as the body may noght throu'.

2322–4. 'Have you not seen how bribes see men through, and how gifts can set right awkward situations? It sometimes happens that a ⟨mere⟩ hen makes it possible for a man to keep his cow.'

2346. *unroikit*: an infrequent usage, primarily Sc., presumably signifying 'loudly', as a child in an unrocked cradle.

2347. *The devill*: with negative force; thus 'Not by the devil'. See *OED*, s.v. 'Devil' *sb*. 21.

2357. 'The wolf asked: "Is this what you advise me to do—⟨namely that I consent that . . .⟩".'

2362. *neip*: turnip. The simile in l. 2395 is thus ironic.

2366. *ye tak it in nane evill*: 'you must not resent this'.

2372. *hous*: the reading from S and HT to replace *hors* in BS (and H) which shows evident scribal error. See l. 2374, where the man is said to have guarded actively his house-door until dawn.

2383. *bellie-blind*: 'blindman's buff', where *bellie* is of uncertain origin but perhaps connected with 'billie' (fellow, comrade), a word chiefly in Sc. and north. use. See p. 119 in I. and P. Opie, *Children's Games in Street and Playground* (Oxford, 1969).

2402. *dart-*: perhaps 'draught'. Harvey Wood suggests evolution from 'dra', with scribal abbrev. and metathesis. See *DOST*, s.v. 'Dart', 'Dairt' *a*.

NOTES

11

2468. *with*: for *wit* in BS.

2473. *off toun*: 'away from this farmstead'; see note on l. 426.

2474. 'For all the wild creatures up to now kept subdued.'

2476. *wichtlie*: for original *wrechitlie*, which hardly fits the over-confident wether. HT has 'wightlie'; and cp. *Fabillis*, l. 553. The emendation is suggested by T. W. Craik (*N & Q*, Mar. 1969, 88–89).

2490. *This come of ane gude wit*: 'This suggestion is sensibly made'.

2538. *bind* may be the hawking-term 'to close with'; see G. G. S. and *OED*, s.v. 'Bind' *v*. 10.

2548. *Syne*: from C and H to replace the obvious misreading *Tyne* in BS.

2550. *freir*: i.e. a Carmelite or 'white' friar.

2551. 'Now that I know the truth of the matter it is obvious that I have fled a deal too far.'

2559. *nane uther*: 'nothing but this'.

2577. *In play or ernist*: 'In one circumstance or another'.

2591–4. 'Providing instances moral and prudent—consideration of which is truly meritorious: by virtue of its fitting symbolism it [the 'parable'] has never to this day failed to provide its readers with a lesson.'

2597. *be thay als gay*: 'once they have become as finely attired ⟨as their betters⟩.' Cp. ll. 2611–12.

2608. *hall-benkis ar rycht slidder*: 'high places are slippery enough', 'the favour of great ones has no certainty about it'.

2613. 'It is not fitting for any servant to oppose actively ⟨his superior⟩.' *uphald weir*: lit. 'maintain feud'.

12

2632. *fyle and bruke*: 'pollute while you are making use of it'; the corresponding line in B, S, and HT shows 'bruke' as a noun (stream).

2645. Signifies hardly more than 'And the facts of the case'.

2659. *and I brukit my heid*: 'if I could have use of my head'; little more than a tag signifying 'and I gave him my solemn word', &c. 'Brook' is a favourite verb for such expressions: see even in Chaucer, 'browke ... myn hed' (*HF*, l. 273), 'brouke my tresses' (*MerchT*, l. 2308), 'brouke ... eyen' (*NPT*, l. 3300), &c.

2671. *Yit pleyis thow agane?*: 'But now you are back to your wrangling again?'

2678. *thay twa*: 'those two statements'.

2683. *Quhilk*: 'Which person', i.e. the *adversar*.

2690. *instant gyis*: 'procedure at present recognized'.

2692. *to gif ressoun and tak*: 'for the purpose of making the relevant statements and receiving those of others'.

2694. *duell in propertie*: 'be in possession', 'hold sway'.

2708. *maill-men*: 'small tenant-farmers', those paying the *maill* (see l. 2754) or 'money-rent', and so also the *mailleris* of l. 2744. In l. 2734 the *mailling* signifies the farm-holding for which such rent is paid.

2710. 'In the task of securing by honest means such livelihood as is fitting even to their station.'

2713. *craft in facultie*: 'by using wrongfully their understanding of human nature'; something more subtle than 'violence'. Lit. 'skill in disposition'.

2716. *poleit*: the reading from B to replace the apparently accidental form *poete* in BS (also in H; C shows 'Poet'). Cp. l. 3.

2744. 'And to the tenants grant a right of pasture.' Cp. quot. from Du Cange in G. G. S.: 'Villagium: praedium rusticum.'

2745. 'And the entering-fine appropriate to a specified period is paid and acknowledged.' *gressome* is a var. of 'gersum', used in its chiefly-Sc. sense of a fine paid by a tenant to his feudal superior on entering upon a holding (as here) or upon renewal of tenure (see l. 2748).

2750. *court*: a workaday cart ('cairt' in B) for stones, sand, &c., in apt antithesis to *cariage*. See *Middle English Dictionary* (ed. H. Kurath; 1954–) s.v. 'Cariage' *n.* 2a, and 'Court' *n.* (2).

2753. *Thus how*: 'To such a degree', &c.

2760. 'You ought to stand afraid of incurring the righteous God's wrath.'

2769. *slane*: correction of original *had slane*.

13

This fable is referred to in Dante, *Inferno*, xxiii. 4–6.

2789. *rauk*: a more fitting epithet for *voce* than the *rank* of BS, probably a form with turned -*u*-. Cp. 'rauk' in G and H, and 'rawk' in B.

2790. *Schir*: also in C and H; in this almost neutral sense applied to females it is genuinely dialectal; see *OED*, s.v. 'Sir' *sb.* 9.

2826–9. 'For scholars declare that in the majority of cases a man's intentions—inclining either to good or evil precisely as his nature predisposes—will match his bodily appearance.'

2831. *lorum*: a clipping of *culorum* from *in secula seculorum*, thus signifying 'conclusion'.

2842. *as jolie Absolon*: a stock medieval comparison for remarkable manly beauty, deriving from 2 Samuel xiv. 25. See, for example, Thomas de Hales, 'Luve-ron', ll. 83–84, and Chaucer, *LGW*, F. 249.

2853. *yone yonder*: chiefly a Sc. and north. collocation not necessarily duplicating but with *yone* perhaps in its reduced sense of 'that'.

2860. *preif that play*: 'embark upon that venture'.

2865. *murthour-aith*: a swearing to keep away peril from the person to whom the oath is uttered. For similar form but unlike meaning, cp. OIc. *morðs-eiðr*, the oath of compurgation in a case of murder.

2869. Cp. *TC*, ll. 170-1. Jupiter was regarded as the highest god and one with special potency in natural phenomena.

2904. *belliflaucht*: 'pulling the skin off whole over the head'. See entry in *DOST*, s.v. 'Belly-flaucht'.

2915-17. 'Better for you to be a humble labourer—to be a mere delver all the days you endure here—than to make up with a worthless mate.' *barrow*: the hand-barrow as distinct from the wheeled kind.

2945. 'Now with garments that delight, now with mere rags tended with a pathetic care.'

2946. *fitche* = 'fitchew', the polecat. The meaning 'fish' (B shows 'fysche') is favoured in G. G. S.; but polecat as gorging beast is aptly described by *full*. Cp. *Lear*, IV. vi. 124-5.

2971-2. The friars were addicted to the use of *exempla* in their sermons.

The Testament of Cresseid

Text: C*. 'THE TESTAMENT OF CRESSEID, Compylit be M. Robert Henrysone Sculemaister in Dunfermeling.'

1-2. In accordance with medieval poetic theory, the work begins with a *sententia*.

4-7. In part, Henryson is making use of the traditional spring opening, for the sun would move through the sign of Aries between 13 March and 11 April. Conventionally that season is associated with the renewal of life and love in man and nature. Cp. the Harley Lyric 'Alysoun', ll. 1-5, and Chaucer, *Gen Prol*, ll. 1 ff. (and Robinson's note); also R. Tuve, 'Spring in Chaucer and before him', *MLN* lii (1937), 9-16. But in Henryson's poem, the spring has been blasted most unseasonably and has become scarcely distinguishable from winter. The poet is thus playing ironically upon literary convention; this particular spring is *doolie*, and so *equivalent* to the 'tragic' theme of love.

As for *Lent*, MacQueen seems right in suggesting that the word here retains some of its earlier connotations with spring and love, and he refers to the opening of another Harley Lyric, 'Lenten ys come wiþ loue to toune'. D. Fox prefers to see 'connotations of deprivation and death—if also of rebirth'.

tragedie: to be taken, says Harvey Wood, in the medieval sense—'a fall from felicity to misery, implying no sense of dramatic construction'. The two other elements of the medieval concept of tragedy, the use of elevated style and restriction of theme to significant events in the lives of eminent persons, are also present in the poem. See Karl Young, *The Drama of the Medieval Church* (Oxford, 1933), i. 6.

can . . . discend: 'caused to fall'.

13–14. In regular astronomy Venus and the sun are never in opposition. But, as D. Fox notes, the unnatural astronomy may well carry a thematic point: 'Opposition . . . is extremely malignant: Venus in opposition to the Sun suggests an impossibly great malevolence.'

25. *humbill reverence*: a stock collocation, frequent in Lydgate. See *Fall of Princes*, vi. 298, ix. 908, &c.

26. *hie magnificence*: another recurrent phrase favoured by Lydgate. See 'The World is Variable', l. 101, &c.

33–35. 'For which condition, recourse to some external heat is best remedy; in helping by way of medical science when the natural processes have lost their vigour I have skill, for I am acquainted with both.' *phisike* is used with a touch of innuendo; see next stanza.

36. *beikit*: a marginal gloss in K reads 'warmed or tosted'.

42. *worthie*: the common emendation to T's 'lusty' is hardly necessary; 'worthy' is essentially Chaucer's epithet for Troilus.

43–46. Obvious reminiscence of the events described by Chaucer, *Tr*, v., and similar in style.

48. For discussion of the validity of *Esperus* and of *esperance* (with an attempt to justify retention of the former signifying a general comforter, or the gladdening Evening Star or even the solacing Morning Star) see C. Elliott, *JEGP* liv. 241–7.

61. Probably poetic fiction to provide Henryson with a show of objectivity; cp. the somewhat dark allusions by Chaucer to 'Lollius' (*Tr*, i. 194) and 'Trophee' (*MkT*, l. 2117). It seems not to be a reference to the *exemplum* in the third part of *The Spectakle of Lufe* concerning Cresseid's treachery, abandonment, and misery: that work is part of the Asloan MS., generally dated several years after the most probable date of Henryson's death. See B. J. Whiting, *MLR* xl. 46–7; J. Kinsley, *TLS* (1952), p. 743; J. Gray, *TLS* (1953), p. 176.

62. *fatall destenie*: 'lot decreed by fate'; an echo of *Tr*, v. 1.

65–68. 'Nor do I myself know whether this particular story has any proper sanction, or is something devised by a new poet, imaginatively conceived with the purpose of describing the lamentation. . . .' Obviously further 'fiction' adding piquancy to the situation.

74. 'And he formally repudiated her.' *lybell of repudie* is the *libellum*

repudii of the Vulgate. In the Wiclif Bible, Matthew v. 31 reads 'Forsothe it is said, Who euere shal leeue his wyf, ʒeue he to hir a libel', with 'libel' glossed as 'a litil boke of forsakyng'.

77. *court* may suggest the royal court (as traditionally the haunt of loose women), and *commoun* (modifying *scho*) 'promiscuous'.

78. For a similar yoking of the somewhat conventional *flour* (choicest bloom) and *A per se* (the peerless one), see Dunbar (?), 'London, thou art the flour of Cities all', ll. 1–8. The second expression is fig. and shortened use of the printers' 'A per se, *a*' = '*A* by itself makes the word *a*'.

85–91. The tolerance and sympathy are kept decorous by the qualification in l. 87 and the distinction between moral failing (*brukkilnes*) and 'secular' attributes (*womanheid, wisedome, fairnes*).

89. *quhilk*: for erroneous *quhik* of the original.

106. *efter the law was tho*: 'in keeping with the custom of the time'.

108. Var. on the situation in Chaucer's *Tr* and in classical accounts generally, where Calchas is priest of Apollo.

115. 'Intending to do their form of pious sacrifice.'

133. *as abject odious*: 'like one repulsive and banished creature'.

135, 283. In Gower, *Confessio Amantis*, iii. 1462 ff., Thisbe addresses both Venus and Cupid as blind. Here Henryson's detail seems to anticipate and underline the equating of Venus with the dark, indiscriminate, and restless powers of Fortune in ll. 218–38.

137. Cp. the Chaucerian *Rom*, ll. 1616–17; but for so conventional an idea no direct borrowing need be assumed.

138. *And ay grew grene*: 'And that it should flourish always'.

140. *forlane*: probably *passé*, 'abandoned', supporting *left*. See *DOST*, s.v. 'Forlane'.

141–2. 'When this was said, spent in spirit ⟨and⟩ in excited state, she fell down in a swoon.'

144. In late antiquity Cupid was sometimes represented with a bell.

149. *influence*: means whereby the stars act on man and sublunary things.

150. *coursis variabill*: probably 'fluctuating patterns of events'.

155. *fronsit*: cp. *MF*, l. 2819. Original *frosnit* taken as 'frozen' fits the context but is hybrid, having weak suffix added to a strong. SJ and T show 'frounsed'; K has 'frownced', glossed as 'wrinkled'. *leid*: the metal assigned to Saturn in astrology.

162–3. 'Down over his belt his silvery-grey locks lay matted in untidy fashion, sprinkled with hoary frosts.'

164. *gyis*: its use here and in ll. 178, 260 is usually queried, mainly because of variant readings apparently deriving from OFr. *guite* (gown, dress). Thus at l. 164 K shows 'gite', and SJ, T have probable corruption

of this to 'gate'; at ll. 178, 260 these three texts read 'gyte'. The customary sense of 'gyte' is 'garment', which duplicates *garmound* in ll. 164, 178. Further, the suggestion that 'hat' is the meaning in these two lines (see G. G. S.) is forced and without real support. The reading from C* can stand in all three cases, signifying 'whole manner of attire'. See *DOST*, s.v. 'Gys(e)', *n.* 2.

177. An established simile; see, for example, Laȝamon, *Brut* (*c.* 1200), l. 7048, where it forms part of the description of King Pir. Lydgate makes extensive use of the same figure; see E.E.T.S., E.S., 60 (1891), pp. 88–89.

178. *gay*: supplied from SJ, T, and K; also in l. 218.

179. Lit. 'With golden selvages gilded on every gore'; i.e. 'With each seam edged with gold'.

187, 188. *roustie*: Harvey Wood suggests 'bronze', 'as red as rust' as the meaning, while acknowledging that bronze is not Mars's metal (see Chaucer, *HF*, ll. 1446–7). D. Hamer (*MLR* xxix. 344) defends the sense 'rusty' as indicating the discoloration of fighting-blades by the victims' blood, this not being wiped away but left to stress the prowess of the sword-men. Cp. the apparent Germanic belief that battle-blood brought hardness to the blade; thus Unferð's sword Hrunting is *ahyrded heaþoswate* (*Beowulf*, l. 1460).

194. *tuilyeour-lyke*: 'in bullying fashion'. K has this note: 'Propter ignorantiam veræ significationis Scotici vocabuli Tullieur erratum est fere in omnibus impressionibus in quibus perpæram describitur *Tulsur.* vox hæc apud Scotos hominem trucem & efferum significat qualem nos Angli vocamus *a Swaggerer*, & Itali *vno Brauo*.'

205. *upricht*: SJ, T, and K show 'unright' (amiss) which at first sight seems a correction to accord with Phæton's fate. Yet in *MF* l. 470 *upricht* signifies 'true', 'undoubted'; in Holland's *Pliny* (1601), ii. 585, it has advbl. force ('And in truth, if we will consider this pageant upright, we must needs confesse . . .'). The word might stand here with a sense of 'undoubtedly', 'assuredly'.

211–17. *Eoye*, *Ethios*, and *Peros* correspond to the Ovidian names *Eöus*, *Æthon*, and *Pyröeis*; see *Metamorph.* ii. 153–5. *and callit Philogey*: this emendation of original *callit Philologie* preserves metre and rhyme and is supported by Fulgentius' form *Philogeus*: for the traditions behind the terminology of the sun-horses and an attempt to justify the emendation, see C. Elliott, *JEGP* liv. 247–54.

218–38. The significance of Henryson's portrait of Venus lies in the emphasis upon her 'greit variance'. For the identification of Fortune and Love, see H. R. Patch, *The Goddess Fortuna in Mediæval Literature* (Cambridge, Mass., 1927), pp. 90–98, and cp. Chaucer, *BD*, ll. 620–49; also Lydgate, *Reson and Sensuallyte*, ll. 1547–54, 3364–9, 4059–61, 4071–2, where the ideas of love-goddess and of fickle two-sided experience are merged. See too in Lydgate, *Fall of Princes*, vii. 1242, *Pilgrimage of the Life of Man*, l. 13092, *Pageant of Knowledge* (2nd version), ll. 111–12.

220–1. Venus's garments are flaunting to the point of appearing odd (*nyce*) since their colours embrace sober black, and green the hue of inconstancy; cp. 'The Garmont of Gud Ladeis', ll. 39–40. In the Chaucerian *Wom Unc*, the refrain approves clothes 'al grene' for the fickle lady. In *Fall of Princes*, green is the 'chaungable colour, contrayre to sadnesse' (vii. 1239–40).

231. *lauch*, *weip*: perhaps absolute infins.: see T. F. Mustanoja, *A Middle English Syntax* (Helsinki, 1960), i. 511.

236. 'Compact of a hollow delight and a counterfeit pleasure.'

238. *widderit*: correction of original *widdderit*.

239–45. The eloquent, 'poetical', and clerking Mercury is astrologically traditional. See also ll. 268–70. In Martianus Capella, *De Nuptiis Philogiae et Mercurii*, Mercury is portrayed as Eloquence.

241. 'With stylized and delightful manner of expression.'

244–5. Cp. *MF*, ll. 1351–3.

246–9. Possibly echo of Chaucer's description of the Doctor of Physic (*Gen Prol*, ll. 425–6). For the association of Mercury with medicine cp. the identification by the Romans of that god with Hermes, who had skill in doctoring. See also Mercury as physician in Boccaccio, *De Genealogia Deorum*, III. xx, 'De Mercurio quinto'.

250–1. Traditional irony. Medical fees took the form of such garments; cp. the 'sangwyn', 'pers', 'taffata', and 'sendal' of Chaucer's Doctor (*Gen Prol*, ll. 439–40) and the 'furrede hodes' and 'cloke of Calabre' of Phisik in *Piers Plowman* (B Text, vi. 271–2).

252. More irony. Many of the god's mythological exploits are dishonest and improper; e.g. his theft of Apollo's quiver and arrows, of Neptune's trident, and of Venus's girdle. And the god 'who could not utter a single lying word' was especially propitiated by those guilty of frauds and falsehoods.

261–3. In folk-tale, the man in the moon is a peasant banished there for stealing thorns. For the rather complex associations of the legend, see O. F. Emerson, *PMLA* xxi. 831–929; for more particular comment (with special reference to the poem in Harley MS. 2253, 'Mon in þe mone stond ant strit') see R. J. Menner, *JEGP* xlviii. 1–14.

267. *liken*: perhaps a phonetic spelling of 'likand' (choosing); cp. T's 'lykyng' and var. spellings of the same in SJ and K. See also comments in G. G. S. and H. M. Murray.

269–70. 'He might have learned the practice of rhetoric, ⟨and how⟩ to express in ⟨quite⟩ a brief discourse a cogent signification.'

275. *or*: from the other versions to replace original *in*.

290. *injure*: from T and ?AN for original *iniurie*, which as well as doing some violence to metre is not a MSc. form.

293. 'I speak for your sakes as well as mine.'

296. *Schir*: a title of respect formerly commonly applied to king, knight, and priest.

303. 'When they had carefully considered the matter.'

312. *lawfullie*: 'in accordance with the decision reached by the assembly'.

313–14. Cresseid's former beauty is expressed in idealized terms; see also ll. 337, 373, 443 ff.; and on the convention generally, D. S. Brewer, *MLR* l. 257–69.

316–18. The 'poetic' manipulation of astrological data is done with ome skill and subtlety. Saturn is a planet 'Cold and Dry . . . Melancholik . . . Masculine, the greater Infortune . . . a contemner of women . . . he signifieth . . . Beggars . . . quartan Agues proceeding of cold, dry and melancholly Distempers, Leprosies' (W. Lilly, *Christian Astrology*, 1647, pp. 57 ff.). Saturn's 'complexion' of melancholy with its predisposing to leprosy replaces Cresseid's 'moisture and . . . heit', the sanguine 'temperament' of Venus, her former goddess.

322. *as ane beggar*: apparently the detail is Henryson's invention; see also l. 483. Hereafter it is repeated in the Cresseid legend. Cp. *Twelfth Night*, III. i. 63.

327–9. 'Revoke your decision and show some mercy—even though such a course is contrary to your nature; for this way (*sa*) your action seems only a vindictive sentence imposed upon the fair Cresseid.'

334–43. Again unobtrusive use of astrological detail. Luna can take away 'heit of bodie' since she is a 'Cold' planet (Lilly, p. 81); yet her other quality of 'moisture' is excluded, and Saturn, 'the supreamest . . . of the Planets' (p. 57), unrestrictedly imposes his melancholic 'complexion'. As well, the Moon, like Saturn, was sometimes associated with the onset of leprosy; see J. Parr, *MLN* lx. 487–91, and espec. his quot. from Joannes Baptista Porta. Realization of the full extent of Cresseid's punishment suggests further subtlety: the yoking of Saturn and Luna (l. 300) is a union of fundamentally unlike planets, the first being distant, dark, masculine, &c., and the second near, signifying white and feminine, &c. (Lilly, p. 82). Yet the association regarded astrologically was also thought to engender leprosy; see Parr's quot. from Fabian Withers's transl. of Joannes ab Indagine. Further, Cresseid is stricken with the disease at a time between noon and supper (see ll. 114, 359), during which third set of hours of the natural day melancholia was assumed to prevail. Again, Saturn 'causeth Cloudy, Darke, obscure Ayre, cold and hurtfull, black and condense Clouds' (Lilly, p. 60) such as appear when Cresseid enters the leper-house.

The depiction of her leprosy shows a similar care for detail; general deformity is implied (ll. 308, 341, 394, 501); ulcerations, tubercles, or spots are referred to (ll. 339–40, 349, 372–3, 395, 448); the eyes undergo change (l. 337); there is suggestion of morbid alteration of the skin (l. 396), and the voice becomes harsh (ll. 338, 443, 445). Such characteristics of the disease are frequently found in the significant medical works of the fourteenth and fifteenth centuries (again see Parr). J. Y. Simpson points out that the changes here described 'are exactly the most marked symptoms of Greek elephantiasis' (*Edinburgh Medical and Surgical Journal*, 1842, lvii. 139–40).

343. *cop*: the leper's begging-bowl; *clapper*: the clap-dish, the wooden lid of which was rattled in warning of approach.

348. *poleist glas*: 'hand-mirror'.

350. 'God knows, at heart she was miserable enough!'

364. A simple yet effective variation on the device of irony, for Cresseid as well as the reader understands the other and compelling truth of the statement.

372–7. The father who recognizes the disease as incurable is also a priest, and in medieval times it was sometimes the duty of the clergy to inspect and report lepers. In the register of Bishop Bronescomb of Exeter it is stated that 'it belongs to the office of the priest to distinguish between one form of leprosy and another' (see R. M. Clay, *The Mediæval Hospitals of England*, 1909, p. 60).

382, 388, 390, 391. 'The Secret Yett, or postern gate, refers to a gate in the south wall of the Monastery, Priory Lane, long since removed. "Ane village, half ane mile thairby" undoubtedly refers to the Nethertown, and the "Spittail house" to St. Leonard's Hospital' (E. Henderson, ed., *The Annals of Dunfermline*, Glasgow, 1879, pp. 169–70). But the references may not be deliberate on Henryson's part.

386. *bawer hat*: presumably a cast-off hat of beaver-fur, to be taken, with the bowl and clap-dish, as the marks of Cresseid's altered circumstances. Change of garb to accompany change of fortune was something of a literary convention; cp. *Orpheus and Erudices*, ll. 157–9. However, Professor Bennett suggests that since, syntactically, the line can refer to Calchas, and beaver-hats were usually worn by men, *his* wish to leave unrecognized, with face obscured by such a head-covering, is meant here.

392. Perhaps another detail echoed from the contemporary scene; 'kirkmen' were often supported by gifts in kind from their parishioners. See Bellenden, *Hystory and Croniklis of Scotland* (Edinburgh, 1536), II. iii. 38, X. v. 141, XII. iv. 262; also A. Abram, *English Life and Manners in the Late Middle Ages* (1913), p. 53.

413. *thy baill on breird*: 'your misery grows apace'.

414–15. 'Would to God that I were buried in my grave, and that none of Greece or Troy had heard of me!' Lit. *heird*='hear it'.

417. *bankouris browderit bene*: 'coverlets beautifully embroidered'.

440–1. The essential contrast is between the simple diet of the lazar-house and the highly seasoned food and drink of better days. Parr, quoting Paulus Ægineta, suggests that Cresseid's meagre fare reflects the medical regimen for elephantiasis. Andrew Boorde writes: 'He that is infectyd wyth any of the .iiii. kyndes of the lepóred must refrayne from al maner of wynes, & from new drynkes, and strong ale . . . and . . . from eating of fresshe beef. . . . And in no wyse eate no veneson, nor hare-flesshe, and suche lyke' (*A Dyetary of Helth*, 1542, ch. xxxi). Chaucer's Summoner, whom recent scholarship has shown to be suffering from leprosy of the type 'alopicia' (W. C. Curry, *Chaucer and the Mediæval Sciences*, New York, 1926, pp. 37 ff.), 'Wel loved . . . / for to drynken strong wyn, reed as blood' (*Gen Prol*, ll. 634–5). Hence Parr's opinion that Henryson is here referring to a diet regarded as prophylactic in his day appears reasonable. And the allusions to the incurability of her disease are not thereby invalidated but rather made more piquant.

442. *clapper*: correction of original *clappper*.

461. Such an image of mutability is largely conventional. Cp. Chaucer, *Bo*, iii, pr. viii. 44–45; also Lydgate, *Fall of Princes*, i. 6086, *Pilgrimage of the Life of Man*, l. 41.

463. Again cp. Chaucer, *Bo*, iii, pr. vi. 5–7.

467. The simile is another conventional touch; see Henryson, 'The Abbay Walk', ll. 10–11 and Lydgate, *Pilgrimage of the Life of Man*, l. 14323.

478. *mak vertew of ane neid*: 'make a virtue out of necessity'. The saw is as old as Ovid (*Amor.* I. ii. 10) and occurs in *Le Roman de la Rose* (l. 14217), in Chaucer (e.g. *Tr*, iv. 1586), and in Lydgate (*Troy Book*, ii. 464).

480. *leve*: emending of original *leir*.

481–3. The begging lepers are segregated (see ll. 382, 524). In a note on this passage Laing writes: 'In the old Burrow Lawis of Scotland, cap. 64, it is enjoined that "Leper folke sall nocht gang fra dure to dure, but sall sit at the posts of the Burgh, and seik almes (with cap and clapper) fra thame that passes in and forth." And James the First, anno 1427, Act 106, ordains that "na Lipper folk sit to thig (beg) nouther in kirk nor kirkyard, nor uther place within the burrowes, but at thair awin hospital, or at the port of the towne"' (p. 262). The Edinburgh burgh-records for the period October 1529–July 1531 contain a 'Statute anent the Leper Folk' which ordains 'that na manner of lipper persone man nor woman fra this tyme furth cum amangis uther cleine personis nor be nocht fund in the Kirk fische merket nor flesche merket nor na vther merket within this burgh under pane of burnyng of ther cheik and bannasing off the toune'.

487. *mervellous* appears as *mervellons* in the original.

488. 'In high triumph and with rejoicing over the victory.'

489. *richt* is duplicated in the original.

498. 'Then she glanced up at him full-view.'

505-11. 'It was no wonder that he conjured up her appearance so quickly—and here now is the reason: in certain circumstances the insubstantial mental image of an object may be so firmly imprinted into the imagination that the external senses are deceived, and so shows itself in shape and manner similar to that formed into a picture by the mind.' M. W. Stearns points out (pp. 98-105) that *idole* signifies Aristotle's copy of a sense-impression persisting in the mind after the external object is removed.

518. He fails consciously to recognize the deformed woman, while she, as yet, cannot accept the benefactor and Troilus as being the same man.

521. The line is duplicated in the original, ending one fol. and beginning the next.

523. *he*: supplied; it is missing only from C* among the early versions.

532. *we knaw be his almous*: 'this evident to us by the way in which he has given his alms'.

538-9. 'Through her heart there passed a sudden and a bitter pang of pain more wounding than steel, and she fell to the ground.'

541. Sense is helped by supplying a final subj. and v. 'she declared'. *ochane*: a Gaelic expression of sorrow, equivalent to 'alas'.

542-3. 'Now is my heart beset with cruel pangs; whelmed in grief, a miserable creature devoid of all hope ⟨am I⟩.'

550. *quheill*: the Wheel of Fortune.

563-4. 'I give you to know that there exist few enough from whom you can trust to have true loving in return.'

567. The simile is common property. See Chaucer, *ClT*, ll. 995-6; also *Wom Unc*, ll. 12-13. Lydgate frequently uses it, e.g. in 'A Freond at Neode', l. 71, and *Pilgrimage of the Life of Man*, ll. 14323-5.

568-71. 'Because I recognise that grievous instability, ⟨a state⟩ frail as glass, in my own person, ⟨of myself⟩ do I ⟨now⟩ speak ⟨but⟩ believe there is as much unfaithfulness in others—⟨they are just⟩ as inconstant and lacking in good faith.'

582-3. Cp. Chaucer, *Tr*, iii. 1368-72, where an exchange of rings is mentioned as well as the giving to Troilus by Criseyde of a brooch; and it is the latter that is set with a ruby.

589–91. Chaucer (*Tr*, v. 1661–2) refers to brooch but not belt. Henryson may have deliberately introduced the latter 'as the cincture or girdle of chastity, just as the brooch represents the badge of true love, placed over the heart' (G. G. S.).

603. *merbell gray*: a conventional phrase; see Chaucer, *SqT*, l. 500, and Lydgate, *Troy Book*, i. 1368, ii. 505, 579, 7520, iii. 2201, 2233.

614. *schort conclusioun*: 'untimely end'.

Orpheus and Erudices

Text: A. 'Heir followis þe tale of orpheus And Erudices his quene.' The poem agrees generally with the account deriving from Ovid (*Metamorph*. x) and from Virgil (*Georg*. iv), but is also markedly influenced by the story as given in Boethius (*De Consolatione Philosophiae*, iii, metrum 12). The use of certain technical terms in the description of the harmony of the spheres suggests Henryson's acquaintance with Boethius' *De Musica*, while it is reasonably certain that the account of the nine muses relies somewhat on Boccaccio's *De Genealogia Deorum*. In the *Moralitas*, the relevant sections of the popular Latin commentary on the *De Consolatione* by Trevet are closely followed. See notes on ll. 415 ff. and 421–4.

25. Perhaps 'They took upon themselves the conduct and odour of their forebears'. See *DOST*, s.v. 'Carriage', 'Car(e)age' *n*.

26. *quhilkis* is for original *qulks*.

43–45. Calliope, strictly the muse of heroic epic, is accorded primacy in music here in order that the significance of music in Henryson's theme can be the clearer. See also ll. 67–70.

71–84. For the thematic significance of Orpheus' passivity in this overture and settlement, see p. xviii.

97–98. Aristaeus, son of Apollo and Cyrene, is properly the protector of cattle. Here he is simply a keeper of beasts.

140. *pynnis*: harp-pegs, around which the strings are fastened and which are used for tuning.

156. '⟨Where⟩ in the wilderness I must live out my wretched destiny'.

159. 'My diadem exchanged for a hat of hair'. See note on *Cresseid*, l. 386.

169. *Quhilk* refers to *me* in the previous line.

170. The frequent editorial preference for emendation in this line is unjustified. The original has *face* (not *fate*) and *oursyld* (not *ourfyld*).

171. *less*: 'without ⟨it⟩'.

188. *Wadlyng Streit*: Watling Street, the Milky Way. See Chaucer, *HF*, ll. 935–9; also note in G. G. S.

198. *Phebus* appears as *Phe* in the original.

223–5. *Quhill* from CM for original *Quhilk*. *Quhilk* in l. 225 is unnecessary syntactically. Thus 'Which harmony pervading the world, in perpetual unison, until ⟨all⟩ motion ceases, is called by Plato the soul of the world'. *Plato* is for *Pluto*, a reading found in all manuscripts. There is an obvious Platonic reference here to the Anima Mundi of the *Timaeus*.

226–39. The first stanza refers to the six arithmetical ratios fundamental to early musical theory: *duplere*, 2:1; *triplere*, 3:1; epitritus (Henryson's *emetricus*), 4:3; emiolius (the poet's *enoleus*) 3:2; *quadruplat*, 4:1; epogdous (original *epodyus*), 9:8. In the second stanza, the five corresponding musical intervals are listed. Three of these are basic: *diatasseron* (epitritus, a fourth), *diapason* (*duplere*, an octave), *diapente* (emiolius, a fifth). The other two are these 'multiplied': *diapason . . . duplate* is bisdiapason (double octave) and *diapente . . . with a dis*, which latter is probably for 'disdiapente', is *triplere* (diapente and diapason, a double fifth). See in Grove, *Dictionary of Music and Musicians* (1954), articles on Greek music (iii. 770–81) and Intervals (iv. 519–24).

The notions the poet raises here are strict, arithmetical, and *proporcionate*; yet each ratio and interval yields the aesthetically pleasing, perfect consonance or *proporcioun*. And later Orpheus achieves this; see l. 368.

231. The original has *symonis*.

261–7. Alecto, Megaera, and Tisiphone (original has *Thesphonee*) are the deities of vengeance, the Erinyes, in Greek mythology. Here they deal out retribution to Ixion (spelt *Exione* in l. 514), the Greek Cain, the first to murder one of his kin and guilty of other crimes too. See note to ll. 489 ff.

277. *Tantalus*: see note on ll. 519–26.

289 ff. The immediate and remote figure in this description of the road to the underworld. From 'local' touches (ll. 289–92, 303–6) the poet progresses to something Dantesque (ll. 310–16).

295. The original has *Theseus* here and in ll. 302, 559.

307. *That* for original *Thai*.

321. In Greek mythology, Priam, son of Laomedon, was the last king of Troy. Hector, his eldest son by Queen Hecuba, is the chief warrior of the Trojans in Homer.

322. Alexander the Great, 356–323 B.C., king of Macedonia. He overthrew the Persian empire, carried Macedonian arms into India, and

thus laid the foundations of the Hellenistic world of territorial kingdoms. *wrang conquest* may refer to the savagery associated with some of his achievements; for example, the sack of Thebes, 335, the storming of Tyre, 332, and the expedition against the Cossaeans, 324.

323. Antiochus I Soter of Syria, 324–262 or 261 B.C., married Stratonice, the young wife of his father Seleucus.

324. Gaius Julius Caesar, 100–44 B.C., the Roman general, statesman, and dictator.

325. Herod Antipas, *c.* 21 B.C.–A.D. 39, had an incestuous union with Herodias, wife of his brother Herod Philip. John the Baptist met his death for denouncing this.

326. Nero, A.D. 37–68, was supposedly guilty of many 'great iniquities'. Here Henryson may be thinking, in a context of moral transgression, of his over-fond attachment to Poppaea Sabina, wife of Otho.

327. Pontius Pilate, the Roman procurator of Judaea, who passed the death-sentence on Christ. The *breking of the law* presumably refers to Pilate's decision to elevate political legality over moral dictates. See John xix. 12.

329–30. Croesus reigned as last king of Lydia *c.* 560–*c.* 546 or 540 B.C. He was famous in antiquity for his wealth and later came to be regarded as the type of acquisitiveness.

331–2. The Pharaoh of the Oppression was probably Ramses II, 1304–1237 B.C. See *Encycl. Brit.*, s.v. 'Exodus'.

333–4. Saul reigned as first king of Israel *c.* 1020–1000 B.C. For his 'rejection of the word of the Lord', see 1 Samuel xv, especially 11, 19, 24, 26, 35.

335–7. Ahab coveted Naboth's vineyard, and Ahab's wife Jezebel brought it about that Naboth lost his life and her husband gained the vineyard. See 1 Kings xxi.

369–70. *Ypodorica*: Hypodorian, a plagal mode in medieval music a fourth below the Dorian. *Ypolerica*: Hypolocrian, a rejected plagal mode a fourth below the Locrian. See Grove, *Dictionary of Music and Musicians*, v. 797–804.

394. In the original *rycht* is written above the line.

409. The paraphrased sense is: 'Willy-nilly, possessions attract our concern, just as a sore place draws the finger.'

415 ff. See Robinson, prefatory remarks on Chaucer, *Bo*, for useful information on Boethius, the Roman senator and consul executed in 524. The *gay Buke* is, of course, the *De Consolatione*, the 'vade-mecum' of the Middle Ages.

421–4. Nicholas Trevet (? 1258–1328); an English Dominican theologian, biblicist, historian, and classicist. His best-known work is the

Anglo-Norman Chronicle, familiar to Chaucer and Gower. Henryson is here alluding to his commentary on Boethius, *In (librum) Boetii de Consolatione Philosophiae.*

480. *outwart*: 'outwardly expressed'.

484. *is . . . say*: 'which means only'.

489 ff. In regular accounts of Ixion's attempt to seduce Juno, the cloud (l. 498) has the latter's shape; and it is from Ixion's embraces that the centaurs are begotten.

509–14. These lines, missing from A, are supplied from B. *seissis* is for original *seisss*.

519–26. Traditional versions of this happening state that Tantalus, in a desire to test the divinity of the gods, killed his son Pelops and served up his limbs for them. Henryson refers to one god only. He may intend this to be Plutus. The variation may imply that the exemplar of greed (Tantalus; see ll. 531–4) is punished because his stratagem is directed at the 'true' god of riches. A link with the more usual account may lurk beneath the change, for Plutus is the son of Demeter, the only deity to eat off Pelops. In l. 525, something like 'then put him' needs to be supplied.

533. *ar* is from B for original *is*.

541. The paraphrased sense is: 'to find all possessions a source of anxiety'. *bak and burd* is a stereotyped expression for possession of clothing and bedding.

547–50. Missing from A, supplied from B. Sense is helped if *Schawand to us* is taken with finite force, 'we are shown' &c. In l. 548 *will* is deleted and *thai* interlined in the original.

There is no ascription in either A or CM. In B occurs the colophon 'q m̄r R H'. In his *Eneados* Douglas glosses the word 'Muse' thus: 'Musa in Gre [Greek] signifeis an inuentryce or inuention in our langgage. And of þe ix Musis sum thing in my palys of honour and be Mastir robert hendirson in new orpheus.'

The Garmont of Gud Ladeis

Text: B. No heading is given, but the colophon reads: 'ffinis of þe garmont of gud ladeis q M̄r ro᷒ Henrysoun'.

Lord Hailes wrote of this piece that it was 'a sort of paraphrase of 1 Tim. ii. 9–11; but the comparison between female ornaments and female virtues is extended throughout so many lines, and with so much of a tire-woman's detail, that it becomes somewhat ridiculous'. Even when allowance is made for critical canons observed in the 18th cent. the statement seems inadequate. If a biblical reference is thought necessary, then one to Ephesians vi. 14–17 seems more apt. Yet Henryson is not only 'moral' here, concerned solely with general 'female virtues': his picture is tinted with chivalric colours and he finds room for qualities belonging to the perfect object of courtly love. Nor is the method one of 'comparison'; it is an instance of the abiding medieval concern with the 'sentence'. The process here hovers near transparency (real and abstract images tend to clash); but when the ideas are sympathetically synthesized, the 'conceit' appears successful (the particularized physical functions of the items of apparel regulate the sequence and potency of the corresponding virtues). Neither is the treatment 'extended'; the *Triumphe des Dames* of Olivier de la Marche (dead by 1502), suggested by some as the source of Henryson's device here, is over thirty times as long. *Garmont* (*garmond* in ll. 3, 37) has its collective sense of 'attire'; cp. the entries 'garment of claise', &c., *s.v.* 'Garment' 2 in *DOST*.

8. 'That there would be no grounds for ill report which would vex her.' Cp. l. 11.

11. *schame*: 'modesty'; *dreid*: 'fear of ill-repute'.

15. 'The eye-let holes formed from steadfastness.'

19. *Purfillit*: 'Decorated'. W. Tod Ritchie (S.T.S., 1928–34) reads it as *Pursillit*, which he regards as an eccentric form: *plesour*: moral attractiveness; that which gives virtuous pleasure.

27. 'Her ruff made of a commendable meditation.'

34. 'Signifying that she shall not be found at fault.' Cp. *The Owl and Nightingale* (*c.* 1200), l. 1390: 'For flesches lustes hi makeþ slide.'

38. *by my seill*: probably fig. use of 'seal', the symbol of attestation and conviction, and aptly following *sweir*.

39–40. 'That she at no time dressed in garments gay or sober becoming her half as well as would these just envisaged.'

The Annunciation

Text: G. The manuscript gives no title. Laing uses 'The Salutation of the Virgin'. He also suggests that this is an early piece; yet its effect is both competent and finished. Not only is there technical achievement (fluent handling of a limiting rhyme-pattern, a subtly varied metre, and functional alliteration), but the feeling is given a restrained, effective modulation (the method is narrative at base, sweeping from Annunciation to Resurrection, yet with brief eddyings of contemplation which reach a soaring climax in the apostrophe of the final stanza).

1–2. 'Love gratefully received can be as strong in its power to drive out all ills as is death in its destructive force.' Lit. *likand* = 'pleasing'. The original runs together *suet* and *is*.

3–4. Cp. 1 Corinthians xiii. 7. *letis*: lit. 'tarries' = 'dwells with', &c.;

NOTES

cp. 'At luvis law a quhyle I think to leit' (Henryson, 'The Ressoning betuix Aige and Yowth', l. 34).

6. *Quhen*: a loose connective best taken as 'So it was when'.

12. As the line stands, 'In Him set thy resolves' = 'Let Him alone guide you'. But in view of the coalesced forms in ll. 2, 24 (*croundis*) and 28 (*applidis*), *decretis* may well be for *decret is*, 'destiny is'.

22. *begild*: 'robbed of her chastity'; obvious reference to the Immaculate Conception.

28. *applid is*: 'hearkens, or consents, or conforms herself' (G. G. S.). See *OED*, s.v. 'Apply' *v*. III, and cp. *MF*, l. 2829.

38. 'Which have their source in the abundance of Divine Love.'

39–40. Reminiscence of the familiar symbol of the burning bush figuring the Virgin Birth; see Robinson's note, *PrT*, ll. 453 ff. and 461.

43–48. An equally common symbol. Just as Aaron's rod budded mysteriously (Numbers xvii) and without natural supply of sap (*dry but wete*) became moist-stemmed and fecund (ll. 45–46), so did the Virgin conceive.

57. *bacis*: G. G. S., referring to *The Mirrour for Magistrates*, xl ('By bloudshed they doe . . . bace . . . their state') conjectures 'establishes (bases)'. But it may signify 'moistens'; see *DOST*, s.v. 'Bais' *v*.[2]

68. *Termigant*: extension of original sense (a god thought by the Crusaders to be worshipped by the Saracens) to signify the Devil.

The colophon reads: 'q Ro. Henrisoun'.

The Bludy Serk

Text: B. The marginal title is in a later hand. The outlines of Henryson's narrative material resemble the story of Emperor Frederick's daughter in the *Gesta Romanorum*. (For discussion of the poet's possible acquaintance with one of the vernacular versions of this work, see G. G. S. i. lix–lxiii.) The narrative is in itself satisfying, with its traditional extravagances and confident rightness of movement, though the lengthy articulating of the 'sentence', where the romantic story is used as the lesser element in a direct allegorizing process, produces a bifurcated effect.

1. *betald*: 'narrated', 'told'. The manuscript separates *be* and *tald*; but see *OED*, s.v. 'Betell' *v*. 2.

9. *bur the flour*: 'was excellently endowed'.

11. 'With a pleasing demeanour and a deep sense of honour.'

16. *our allquhair*: 'over everywhere' = 'throughout the world'.

38. *his persoun*: 'him in person', 'face to face'. Cp. l. 51.

58. *deir*: an imperfect rhyme, acceptable as assonant; cp. *wame*, l. 24.

Craigie (referred to in G. G. S.) suggests substitution of 'fre' (noble).

96. *mak*: taken as 'to make' it syntactically harasses *With*, while such identical rhyming with l. 92 is abnormal usage for the period. It may be 'made' in exigent rhyme-form; or perhaps the dialectal *mak* signifying 'apt', 'seemly'; see entry in *Promptorium Parvulorum* (1440): 'MAK, or fytte *and* mete . . .' ('men should remember their Saviour with prayers fitting to Him').

112. 'Where laws are strictly led' = 'Where full justice is effected'.

117. If preciser significance than that of man saved by Christ must be looked for, then presumably there is reference to the angel-functions connected with the Redemption, probably those of Gabriel, the angel of the Incarnation and of Consolation. See *Cath. Encycl.*, s.v. 'Angel'.

The colophon reads: 'ffinis q $\overline{Mr}$ R Henrici'.

The Thre Deid-Pollis

Text: B. 'ffollowis the thre deid pollis.' An insistent yet stylized expression of the common medieval 'tension' between the attractiveness of earthly plenitude and the strong realization that 'man is at the last mete for worms' and to be judged. See R. Woolf, *The English Religious Lyric in the Middle Ages* (Oxford, 1968), p. 320.

3. *With gaistly sicht*: 'With eyes of terror'; applicable, as indicated in G. G. S., to the skulls and to 'sinful man'.

14. The line is duplicated in the manuscript, concluding one fol., beginning the next.

22. Cp. note on *TC*, ll. 313–14.

26. *Poleist*: 'Decked out', 'Adorned'; a development of the basic sense 'brought to a finished state'. Cp. R. Greene, *A Quippe for an Vpstart Courtier* (1592): 'that pinch their bellies to polish their backs' (ed. A. B. Grosart, 1881–3, xi. 236).

27. The metrically necessary *so* is from MT.

29. *quhailis bane*: ivory from the walrus or similar animal confused with the whale. The simile is common in ME poetry; see *Secular Lyrics of the XIV and XVth Centuries*, ed. R. H. Robbins (Oxford, 1952), Nos. 129, 130.

42. *phisnamour*: the physiognomist, one reading the character from the face; *palmester* is the palmist.

45. *science* suggests a 'personal' pursuit (the acquiring of knowledge by study) and *lare* a 'public' action (the imparting to others of such knowledge).

49. *ay*: again from MT.

55–56. 'And then on our souls awaiting His divine judgement, to be given when He shall call and summon us.'

In B the ascription is to 'patrik Iohnistoun' (known to have produced interludes at the Sc. court, 1476–7, 1488–9); but there seems to be no positive reason for rejecting the naming of Henryson as author in MT. Similar sentiments are expressed in the same metrical and stanzaic patterns in his 'The Ressoning betwixt Deth and Man'. The cadences of the apostrophizing firmly recall those of Cresseid's 'Complaint', and the linear use of head-rhyme (especially in the sequence aa/bb) is a frequent stylistic device of his (see *TC*, l. 19, 'The Bludy Serk', l. 11, 'Nerar Hevynnis Blyss', l. 11, 'The Want of Wyse Men', l. 7).

Nerar Hevynnis Blyss

Text: M. No version entitles the poem; the usual title, 'The Prais of Aige', hardly indicates the theme. The piece shows progression from the awareness explicit in 'The Thre Deid-Pollis'. Here is no 'tension', but unsubtle thought-play on the theme of resolution and resignation.

2 *Ane*: for original *and*.

5. *to my dowme*: 'to my mind', 'as I could make out'.

6–7. 'For I desire rather not to be young again than to become lord and master of all this world.' Lit. *for my wys* = 'in favour of my wish'.

11, 12. *his*: a form of 'hes', part of 'hef' the var. of 'haif'; see l. 29.

17. *repit*: a misread or idiosyncratic form of the 'reput(e)' in CM, B, and B★.

28. 'Today a kingly state, tomorrow lacking all possessions.' Lit. *spend* = 'put to use'.

29. Grace is God's mercy and favour, hope of which can sustain (*defend*) dwellers in a mutable world.

Ascription occurs only in B★ and B, the latter stating 'q Hendersone'.

Ane Prayer for the Pest

Text: B. The title is given in the manuscript. In this supplication 'against' the plague (which occurred too often in the later Middle Ages for the poem to be dated precisely) spirit and letter of God's governance are differentiated with pert bluntness and easy recourse to 'legalistic' argument.

3. *or sal be, is perfyt*: from B★, giving better sense and metre than B's *or evir salbe perfyt*.

22. 'So that none dares go and remain with another.' Obvious reference to the contagion.

36. 'Withdraw this decision, though we know that it is in accord with true judgement on Thy part.'

45. *Thyne awin symilitude*: 'us made in Thine own likeness'.

46. 'Carry out punishment with clemency, not violence!'

49. *Thow grant*: a prayer (*imp.*).

53. *bot dreid*: 'without fail'; B★ reads 'be deid' (by death).

54. *law*: God's ordinances.

55–56. It is God's desire to protect, but the effecting of that wish waits upon man's observing his own code of justice.

65. The three stanzas beginning here, with their internal rhyme, and exotic diction culled chiefly from a common corpus of patristic writing, have several parallels in MSc. poetry concerned with similar themes. The most obvious is Dunbar's 'Hale sterne superne, hale in eterne'. *Superne* = 'supernal' (high, exalted). *Lucerne, guberne*: adapts. of Lat. *lucerna* (lamp) and *gubernāre* (govern).

68. *O Trewth*: 'Oh Fount of truth'.

69. 'Were we once penitent our suffering would straightway cease.'

70. 'Whoever has sought Thee has never been abandoned.'

71. *with space*: 'after a while' = 'at a time fitting to Thee'.

74. *distort it in exyle*: 'turn it aside into exile' = 'put it utterly down'.

75–76. 'Unless Thou givest help, death by such means can seem only a stratagem to deceive men and cheat them of their lives.' *the laif*: lit. 'the remainder', i.e. those yet with lives to be ended by the plague.

79. 'Unless Thou canst find it in Thee to disregard our sinning by way of wealth ill-gotten?' *oursyll*: lit. 'cover over'.

83. *we not suspect*: 'we do not hold in doubt' = 'we have hope of'.

84. *deluge*: 'remove from'; less familiar in form than the 'dislug' in B★.

85. 'Grant us Thy timely aid before we are overcome by such a death.'

86. 'We ourselves repent and regret our time ill-used.'

The ascription to 'henrysone' is in a later hand.

Robene and Makyne

Text: B. The manuscript gives no title.

In terms of *genre* the poem primarily resembles the OFr. *pastourelles*. W. Powell Jones (*MLN* xlvi. 457–8) goes so far as to suggest as Henryson's 'source' a *pastourelle* by Baudes de la Kakerie found in a 13th-cent. manuscript, a view validly criticized, chiefly by reference to technical considerations, by A. K. Moore (*MLR* xliii. 400–3); he suggests as a more decorous designation of Henryon's poem 'pastoral ballad'. Another and telling difference is to be found in the agent affecting Robene; for the Frenchman it is a second girl, but for the Scot a flock of sheep—a typical vivifying of convention.

Makyne, along with its variants *Mawkin, Malkyne* (see ll. 67, 121, &c.) is the diminutive of some such name as 'Matilda', 'Maud' and 'Mald'.

7. *in dern*: 'concealed', qualifying *dule*: see l. 22; in l. 39 *I* = 'In'.

11. *wude*: for original *wid*.

12. *raik on raw*: a common allit. expression, lit. 'pass in a row' = 'wander afield'.

19–20. 'Be gentle and gracious and of a pleasing demeanour, with discretion, valour and liberality.' Such qualities, along with those named in l. 24, are the stock attributes of the courtly lover. Cp. Chaucer, *NPT*, ll. 2908–17.

21–23. 'So that no disdainful attitude may harass you, no matter what secret sorrow consumes you, strive with all your means ⟨for her good-will⟩.' Here *denger* is used in its 'courtly' sense, that quality in the loved one that manifests disdain and reluctance. The lover here is advised not to aggravate his longing-grief by causing the woman to become intractable.

30. *gois haill aboif*: 'go altogether above' = 'are all around me on this hill'.

31. *play us*: 'dally', probably with a sexual connotation; cp. *Venus and Adonis*, ll. 123–6.

39. 'Unless concealed here you will gratify my longing . . .' *with* . . . *daill* = 'have to do with sexually'.

43–46. 'It might be possible for my sheep to fend for themselves until we have taken our full pleasure—though I do become uneasy if I hold back once they have begun to stray.'

47. *Quhat lyis on hairt*: 'My innermost feelings'.

49. *roif and rest*: a common allit. tag, *roif* signifying 'ease'. Cp. 'The Annunciation', l. 10.

56. *lue*: 'care for'. The manuscript reading is obscure, though it seems most like *lue* (a form of *luw* = 'love'), which in sense satisfactorily balances *lufe* in the previous line.

85–86. 'My one desire is to gain completely your heart.'

89. *say*: probably an exigent rhyme-form of 'said'.

93–95. 'It is my constant prayer that God may heap chilling sorrows upon those who eagerly seek to win you to love-making.'

96. Another common allit. pattern. 'In wood, forest or enclosed field' = 'In any place'.

112. *I think to mend*: 'I am bent on quite a different course'; lit. *mend* = 'amend'.

122, 128. *holt(t)is hair*: again a stereotyped allit. expression, lit. 'grey woods'; in view of earlier hints of the *locale* of the action (see l. 99 e.g.) Henryson is apparently using it conventionally. Some such force as 'the now-saddening woods' is required to bring out the touch of pathetic fallacy.

The colophon reads: 'q n̄r robert Henrysone'.

GLOSSARY

In the main, only words unfamiliar in terms of spelling and meaning, and not explained in the Notes, are included. The following orthographical variants should be noted:

(1) *Internal* (according to MSc. conventions): *a/e, marvale, mervell; a/o, mane, mone; ai/a + e, wait, wate; d/t, fraward, frawart; e/-, carle, carll; e/e + e, suet, swete; f (ʃ), gif(ʃ); f/v, belyif, belyve; i/-, tho(i)lis; -ie/-y, halie, haly; o/u, corage, curage.*
(2) *External* (between MSc. and modern conventions): length shown by added *i* or *y* (*mair, cleyr, blyith, scoir, cruikit*); *a: ai, e, ea, o, ou* (*remane, rajoisit, hartis, gat, fand*); *e: a, ea, i, ie, o, y* (*wes, ernist, wedow, le, werkis, hempyn*); *i: e, ea, u* (*yit, grit, injust*); *o: oi, oo, u* (*voce, wod, sone*); *ow: u* (*dowkit*); *u: o, oo* (*lufe, guse*); *y: i, ui* (*fyn, gyle*); *c: s* (*defense*); *ch: gh* (*flicht*); *d: t* (*gallandis*); *d(d): th* (*gaderit, togidder*); *k(k): ck prikkit, lok); n: m* (*confort*); *quh: wh* (*quhen*); *s: ss* (*mis*); *t: c, d* (*pretious, wicket*); *th: d* (*murther*); *u: w* (*grouis*). Excrescent *d, e, g* and *s* are occasionally found (*suddand, pairte, garding, discyde*). In places *on-* = *a-* (*onfar, onsyde*).
Noun-plurals are generally in -*is*, -*ys*. In verbs, when the *pers. pron.* is used with the *pr. ind.*, the 2nd person only ends in -*is*; in other usages all persons end in -(*i*)*s*; the *pr.p.* ends in -*and*, -*ing*, -*yng*, and the gerund in -*ing*, -*yng*; the *pa.t.* and *p.p.* of weak verbs usually end in -*it*, -*yt*, and the *p.p.* of strong verbs in -*in*, -*yn*. (The phonology, orthography, lexicology, and grammar of MSc. are fully discussed in G. Gregory Smith, *Specimens of Middle Scots*, 1902.)
Minor orthographical variants are generally ignored, the head-word representing the commoner form. Obvious derivatives are also ignored (e.g. *cairfull* from *cair, laichly* from *laich*), as are slight modifications of roots when given affixes (e.g. *clud/-ie* for *cluddie*). Words identical in form but different in meaning are put beneath the same head-word and the senses distinguished by arabic numerals.

abaid, (*n.*) delay.
abak, back(wards).
abasitlie, humbly.
ABC, instructive statement.
abone, above.
about, (a)round (about), thoroughly; **all ~**, from any direction.
abraid, took leave.
abreird, on breird, into its first shoots (also *fig.*).
absence, absentees.
abstractit, withdrawn.
abufe, above, in the air.
abusioun, malpractice, misuse.
abyde, remain, stay with.
accord, agree, suit, yield.
Acheron, river of the Greek underworld.
actand, (*pr.p.*) actuating.
addrest, went.

adoun, down.
adversar, adversary.
advertence, warning, heed.
affectioun, effectioun, disposition, fondness, passion, selfish interest.
agane, aganis, again(st), as well, as provision for, for (your part), in full view of, in reply.
ago, fallen, gone, past.
agreabill, apt.
aill, (*n.*) distress.
aip, the ape.
air, (1) heir; **-schip,** inheritance. (2) oar. (3) beforehand, early, earlier; **airlie,** early, just now; **air and lait,** without ceasing.
aith, oath.
aitis, oats.
alis at, has against.
alkin, all kinds of.

all, every, plainly, quite; **at ~,** in every respect.
allegit to, claimed.
allow, commend.
al(l)quhair, everywhere.
almous, alms(giving), kindness, sustenance; **-deid,** alms.
a(l)s, as, also, so; **-wele,** as well.
alsone, straightway.
alswa, also.
alterait, changed.
alway, increasingly.
amang, among; **ay ~,** every now and then; **amangis,** amongst.
amendis, tak ~, exact redress.
amiabill, friendly, loving.
amorous, affectionate, loving.
and, if.
ane, a, one, (a) certain; **~ and ~,** one by one; **of ane,** exceedingly.
aneuch, anew(ch), yneuch, enough.
anis, (1) (for) (just) once. (2) ones.
anone, at once.
apon, given to.
apostata, apostate.
apparitour, court beadle / crier.
apperance, be ~, so it seemed.
appetyte, inclination, lust, desire, will.
applicate, applied.
Aquarie, Aquarius the zodiacal sign.
areir, behind, of the past.
ark, box.
armit, protected.
array, clothing (*n.*); **-it,** decorated.
arreist, apprehended, check (*v.*).
as, (1) ashes, dust. (2) as if, as is the case with, like those, such as; **~ now,** now; **~ than,** then.
ascence, ascent.
as(e), ask.
assaill, make love.
assay, find out.
assent, aid (*n.*); **with ane ~,** unanimously.
assessouris, assistants to judge.
assure, be sure of.
ather, recent.
at(t)our, about, across, above, (down) over.
atteichit, attached (*legal*), inflicted, visited.
attent, (*n.*) heed.

aucht, ought.
Aurora, the dawn-goddess.
auster(ne), (*adj.*) stern.
autentik, fully qualified, important.
availl, value (*n.*), be of use.
aventure, danger, destiny, happening; **be/throw ~,** by chance.
avise, think over; **-itlie,** after reflection.
aw, (1) owe. (2) (in) awe, fear.
awfull, stern; **-ie,** gravely.

Bacchus, god of wine.
bad, commanded.
baid, (*n., v.*) delay, halt, stay.
baill, sorrow (*n.*); **-full,** dangerous.
bair, (1) boar. (2) bare. (3) bore, carried.
bait, (1) halt (*n.*). (2) enmity.
bak, the bat.
balandis, (*n.*) balance.
balk, unploughed strip of land.
ballet, short poem.
band, encircled.
bandoun, durance.
banes, banish; *p.p.* **baneist.**
banestikill, stickle-back.
barnage, time of youth.
barret, (*n.*) sorrow, trouble.
bastoun, stave.
battis, (*n.*) blows.
Bawdronis, a Sc. name for a cat.
ba(y)th, both.
be, by, around, because of, before, beside, by the time that, for, near, of, to, when, concerning.
be, bee.
beand, (*pr.p.*) being.
befoir-the-hand, already, earlier.
beforne, in front (of); **off ~,** earlier.
begouth, began.
behest, (*n.*) promise.
behind, in the background.
behufe, needs (*n.*); **-it,** it was necessary for, was destined.
beik, (*v.*) warm, bask.
beild, refuge; **-it,** constructed.
beinly, (*adv.*) well.
beir, (1) the bear. (2) bier. (3) outcry. (4) bring, carry; **~ by,** divert from.
beis, is, are.
beit, (1) beat. (2) small bundle.

bek, (*n.*) bow.
bely(i)f, straightway.
bene, (1) are. (2) fair, protecting, well-provided.
bening, benign.
benit, filled.
bent, grassy patch, ground, field, heath.
berk, (*v.*) bark.
berne, man, fellow.
bes, beasts.
beschrew, (*v.*) curse.
beseik, beseech.
besene, adorned.
besie, diligent; **-nes,** activity.
bestiall, animals.
bet, beat (*pa.t.*).
betakin, signify.
beteiche, bequeath.
betis, relieves.
betra(i)sit, betrayed.
betuix, between.
beuch, bough; *pl.* **bewis.**
bever, the beaver.
bid, (*v.*) desire.
big(ly), pleasant, well endowed.
bill, formal document.
binge, bow of obeisance.
bir, (*n.*) whirr.
birkin, birchen.
birn, (*v.*) burn.
birth, rank (in respect of parentage).
bittill, beetle (for striking flax).
bla, bluish, livid.
blaberyis, bilberries.
blaiknit, pallid; ~ **bair,** made destitute.
blenk, glance (*n., v.*); **-ing,** expression; **blent,** glanced.
blis, (1) beauty, splendour. (2) bless.
blom, blossom (*v.*); **-is braid,** widely flourishes.
bluddie, bitter.
blude, descent, family.
blunder, error.
blyith, content, fair, gay; **-lie,** readily.
blyn, cease.
bocht, bought, redeemed, recovered.
bodie, person.
boig, bog.
boist, (*n.*) menaces.
boit, boat.

bollis, flax-pods.
bolnyng, (*n.*) swelling.
bonat, (*n.*) cap.
bond, husbandman.
bone, bane.
bore, pierce; *pa.t., p.p.* **bord.**
boreall, northern; **Boreas,** north wind.
borrow, surety, redeem.
bot, but, but, just, only, without, except (for); ~**and,** and also; ~**gif,** unless; ~**only,** without.
boun(e), on the point of, ready.
bourding, (*n.*) jesting.
bowche(ou)r, 'butcher', executioner.
bowellit, disembowelled.
bowsumest, most compliant.
bra, hillside; *pl.* **brais.**
bracis, (*v.*) embraces, secures.
brag, (*n.*) blast.
braid, (1) broad. (2) jerk (*n.*), pull (*n., v.*), bounded, darted, stretched; *pa.t.* also as **braidet, braided.**
brak, broke (open), unfolded.
bred, spring up.
breid, (piece of) bread.
breir, briar.
breird, spring up, sprout.
brek sleip, keep awake.
brent, lofty, smooth.
bricht, fair (one).
brig, (*n.*) bridge.
brist, (*v.*) break; *pa.t.* **birst** (also **brast,** pierced).
brocht, brought.
broddit, prodded.
brok(e), the badger.
broun, dark.
bruke, have use of.
brukill, broukle, unstable, morally weak; **-nes,** frailty.
brutall, unreasoning.
brybouris, rascals.
Bryde, Bridget.
brym, (*n.*) water.
bud, gift, bribe.
bufe, above.
bugill, (1) wild ox. (2) horn.
buk-heid (-hude), blindman's buff.
bull, (*n.*) document.
bullar, (*n.*) bubble.
bunche, (*n.*) bundle.

GLOSSARY

bund(in), (*p.p.*) bound.
burde, (*n.*) feast, table.
bure, carried, suffered.
burelie, goodly, stout, well-wrought.
burges, (*adj.*) town.
burioun, (*v.*) bud.
burn(e), brook, stream.
bursin, destroyed.
busk, bus, (1) bush. (2) adorn, dress.
bust(e), small box or case.
busteous, bustuos, noisy, rough, rude, stout, wild.
bute, buit, (*n.*, *v.*) help, remedy.
butt(e)rie, larder (also *fig.*).
byde, dwell, tarry; **-and,** awaiting; **biddin,** remained.
byle, outbreak; **bylis,** boils (*medical*).

cabok, cheese.
cace, ca(i)s, circumstances, fortune, happening, matter, situation, station; **off/(up)on ~,** by chance; **I put the ~,** suppose.
cadgear, itinerant dealer in fish.
caff, calf, beasts.
cair, (*n.*) sorrow.
calf(f), chaff.
ca(u)ld, baleful, coldness.
campis, hairs.
can, can (do), did, know (how to).
canker, corruptions: **-it,** corrupt (*adj.*).
cant, lively, merry.
capill, horse.
carie, make one's way.
carioun, body, lifeless frame.
carll, 'fellow', man.
carp, chatter, talk (*vs.*); **carpin,** declaration.
carrolling, singing and dancing hand in hand.
cassyn, thrown, cast.
cast, seek out; **-in,** thrown: **caist,** threw.
cative, wretched.
cause, case (*legal*); **-les,** needlessly.
cavillatioun, trickery.
cawtelous, (*adj.*) cunning.
ceder, cider.
celsitude, high rank, sovereign state.
certane, inevitable; **in~,** indeed.
certify, be certain.
chair, chariot.

chalenge, (*v.*) claim.
chalmer, chaumer, chamber; **-glew,** love-making.
chambelate, fine cloth.
chanceliary, office of chancellor.
cheir(e), cheer, comfort, countenance (*ns.*), manner, mood; **mak~,** be content; **quhat~?,** how is it with you?
cheis, (1) cheese. (2) choose.
chemeis, loose robe.
cherising, prosperity.
cherit[i]e, magnanimity; **of/for~,** out of kindness.
chevalry, valour, knightly prowess.
cheverit, shook.
chuff, peasant.
churll, labourer, man.
chyld(e), young servant, youth.
cirkill, (*n.*) orbit.
citatioun, summons.
clais, claithis, clays, (*n.*), clothes.
claucht, snapped.
cled, clad, covered.
cleir, bright, fair, sweet.
clemens, clemency.
clene, fully, spotless, utterly.
Cleo, the muse of history.
clergie, learning, skill.
clerk, scholar.
clinscheand, (*pr.p.*) limping.
clois, hald ~, keep still.
clout, small piece.
clud, cloud (*n.*); **-ie,** misty.
cluke, (*n.*) claw, clutch, talons.
clym, climb; *pa.t.* **clam.**
clynke, make a clinking sound.
codices, codes (*legal*).
coffer, box.
coft, paid for.
coif, (*n.*) hollow.
collatioun, late-night refreshment.
colour, cullour, complexion, hue.
columbie, columbine.
come, came.
comfort, (*n.*) service.
commounis, humble folk; **commountie,** common people.
communnit, commonnit, conversed.
compeir, appear.
complexioun, bodily constitution, appearance, nature.

compt, (v.) care, reckon, value, number.

compylit, concluded, described.

con, squirrel.

conding, excellent.

conditioun, state (n.); **off his ~,** as far as his qualities were concerned.

confectioun, medical preparation.

confidderit, in league.

confidis, believes.

conqueis, acquire; **conque(i)st,** gain (n.).

consave, conceive.

conserve, protect.

consonant, according in sound.

constance, steadfastness.

constellatioun, stellar effects.

consuetude, custom.

consumit, dispelled.

contagious, harmful, tainted.

continence, chastity, self-restraint.

contra and pro, against and for.

contrair, opposed (adj.); **-ie,** oppose.

contrufit, thought-up.

contumax, guilty of contempt of court.

convenient, morally apt.

conversatioun, dealings with others.

convocatioun, assembly.

convoy, accompany.

cop, (n.) cup; pl. **coppis, cowpis.**

corage, demeanour, disposition, sexual desire.

Corbie Ravin, the raven.

coronate, crowned.

corruscant, radiant.

cotidiane, daily.

couch, cower, lie down.

counterfeit, imitate.

courtlie, graceful.

courtyne, curtain.

couth, (1) familiar, known. (2) could, did (also **culd, coude, cowd**).

covatyce, covetousness.

crab, provoke; **-it,** perverse; **craibit-lie,** ill-naturedly; **crabbing,** state of annoyance.

craft, means (of livelihood), way of life; gain; **-ie,** skilful.

crag, neck.

craig, hillock.

craikand, (pr.p.) croaking.

crampand, curly.

cran, long (like a crane's neck).

craw, (v.) crow; pa.t. **crew.**

creill, wicker-basket.

creip (v.) creep; pa.t. **crap.**

croip, (1) crops. (2) tree-top.

crose, make the sign of the Cross over.

croun, beir the ~, be acknowledged as best.

crous, bold.

crowna(i)r, coroner.

cruikit, deformed.

cry, (n., v.) command.

cule, slake.

cummit, came.

cún, learn; **-ing,** knowledge, skill(ed).

cunnand, arrangement, covenant.

cunning, coney.

curcheis, kerchief.

cure, (1) intention, responsibility; **-is,** efforts. (2) cover (n.).

curios, elaborately modulated.

cuvating, (n.) desire.

Cynthia, the moon.

da, doe.

daft, foolish.

dait, (n.) time.

daly, from day to day.

dansand, gambolling.

dawing, (n.) dawn.

de(e), dy, die; pa.t. **deit,** pr.p. **deand.**

debait, argument, resistance.

declair, decide, explain, clear.

declyne, lessen, object to.

decreit, decision, decree (pl. **decreis, decreitis**); decreed.

ded-lyke, death-like.

defence, off grit ~, very secure.

defend, (make) defence, protect one's self, support.

defy, reject.

degre, position, rank; **in all ~,** in every respect.

deid, (1) dead, death, heavy; **-lie,** sinful. (2) action, deed.

deif, deaf.

deificait, deified.

deill, (v.) associate, hand out.

deiplie, solemnly.

deir, dearly, precious.

dele, (*n.*) part; **ilk ~,** entirely.
delectioun, (*n.*) indulging.
delicate, (*adj.*) choice.
delictacioun, enjoyment, delight.
delitious, charming, refined, sweet, tasty.
deme, adjudge; **-ing,** suspicion.
deminute, (*adj.*) slight.
denude, naked.
denye, deign.
depa(i)rt, divide (*v.*); **withowttin depairting,** wholly.
deray, disturbance.
derenye, put on trial.
derne, concealment, secret place.
desait, deceit; **desave,** deceive.
devoyd, get rid of, relieve, shun.
devydit nicht, called out at the ending of darkness.
devyne, (1) divinity. (2) devise.
devyis, (*n.*) plan.
dew, apt.
Diana, Diana, goddess of chastity.
dicht, done, made, ornamented, treated.
different, distinctive.
diffinityve, final.
dill, relieve.
ding, worthy.
dirk, uncertain.
disagysit, disguised.
discence, descent by lineage.
discend, descend.
dische-likingis, plate-leavings.
diseis, (*n.*) discomfort.
dispens, grant remission of penalty.
dispisit, demeaned, made an object of scorn.
disponyng, bestowal.
dispyte, contempt.
dissever, (*v.*) part, vanish.
dissumlait, (*adj.*) dissembling.
dite, dyte, poetry, lay; **-yng,** (*n.*) composing, singing.
do, carry out, provide.
doctryne, edification, lesson, opinion.
document, warning.
doggitly, cruelly.
doif, dull, lifeless.
dome, judgement, opinion.
donk, moist.
dosinnit, dazed.

dote, think/act foolishly.
douk, dowk, dulk, (*v.*) dowse, duck, plunge.
doun, hillock.
dout, fear (*n.*, *v.*), misgiving; **but ~,** indeed.
draf, leavings; **-troich,** swill-trough.
draif, hurried on.
draw, let ~, set about making off.
dreddour, terror.
dreid, fear (*n.*, *v.*); **but ~,** assuredly, indeed; **haif ane ~,** have doubts.
drerie, sad.
dres(si)t, proceeded, resigned, whelmed.
drewch, drew.
drift, (1) impetus. (2) drove (*n.*).
drop, village.
drounit, inundated.
drowbly, clouded, turbid.
drowpit, downcast; **~ in dout,** were overawed.
drowrie, love-token, loved one.
drug, (*v.*) pull.
dry, dryness, lacking affection.
dub, (*n.*) pool.
dude, duid, do it.
dule, sorrow(ing); **-full,** disastrous, miserable; **dolly, doolie, dully,** sad, woeful.
dullis, becomes slack.
dungin, beaten.
duschit, dashed.
dyat, (*n.*) diet.
dyke, ditch(es), mound, low wall.
dytis, indicts.

e(e), eye; *pl.* **ene, eyne; hes ee,** looks (*v.*).
effek, (*n.*) end, purpose.
effe(i)r, befitting, be proper; *pa.t.* **aferit, effeird.**
ef(f)eird, effe(i)rit, afeird, afraid.
effray, (*n.*) fright.
eftir, according to, after; **~syne,** afterwards.
e(i)k(e), add to, augment, also, as well.
e(i)ld, (*n.*) age.
e(i)rd, ground, soil, world; **-lie,** earthly.
eir, (*v.*) plough.

eit, eaten.
eith, easy, easily.
elderis dayis, days of our forefathers.
electuairis, medical conserves.
Eliconee, Mount Helicon, sacred to the muses.
enchessoun, (*n.*) reason.
endytit, uttered.
ene, evening.
entre(s), entrance.
Eolus, Aeolus, god of winds.
(e)schaip, (*v.*) escape.
eschame, be ashamed.
esperance, (*n.*) hope.
estait, condition, rank, state, way of life.
everilk, every.
evin, (1) evening. (2) even, fairly, justly, precisely; **ful ~,** with pleasing symmetry.
exild, exylit, driven out, free.
expence, money spent on food.
experience, be ~, in fact.
expert, am ~, have (sorrowful) experience.
expone, explain.
extasy, frenzy, swoon.

fa, foe.
fabill, but ~, frankly.
fachioun, curved blade.
facound, eloquent.
facultie, method, profession, disposition.
fa(i)d, wither; **-it,** dulled, unfeeling.
faikin, deceitful.
failye, fail.
fair, (1) food(-taking). (2) go, live, fare. (3) beautiful, pleasing; **-heid,** beauty; **fairlie,** securely, smoothly.
fald, (1) swerve from truth. (2) embrace (*v.*).
fall, befall, come by, happen, enter, be effected; **~ in ressoning,** argue.
fallow, companion, associate with (*refl.*).
fall-trap, snap-trap.
fals, guilty; **-et,** falsehood, fault.
falt, blame, default, lack (*ns.*); **-it,** did wrong.
fame, reputation; **in ~,** of renown.

fane, eagerly, glad(ly).
fang, (*n., v.*) catch.
fant, weaken.
fantasie, act of magic, illusion.
far furth, (*adv.*) best.
farie, fary, act of magic, fairy folk, fairyland.
farne, fern.
fassoun, (*n.*) style.
fast, close, copiously, quickly.
fauld, sheep-fold.
faw, variegated.
fay, faith, 'word'.
fayest, those utterly fated.
fax, hair.
fe, (1) sheep. (2) reward (*n.*).
fecht, (*v.*) fight, struggle.
feddram, plumage.
feid, (1) enmity, wrath. (2) feed.
feill, fele, (1) feel, smell, knowledge, seek to know. (2) many.
feind, devil.
fe(i)nyeit, faynit, fictitious, deceitful, invented, pretended, supposed.
feir, (1) companion. (2) doings. (3) fear (*n.*); **-full,** inspiring reverence; **feiritnes,** terror.
fe(i)rd, fourth.
fe(i)rlie, strange(ly), so very, suddenly; **ferliand,** amazed (*adj.*).
feitho, fitchew.
fell, (1) hill. (2) cruel; **-oun,** deadly, desperate.
fellowschip, company.
fent, (opening in a) garment.
fer, far; **-er,** further.
fervent, very hot, ardent.
fettillie, skilfully.
fibert, the beaver.
figour, appearance, body, bodily shape, example, symbol(izing); **be ~,** through *fig.* representation; **figurall,** allegorical; **figurate,** likened, symbolized.
firth, wooded country.
fitchis, vetches.
fla, flay; *pa.t.* **fled, flew;** *p.p.* **flane.**
flaill, well-beam.
flane, arrow.
flang, tossed about.
flasche, sheaf.
flat, expanse; **-ling(is),** full length.

GLOSSARY

fle, (1) fly (*n.*). (2) fly, race (*vs.*), flee; **-ar,** one who flees; *pa.t.* **flaw; flowen,** flown down.

fleidnes, fright.

fleit, (1) flow, swim. (2) scared off.

flemyt, driven away.

flesche, meat; **-lie,** sensual.

flet, in the ∼, indoors.

flewer, odour.

flit, move elsewhere.

flocht, on ∼, (*adj.*) upset.

Flora, goddess of spring and flowers.

flure, floor.

flurischand, growth, well endowed.

flyte, argue.

fog, moss.

foirfalt, be forfeited.

foir-run, (*adj.*) exhausted.

foirse, be aware, see first.

foirspeikar, speaker, 'chairman'.

fold, earth, world.

fontale, coming from a fountain.

for, as (aid to), by reason of, from, in place of, in spite of, of, out of, to avoid, with, inasmuch as.

forbeir, show deference to, give up.

force, fors, strength; **on/off ∼,** of necessity, indeed; **forcelie,** strongly; **forcit,** compelled.

forfaut, condemn.

forgif, release to.

forlore, (*p.p.*) lost.

formest, fastest.

forquhy, since, because, for this reason.

forrow, in front of.

forsu(i)th, indeed.

forthink, repent.

forthy, therefore.

fortunait, dealt with by fate.

foryeild, (*v.*) reward.

foryet, forget.

foull-carpand, evil-tongued.

fowlis, birds.

fowmart, polecat.

fra, fro, from (the time that), of, when, with respect to; **∼ that,** because.

frank, at liberty.

fraucht, passage-money.

fraward, frawart, adverse, perverse.

fray, (1) from. (2) fright.

fre, generous, noble.

freikis, 'creatures'.

freisit, became severe.

fresch, delightful, fair, gay, tidy.

frivoll, miserable; **-us,** paltry, worthless.

from, with.

fronsit, (*adj.*) wrinkled.

fructous, fruitful.

frute, harvest, worthwhile matter.

fude, food, living.

ful(l), quite, very; **-ely,** wholly.

fulminait, issued.

fundin, found.

fur, (*n.*) furrow.

fure, went, (has) fared.

furrit, trimmed.

furth, along, on(wards), out.

fute for fute, keeping step.

fyft, fifth.

fyle, defile, pollute; *pa.t., p.p.* **fyld, fylit.**

fyn(d)e, find; **-ar,** discoverer; **fand,** found, reached, experienced.

fyne, artful, 'superior'; **-lie,** completely.

ga, gane, gay, go, be incumbent; *pr.t.* **gais.**

gadman, ox-driver using a goad.

gaif, gave.

gaip, strive, open the mouth.

gait, (1) path. (2) fashion. (3) goat(s).

galay, ship.

gam(e), joy.

gane, be of use, suit.

gane-come, (*n.*) return.

gane-say, refuse, resist.

gang, go; **∼ between,** intervene.

gansell, sauce.

gar, make, cause; *pa.t.* **gart.**

garneist, garnischit, adorned.

garth, garden.

gay, beautiful (one), brilliant, delightful, fine, handsome, strong, excellent.

geill, jelly.

geir, (*n.*) attire, treasure.

gemynyng, two-part harmony in simple form.

generabill, capable of being generated.

general, in ~, with common purpose.
generatioun, begetting.
generit, begotten.
gent, beautiful.
gentill, fine, good, noble, obedient, well-born.
gentrace, gentrice, kindness.
gers, grass; **greissis** (*pl.*) lawns.
gest, (1) guest. (2) romance (*n.*).
geve, if, whether.
gif(f), (1) give (also **geif**); **God ~,** would that; *pa.p.* **gevin.** (2) if, whether.
giglotlike, like a strumpet.
gillet, mare.
gimpis, subtleties.
gin, device.
gird, moved, rose, struck.
girnand, (*adj.*) snarling.
glar, make muddy.
gled, the kite.
gleid, ember.
gloir, glory, splendour.
gloming, twilight.
glose, (*n.*) gloss (*legal*).
glowmand, (*adj.*) frowning.
glowrand, (*adj.*) staring.
glyde, go.
goikit, stared foolishly.
gorrit, pierced through.
gostlie, spiritual.
governance, authority, good demeanour.
grace, kindness, favour, fortune.
graip, vulture.
gra(i)thit, equipped.
grane, point, particular.
grant, agree.
grantschir, grandfather.
gratious, luxuriant, with grace.
gravis, groves.
greif, vexation, distress.
gre(i)t, lamentation, weep.
grene, (1) sward. (2) apace, fresh; **mak ~,** revive.
greting, (*n.*) praise.
grevand, grievous.
Grewe, Greek.
grew-hound, greyhound.
grimmit, befouled.
grislie, horrible.
grottis, groats.

grouf, on ~, prostrate.
groundin, sharpened.
ground(is), bottom, ground; **groundit,** based; **groundless,** bottomless.
growand, (*adj.*) carpeted.
growis, wrinkles in terror.
grunching, (*n.*) grumbling.
grype, vulture.
gud(e), goods, possessions, suitable; **-lie,** excellent(ly), lushly, very.
gukkit, stupid.
gule, bitter weeping.
gust thair mouth, give them relish.
gyd, protect.

habirgeoun, sleeveless armour-coat.
hace, hoarse.
ha(i)f, have; *pr.t.* **hais, hef.**
haikit, went.
haill, (1) perfect, (al)together, whole; **-sum,** wise; **all haill,** entirely. (2) (*v.*) draw, pull, rush.
hair, (1) the hare. (2) hoar.
ha(i)rt, hert, heart, courage, resolution; **-lie,** heartfelt, earnestly; **with hairt,** from the heart.
haist, speed (*v.*); **-elie,** without reflection.
hait, hate, hot, passionate, warm.
hald, contain, go, keep, protect, regard, reign, set (about), support; **~ of,** be subservient to; **~ thair heid,** show their faces.
halfheid, the side of the head.
halie, devout; **-dayis,** gayest.
halkis, (*n.*) hawks.
hals, neck.
hame, home; **-lie,** familiar.
hanche, hip.
hand, power, signature; **fra the ~,** when unleashed; **hand-breid,** handbreadth.
hankit, became entangled.
hantit, accustomed, practised.
hap, (1) luck, fortune; **-innit,** (it) chanced. (2) protect.
harberie, herbery, lodging, shelter, refuge.
hard, (1) heard. (2) stout.
harlet, rascally.

harlit, dragged (away).

harnes, armour.

harrowis, field-harrows.

harsky, rough.

having, demeanour.

haw, dull-coloured, livid.

he, high.

hecht, hicht, (be) called, undertook; (*n., v.*) promise, vow.

heiddismen, those in authority.

heidit, (*adj.*) tipped.

heif, (*v.*) lift.

heill, (1) hide. (2) well-being. (3) heel (*n.*)

heir-foir, for this reason.

hekill, (*n.*) hackle; (*v.*) dress with a hackle; **heklit,** lying fringed; **on hekillit-wyis,** with edges cut in a fringed pattern.

hellis, infernal.

he(i)thing, mockery.

helthsum, prudent.

hend, gentle.

Herato, Erato, muse of lyric poetry.

herd, guardian.

heritage, inherited possessions.

Hesperus, Evening Star.

heuch, huche, cliff, cleft.

hevie, dispirited, sad; **-lie,** sorrowfully; **hevines,** grief.

hewmound, helmet.

hicht, aloft; **of/on ~,** high.

hiddeous, horrible.

h(i)e, high, proud, raise; **(up)on ~,** loudly.

hindir, recent, other.

hing, hyng, (over-)hang; *pa.t.* **hang.**

hint, seize(d), snatch(ed).

hir, her(self).

hird, (*n.*) flock.

hirpilland, (*pr.p.*) limping.

hoche, hind-leg, joint; *pl.* **hoichis.**

hoir, rough.

holkit, hollowed-out.

holt, forest, wood.

holyne, holly.

hone, but ~, at once.

hop, (*v.*) jerk.

hostillare, one given to entertaining guests/strangers.

hovit, raised.

how, (*adj.*) hollow.

howp, (*n.*) hope.

humanitie, kindness.

humill, humble.

huny, sweet one.

hurcheoun, hedgehog.

hurd(e), treasure, accumulation.

huresone, bastard.

husband, husbandman.

hy, (*n., v.*) haste.

I ges, indeed.

ignorants, foolish ones.

ilk, each; **-a,** same.

ill, (*n.*) evil.

imbrace (fra), protect (from).

implicate, (*p.p.*) involved.

in, at, for, inside, into, on, with.

incontinent, straightway.

indorsat, endorsed.

indure, last (*v.*); **-ate,** hardened (*adj.*).

infect, replete.

infild, undefiled.

inflat, (*p.p.*) blown.

ingenious, discerning.

ingyne, intention.

inobediens, disobedience.

in-schunder, to pieces.

insolence, licentiousness.

insolent, 'flighty', inexperienced.

instante, with ~, without delay.

intellectif, intellectual.

intent, (*n.*) mind, purpose, thought.

intentioun, accusation, charge.

intermell, meddle.

intill, into, drawn about, of, in, towards.

intraill, belly.

intruse, (*v.*) urge.

inwart, essential, deep, heartfelt.

iwis, indeed.

janglour, tell-tale.

jasp, jewel.

je(o)pardie, device, fortune, trick.

jolie, dainty, fine, gay, pleasant, pretty, smooth-running.

jonit, (*p.p.*) interlinked.

jowall, jewel.

kame, comb (of cock).

katche, (*n.*) chase.

keip, heed (*n.*); protect.

keitching, abode.
kemmit, combed.
ken, know, recognize, reveal; *pa.t.,*
p.p. **kend, kennit.**
kennettis, small hunting-dogs.
kest, cast, pondered, put, sought.
kist, chest.
kith, (*n.*) place.
kittokis, paramours.
knakis, knax, jargon, small talk.
knap, strike down.
knawe, recognize; **-legeing,** know-
ledge.
knichtlie, chivalrous.
kyith, (*v.*) manifest, show.
kynd, disposition, nature, state.

laich, (*adv.*) low.
laid, (*n.*) load.
laif, others, remainder.
laip, (*v.*) drink.
lair, instruction, learning.
lait, (1) seek. (2) formerly.
laith, unwilling.
lak, censure (*n.*); **-it,** disparaged.
lane, gift.
lang eir, early on.
langour, longing, pining.
lans, (*v.*) bound, scramble.
lap, leapt.
laser, leisure, time.
lat, let, ~ **be,** leave (off), renounce;
~ **se,** assay, let it be seen; ~ **wit,**
inform.
lauboraris, peasants; **lauborit,** culti-
vated.
lauch, (*v.*) laugh.
lauchfull, lawful.
laud, (*n.*) praise.
laverok, the lark.
law, (1) hill. (2) low (*adj., adv.*). (3)
abase. (4) justice; **-tie,** fidelity,
loyalty.
lawn, fine clothing.
lazarous, leprous one.
le, (1) field; *pl.* **leis.** (2) tranquillity,
unruffled. (3) lie (*n.*); **but leis,**
assuredly; **learis,** liars; prevaricate
pr.t. **leis,** *pa.t.* **leid, leit, lieit.**
ledder-fute, foot of gallows-ladder.
legacie, (*n.*) bequests.

leid, (1) folk, one, man. (2) lead
(mineral).
leidar of the dance, actuator.
leif, (1) leaf. (2) dear. (3) leave (*n., v.*),
allow, bequeath. (4) exist, live,
remain; *pr.p.* **levand; leving,** way
of life, possessions, food.
leill, le(i)le, loyal, just, true; comp.
lelar.
le(i)r(n), learn, teach; *pa.t.* **le(i)rd,**
lerit.
leme, ray.
lemman, lover.
len, give.
lenand, (*pr.p.*) crouching.
lenth, in ~, length-wise; **on** ~, full
stretch.
Lentring, Lent.
lest, endure; **-and,** (ever-)lasting.
lesum, lawful, pure.
let, lat, prevent; **but lett,** unceasing-
ly.
lettand, making as though.
letter, (1) court-order. (2) last (*adj.*).
lettin, (*p.p.*) shed.
leuch, lewch, laugh(ed).
lever, rather.
levere, liver (of body).
lewer, louvre.
lichorus, lecherous.
licht, (1) bright, easily, frisky, nimbly,
lighten; **-lie,** disparage. (2) alight.
liggand, lying down.
likame, body.
likkin, liken; **be liknes,** symbolically.
lind, loin.
ling, patch of heather.
linget, linseed.
linkis, (*n.*) fetters.
lint, flax; **-bollis,** flax-pods.
lipper, leper; **-ludge,** leper-house.
list, chose; **-is,** is pleased.
loggerand, loosely-hanging.
loif, flatter, praise.
lokker, (*adj.*) curling.
loun, 'creature'.
lour, skulk.
lous, lows, dissolute, free (*v.*),
loosen(ed), unyoke.
lout, bow down.
loving, (*n.*) honour.
low(e), (*n.*) flame.

lowne, unruffled, still (*adj.*).
lude, loved.
lu(i)f, (1) love (*n., v.*). (2) palm of hand.
lu(i)k, luke, appearance, glance, consider, look to/at, search.
lukkin, webbed.
lurker, scoundrel.
lust, pleasure, vice; **-ie,** fair, becoming, handsome, carefree, pleasant; **lustines,** beauty.
lusumest, fairest.
lyart, silver grey.
lyfe hes tane, is born.
lyke, likely, likewise, similar; ~ **as,** as if.
lyking, (*n.*) delight, desire.
lyly, lily-like.
lymmer, rogue.
lyne, flax-stalks.
lyre, hue, complexion, skin.
lyt(e), lyttill, little (way).

ma, (1) may. (2) make. (3) more.
maculait, defiled.
ma(w)gre, displeasure, in spite of.
mair, further, more (ado).
mais, (1) make(s). (2) dish (of food).
ma(i)st, greatest; **-er,** overpower, leading (*adj.*); **maistrie,** evil power.
maith, maggot.
malisone, (*n.*) curse.
man, mon(e), must.
mane, (1) strength. (2) moaning (*n.*).
manesworne, forsworne.
mangerie, (*n.*) feast.
manheid, proof of valour.
manifest, blatant; **-it,** exposed.
mansioun, separate dwelling-place.
manteinans, (*n.*) fostering.
manure-place, manor-house.
mapamond, world.
mark, go, resolve.
marmisset, marmoset.
marrit, perplexed.
massie, solid.
mastress, mistress.
mat, (*v.*) baffle.
mav(e)is, mawis, thrush.
mawe, belly, stomach.
may, maiden, virgin.
meid, (*n.*) bribe(s), reward.
meill, flour-meal.

me(i)nis, method(s).
meir, pure, simple.
meit, (1) food, sustenance; **-is** (*pl.*) dainties, dishes. (2) (close-)fitting, worthy. (3) meet (*v.*).
mekill, mekle, big, great, much.
meldrop, drops of mucous.
mell, (*v.*) mate.
Melpomane, Melpomene, the muse of tragedy.
Memoria, Mnemosyne, mother of the muses.
memour, thought (*n.*); **-iall,** remembrance.
mend, assuage, improve, make amends, remove, made up (a fire).
mene, think, ponder.
menye, (1) family. (2) hurt (*n.*).
merie, mirie, playful, pleasant; **-nes,** diversion.
merk, mirk, wicked, dim, in darkness.
merle, merll, blackbird.
mertrik, marten.
micht, could, power, pressure; **of ~,** mighty.
midding, midden.
middis, midwart, the middle.
ming, meng, intersperse; **-lit with blude,** bloodshot.
minorall, metallurgical art.
mis(s), fault, sin.
mischeif, adversity, hurt; **mischevis,** injures.
misfaire, go astray/wrong.
misknaw, disregard, be unaware.
mister, (*n.*) need.
mo, additional, other.
mocht, could, might.
modelacioun, observance of due measure/proportion (*music.*).
modifie, assess.
moist, (*n.*) damp.
mold, mow, earth, dirt, dust.
monische, admonish.
mony, many (a); ~ **ane,** in plenty.
morne, morning; **the ~,** tomorrow.
mortyfie, bring into subjection.
mot, may.
moving, motion.
mowdemart, the mole.
mowis, (*n.*) quibbles, jests.

mowlit, mouldy.
mude, (n.) mind, 'spirits'.
muf, move.
muke, dirt.
mure, (n.) moor.
mydred, diaphragm, midriff.
myld, pleasant, gentle one.
mynd, thought (n.); **in ~,** to himself.
mynour, metallurgist.

nakit, nakedness.
namelie, especially.
nanis, for the ~, indeed.
nar. See **neir.**
nathing, not in the least.
nay, withouttin ~, certainly.
neidis, it ~, it is necessary.
neidlingis, of necessity.
neir, nere, near(ly), close(ly), almost;
   -hand, almost; **neir be,** within a
   radius of; **nar,** nearer; **neist,** adjac-
   ent to.
nek-hering, sharp blow on the neck.
nethir-mar(e), further down.
new, freshly, recently; **~ agane,** a
   second time.
no(u)cht, not, nothing; **off ~,**
   worthless.
noit, (1) watchful. (2) note (of music).
none, noon.
nor, but that, rather, than.
not, nothing.
noter, notary.
nothir, nouther, neither.
now, as ~, now, for the present;
   nowondayis, nowadays.
noyes, (n.) singing.
nureis, nourisher.
nyse, nice, foolish, odd, subtle.

object, oppose (as evidence).
oblis, pledge (v.); **-ing,** bond.
obsolve, (v.) answer.
occurris, comes back.
ocht, anything, at all.
of(f), against, between, by, cut off, for,
   from, in, made of, of, off, over, with.
oftsyis, often.
okker, usury.
on, against, at, by, during, from, in(to),
   of, (on)to.
once, the ounce.

one-deid, indeed.
one-til, until.
onloft, aloft, loudly.
onpace, quickly.
ony, any.
operacioun, the carrying-out.
opinioun, good name.
oppin, blatant, obvious, unchecked.
or (that), before.
orature, room for private worship.
oritionis, prayers.
orloge-bell, teller of the hours.
ornament, jewels.
o(u)cht, anything, at all, in any way.
oulk, week.
our(e), ovir, over, through.
ourset, overwhelmed.
oursyld, hidden.
outher, either.
out-red, brought to an end.
outthrow, throughout.
outwaill, rejected creature.
outwin, (v.) escape.
over-draif, enveloped.
overheillit, (p.p.) adorned.
over-malapart, impudent.
overpas, pass away.
over-schort, too weak.
oversone, too ready.
ovircome, ourcome, recovered,
   came to.
ovirspred, (p.p.) covered.

Pace, Pasche, Easter.
pace, ane sturdie ~, with firm steps.
pad(dok), frog.
paissit, moderated.
palpis, pappis, breasts, teats.
palyeoun, pavilion.
pane, (1) garden plot. (2) 'pain' (legal),
   torment; **-full,** grievous; **on pane
   off my heid,** on my life; **panit,**
   suffered.
parabole, parable.
paramour, love(r), passionately; **-is,**
   love-making.
parliament, assembly.
part, representative (n.) partly; **~ of,**
   distribute; **parteis,** parties (legal);
   partit, destroyed; **partles off,** free
   from.
passis, surpasses.

GLOSSARY

patill, plough-staff.
paynchis, paunches.
payntit, (*adj.*, *v.*) variegated.
pedder, pedlar.
peil(l)it, plundered, stripped.
peip, (*n.*) squeak.
peir, equal.
peirsing, (*n.*) blinding.
pe(i)s, (1) peace; **peacis** (*pl.*) salvation. (2) peas.
peit-poit, peat-hole.
pellet, (*n.*) skin.
penetryve, cruel, piercing.
pennair, pen-holder.
pennis, (*n.*) wings.
pennit, (*adj.*) quilled.
pennyfull, round and full.
pens, meditate; **-ivenes,** sadness.
pera(d)venture, possibly.
perem(p)tourlie, without fail.
perfay(e), indeed.
perfit, perfect, accomplished.
perqueir, thoroughly.
persoun, (*n.*) rank.
pete, pietie, pity, clemency; **-ous,** pitiful.
p(e)ure, pore, (the) poor.
pew, thin cry.
phisnomy, appearance, physiognomy.
picht, pitched (*pa.t.*).
pith, strength.
place, (high) rank.
plait, platter, plate.
plane, (1) valley, space. (2) clearly, manifest; **-ly,** openly.
play, game, jest (*ns.*), joyousness; **maid it ~,** made light.
pla(y)nt, complaint, lamenting, grief.
pleid, jeopardy, discussion, attack, argument.
plenye, complain, lament.
plesand, gay, pleasing; **-ly,** becomingly, delightfully; **plesance,** (a show of) delight(s); **plesing,** pleasure.
plet, (*v.*) embrace, twist, weave.
pleuch, (*n.*) plough.
pley, plea, pleading.
ply, distress, plight, state; **into ~,** in good condition.
plycht, (*n.*) blame.

point, (1) appearance, detail; **in ~,** about (to). (2) lace (*n.*).
poleit, polite, plausible, stylized.
poll, skull; **deid- ~,** death's-head.
Pollymyo, Polyhymnia, the muse of the stately hymn and religious dance.
pontificall, episcopal vestments.
port, (1) gate, (2) bearing (*n.*).
potestate, potentate.
pow, (*n.*) paw.
practick, practice, experience.
prais, (*n.*) reward.
prayer, (*n.*) petition.
precelling, surpassing.
preclair, renowned.
preiching, lesson.
preif, see, try, prove, taste.
pre(i)s, strive, struggle.
prene, (*n.*) pin.
prent, (1) evidence. (2) imprint (*v.*).
present, represent, show.
presume, suspicion.
pretend, aspire to, seek out, bring action at law.
prettie, 'fine', interesting, well made.
previe, discreet; **-elie,** secretly, stealthily.
prevydit, fore-ordained.
price, pryis, (*n.*) bribe, honour, worth.
privilage, exemption.
professioun, outward demeanour.
progenitouris, ancestors.
prompit furth, burst out.
propertie, quality; **in ~,** in our possession.
propone, propose, state (a case).
proporcioun, harmony, melody; **-ate,** balanced, perfect (*music.*).
Proserpina, Persephone, queen of the Greek underworld.
provisioun, forethought.
provocative, exciting to lust.
provyde befoir, foresee.
pruf, attest.
pu(e)n(e)is, punish; **-ing,** suffering (*n.*).
pungitive, ready to sting, vexatious.
purches, (1) concubinage, plunder. (2) manage.
purfellit, adorned.

purpour, purple.
pursephant, royal messenger.
put, ~ away, suppress; **~ doun,** destroy; **~ in memorie,** record; **~ out,** declare.
pyip, (1) sing. (2) cask.
pyke, fabricate, pick (out), steal; **-eris,** pilferers; **-is,** thorns.
pyme, (n.) cry.
pyne, punishment.

quailye, corn-crake.
quair, small book.
querrell, plea, case.
quert, in ~, alive.
quha(y), who(ever).
quha(i)r, where(by), with which; **-at,** at what; **-of,** of which; **-throw,** by/from which.
quhais, whose.
quham, whom.
quhasill, weasel.
quhat, what(ever).
quhen (that), when.
quhether, quhidder, (1) where, whither. (2) whether **(quhether** also introduces direct quests.).
quhilk(is), who, which.
quhill, in the hope that, until.
quhitret, stoat.
quhrynand, (pr.p.) ?whining.
quhyle, (short) space of time; **this ~,** for some time; **quhylum,** once upon a time; **quhyle (quhylis) ... quhyle (quhylis),** now ... now.
quhyt(e), bright, fair, white, specious; **-lie,** whitish.
quik, (the) living.
quitclame, (v.) release.
quotidiane, daily.
quyet, (n.) comfort.
quyte repay, gone, free, 'clean'.

ra, the roe.
rad, (adj.) terrified.
radicate, rooted.
rage, violent heat; **-yne,** tumult.
raif, rave.
ra(i)p, (n.) rope.
rais, (1) race (n.). (2) rose (v.).
raith, quickly.
rak, heed (n.), think.

raklie, impetuously.
rampand, rearing up.
rank, complete (adj.), loathsome.
rany, rain-laden.
rate, manner.
rather, sooner; **rathly,** quickly.
rattoun, little rat.
raucht, gave, given.
rauk, rawk, harsh.
raw, on ~, in a pack.
rax(e), prevail.
recompens, atone for.
recreat, refresh, revive.
recure, get back, recovery.
red, marked as.
reddie, prompt, on the point of; **-lie,** easily.
refer, apply to; **-it to,** matter for.
refet, recover, recuperate.
refrane, restrain.
refuse, let go, prevent.
regne, prevail, domineer.
regrait, (n.) lamenting, sorrow.
reheirs, tell (at length).
reid, (1) advice, advise. (2) red, hue. (3) reed. (4) read.
reif, ry(i)f, reive, rob (of), tear, destroy, (pa.t. **reft, raif**); thieving.
reik, (v.) grant.
reird, loud noise.
remeid, remedy (n., v.), assuage, remission.
remord, examine, have remorse.
remufe, move away, withdraw.
renewit, made fresh.
rent, (1) income, possessions. (2) (n.) devoured, torn.
renye, govern, rule.
repair, resort (n., v.), contemplation.
report, declare.
repreif, reprufe, shame (n.), reprove.
requyre, ask.
resaif, take (in); p.p. **ressavit.**
ressoun, declaration, inscription, discretion, moderation; **be ~,** with good reason.
restles, on and on.
retour, (n.) return.
reulie, tractable.
reulre, ruler.
reuth, rewth, compassion.

revand, ravenous; **revar,** robber; **revin,** ripped (*p.p.*).

revolve, consult carefully.

rew(e), have pity on, regret (*v.*).

riche, endow.

richt, plainly, precisely, even, extremely, justice, properly.

rin, ryn, continue, follow, drop, run.

ring(e), endure, prevail, rule, come by power.

rink, renk, man, knight-at-arms.

rippillit, removed the seeds from.

rispite, exemption.

rod, path.

Rodomantus, Rhadamanthys, one of the judges in the Greek underworld.

roib, (*n.*) coat.

rois, ros, the rose; **-ing,** rosy.

rok, distaff.

rold, (*adj.*) polished.

roll, hasten, luxuriate.

ron(e), thicket.

roseir, rose-tree.

rotche, (*n.*) rock.

rotting, putrid matter.

rouch, rough (ground).

roun(d), (*v.*) whisper.

roustit, morally foul.

rout, (*n.*) blow.

rowand, abounding.

roy, king.

rude, (1) artless, coarse, poor, unskilful. (2) cross (*n.*). (3) complexion, face.

rufe, tranquillity, shelter.

rug, rend.

ruik, rook.

rumissing, (*n.*) roaring.

runkillit, (*adj.*) wrinkled.

rurall, (*adj.*) country.

ruse, extol.

rusticat, boorish, vulgar.

rute, root (*v.*), source, undergrowth.

ryce, small branches.

ryte, habit.

sa, so, though.

sad, dull, firm(ly), serious, solemn.

Sagittarie, Sagittarius the zodiacal sign.

saif, heal, protect, save; **∼ your mercie,** your pardon.

sa(i)kles, innocent.

saipheron, saffron.

sair(e), soir, hurt (*n.*), grieved (*adj.*), grievous(ly), bitter, disaster; **-ie,** wretched.

sait, (*n.*) seat.

sall, shall; **sauld,** should.

salmes, psalms.

sals, sauce.

salusit, greeted.

salve, remedy (*n.*); **-iour,** Saviour.

samin, same.

sang, music, outcry.

sapoure, savour, quality.

sark, serk, inner garment, shirt.

Sathanas, Satan.

satisfie, carry out.

saull, sawll, soul.

saw, set, sow; *p.p.* **sawin; saweris,** sowers.

sayne, say.

scant(lie), scarcely.

schaddow, reflection, shade.

schaippit, escaped.

schamefull, ashamed.

schankis, legs.

schaw, (1) declare, demonstrate, manifest, reveal. (2) copse, covert.

sched, driven, parted, poured out; **-and,** sweeping through.

scheill, dwelling-place.

schene, beautiful, glittering.

schent, destroyed, unconscious.

schill, shrilly.

scho, she.

scho(i)t, (*n.*) blow, stroke.

schone, shoes.

schore, (*n.*) threats.

schow, (*n.*) thrust.

schrew, (1) rascal. (2) curse (*v.*).

schrink, (*v.*) twitch.

schuik, shook, smashed.

schuir, (*v.*) cut.

schulit, cleared.

schupe, began, set about.

schute, (1) defecated. (2) pounce (*v.*).

science, learning.

scorne, scorning (*n.*), something contemptible.

scra(i)p, scratch (*v.*); **∼ out,** delete.

screit, ? disintegrate.

scrip, food-wallet.

scripture, proverb.
se(e), (1) see that/to, give heed, look at (also as **sy**). (2) sea, water.
secretar, one possessing the secrets.
seill, sell, seal (of office, of Confession).
seith, boil, cook; *p.p.* **soddyn.**
sek, (*n.*) sack.
selcouth, strange thing.
seldyn, seldom, rarely.
self(f), the ∼, itself, themselves.
semis, befits.
sempill, plain, simple.
sen, send; *pa.t.* **send; God sen,** would that.
sen (that), since.
sendill-tymis, seldom.
sent, (*n.*) scent.
sentence, lesson, opinion, pronouncement, thought.
senyeis, (*n.*) marks.
senyeours, fine fellows.
serusite, seriousness.
serve, (1) deserve. (2) aid (*v.*); **–ice,** dealings, happenings; **servitour,** servant.
sessoun, seasoning.
set, compose, determine, intend, employ, value; **∼ by,** refuse.
sete, throne.
severall, separately.
sewe, broth, pottage.
sex, six; **sext,** sixth.
sic, such.
sich, (*n., v.*) sigh.
sicht, (1) sight, eyes. (2) sigh (*v.*).
sicker, firmly, good, quite, safe, steadfast, sure; **–lie,** certainly; **sickernes,** security, stability.
silie, sely, foolish, innocent, poor, wretched.
similitude, likeness.
simonie, buying and selling church preferments.
simuland, (*pr.p.*) feigning.
sirculit, encircled.
sit, (*v.*) fall.
skaith, scaith, (*n.*) damage, harm.
skap, (*n.*) scalp.
skar, sker, take fright, chase.
skelfis, (*n.*) shelves.
skirt, (*n.*) lap.

sklender, ill-nourished.
skrow, scroll.
sla, slay.
slaik, (1) assuage, satisfy. (2) dells.
slavering, slobbering.
sle, subtle, accomplished.
sleuth, sloth.
slewthound, tracking-dog.
slicht, deception, knack, skill.
slidderie, slippery.
slonkis, (*n.*) hollows.
slyde, move quietly.
small, slender, unexalted.
smertlie, quickly.
smoirand, (*pr.p.*) suppressing.
snod, flat ground.
sober, calm (*v.*), humble, simple; **–lie,** solemnly.
so(u)cht, sought out, went.
soft, (*v.*) calm, restrain.
solempne day, festival.
soliter, alone.
sone, (1) son. (2) sun. (3) early.
sop, one steeped in.
sour(e), displeasing.
sowpit, drowned, whelmed.
soyr, reddish brown.
space, distance, time, while.
spairit, avoided, failed.
spamen, prophets, soothsayers.
speid, hurry on, prosper, save, succeed; **gude ∼,** quickly.
spe(i)r(e), (1) spear. (2) sphere. (3) ask (why).
speit, (*n.*) skewer.
speldit, spread-eagled.
spence, larder; **spenser,** steward.
spend, exhausted one's self.
spill, destroy.
spirit, preserving instinct.
spittail-hous, leper-house.
splene, heart.
spoliate, bereft.
sport, diversion.
spreidis, prevails.
spreit, spirit.
spring, (gay) tune.
sproutis, growth.
spurn, hurl, strike.
stair, bewildered state.
stall, stole (*pa.t.*).
stand, endure, be checked, remain in

GLOSSARY

reach; ~ **for it,** assure one; **stand at,** accept.
standfray, opposed (to).
stangis, (*v.*) stings.
stark, strong, severe.
starnis, sternis, stars.
start, moved, turned; ~ **on fute,** got to one's feet.
stationeir, (*adj.*) fixed.
stature, height, standing.
steid, place (*n.*); **-fast,** firmly fixed.
steipit, soaked.
steir, (1) (*v.*) bestir, control, rule, work. (2) stirring (*n.*), disturb, alarm, move (to anger); **-and,** in dispute.
stentit, stretched.
stevin, (*n.*) accord.
stikkand, fastened.
still, (1) fall (*v.*). (2) easily, quiet(ly), restrained; **lowd and ~,** unfailingly.
sting, piece of wood.
stint, (*v.*) pause, stop.
stirk, bullock.
stok, (tree-)stump.
stonist, alarmed.
stoppell, stopper.
stoppit, stuffed.
stottis, bullocks.
stound, pang.
stouth, robbery.
stra, stro, straw; **lay a~,** cease, desist.
straik, stroke (*n.*, *v.*), shot (*v.*), struck (off).
strait, cogent, binding; **-lie,** closely, strictly.
strand, stream.
straucht, straight, put in line, stretch(ed).
streik, (*v.*) stretch.
streit, strete, road.
strenth, validity.
strikkin, struck, cut.
stude, brood(-mare).
studdie, (*v.*) marvel.
stuff, food.
stuffit, (*p.p.*) filled.
stule, (*n.*) place, seat.
styll, plight.
subcharge, extra course at a meal.

subtell, intricate, cunning, strange.
succour, aid (*n.*); **mak ~,** help.
sucker, sugar.
suffrage, (*n.*) help, support.
suggestioun, prompting to evil.
su(i)th(e), (the) truth, truly.
suld, sowld, ought, should.
sumdeill, somewhat.
summoun(dis), (*n.*) summons.
sumtyme, before, once.
superfluous, wordy.
superscriptioun, title.
suppl(i)e, (*n.*, *v.*) aid.
suppo(i)s, although.
supportatioun, sustenance.
sustene, uphold.
sutis, (*n.*) suits (*legal*).
swa (that), as long as.
swak, (*n.*, *v.*) swing, throw.
sweit, (1) cold sweat(ing). (2) beneficial, dear (one), pleasurable, pure, sweet(ly).
swelly, (*v.*) swallow.
swelt, died, fainted.
swing, (*v.*) toil.
swingillit, scutched.
swoping, (*n.*) sweeping.
swy(i)th, straightway.
syde, (1) wide. (2) side; **-lingis abak,** with a movement to the back and side.
syis, a time.
syke, streamlet.
sylit, hidden away.
symphonis, harmonies.
syne, (1) again, then, afterwards. (2) (*n.*) sin, 'shame'.
syte, (*n.*) sorrow.

taid, toad.
taill, advice, words.
tailyeis, portions.
tais, (1) toes. (2) takes.
tait, playful.
ta(k), (1) holding (*n.*). (2) ascertain, convince, keep; ~ **heit,** be warmed; ~ **in gude keip,** centre one's thoughts on; ~ **na labour,** have no concern; ~ **on hand,** accept; ~ **the dew,** wander afield; ~ **in cure,** undertake; *pa.t.* **tuke, tuik,** *p.p.* **tane, tone.**

takin, ta(i)kning, token.
talking, story.
tar, harass.
tarie, tary, (*n.*) delay.
tarrow, tarry
tedderit, (*p.p.*) fastened, caught.
temperance, moderation.
te(y)n(e), anger, fierceness, angry, cruel.
tendouris, attenders, guides.
tennour, purport.
tent, (*n.*) care, heed.
tepat, small shoulder-cape.
terme, (1) period for payment, lease. (2) expression.
Tersitor, Terpsichore, the muse of choral dance.
teuch, tewch, tough.
textual, of the text.
tha(i)r, (1) their. (2) there; **-at,** there, through; **-foir,** by such; **-fra,** from such; **-off,** by, from, in, with such; **-out,** among, of such, outside; **-throw,** thereby; **-to,** as well, to that end.
thame, them(selves).
than, then.
that, in/so that, in those who.
thay, those; **~ dayis,** then.
Thelya, Thalia, the muse of comedy.
thidderwart, in that direction.
thig, beg.
thing, things, matters, creatures.
think, intend, it seems.
thir, these.
this, thus.
tho, then.
thocht, (1) though. (2) thought (*n., v.*).
tho(i)ll, permit, suffer, withstand.
thrawand, (*pr.p.*) struggling.
thrawart, crooked, stubborn.
thrawin, ill-tempered, sour.
thrid, third.
thrist(ing), (*n.*) thirst.
throw(ch), through.
thus-gait, in this way.
thyne, thence, there.
tig, (*v.*) play.
till, at, by way of, for, to, until.
tint, seized, lost.
tippit, (*adj.*) pointed.

tirlit, plucked.
tirrane, cruel.
tit, (1) tips (*v.*). (2) ripped (*v.*).
to, as, at, by (way of), for, too, with.
tod, fox.
tolter, (*adj.*) swinging.
to-rent, torn to pieces.
tour, tower.
towis, (*n.*) paws.
town, owt off ~, to distant parts.
toxicate, (*adj.*) poisoned.
trace, (*n.*) track.
Trace, Thrace; loosely, the mountainous region n. of Greece.
traist, trest, expect, hope, trust.
trampit, stepped heavily.
tratour, traitor(ous).
travell, travall, exertion, pains.
tra(y)ne, (*n.*) snare.
trestly, truly.
tretie, entreaty.
treuth, fidelity.
trew, loyal; **-lie,** indeed.
trig, (*adj.*) trim.
trimmillit, shook.
trip, small flock.
tripe, guts, entrails.
trow, believe, think, trust.
truker, rogue.
trusterie, faith.
tuitchit, touched.
tume, (*adj.*) empty.
tussillit, 'worried'.
twa(ne), tway, two.
twentie, twentieth.
twin, (*v.*) divide.
twist, tree-branch.
twyn, twist.
tyde, hour, season.
tyke, dog, rascal.
tyme, period (for payment); **as for the ~,** for the time being; **in gude ~,** indeed.
tyne, lose; *p.p.* **tint, tynt.**
typis, (*n.*) figures.

uglie, ugl(y)e, gruesome, horrible.
unamyabill, hostile.
unbald, fearful.
unbrynt, unburnt (*sc.* bush).
uncouth, unaccustomed.
underta, undertake, promise.

undir, beneath, on the ground; **-neth,** conditional on.

uneith, hardly, scarcely.

unfane, (adj.) displeased.

unfutesair, comfortable.

unkynd, unnatural.

unlusum, unlovely.

unprovysit, unforeseen.

unsmart, weak.

unsuspect, honest.

untill, to.

unwarlie, unguardedly, without warning.

unwsit, unbroken (of oxen).

up, (adv.) open.

upcast, (n.) taunting.

up-keikis, (v.) peeps.

uponland, in/of the country; **-is,** rural.

upricht, assuredly.

Uranya, Urania, the muse of astronomy.

use, accustom, be used to, custom; **-and,** accustomed; **usit,** customary.

uthir, other(s); **~ ma,** others along with it.

utter, outer.

vaill, (1) valley. (2) avail.

vane, empty; **vanitee,** worthlessness.

variance, uncertainty.

veiling, (pr.p.) lowering.

veritie, truth.

verray, indeed, quite, true, very, utter(ly).

vilipend, (v.) dishonour.

vincust, (p.p.) overcome.

vittell, food.

vocatioun, (n.) summoning.

vult, (n.) countenance.

wa(i)g, become agitated.

waik, (1) weak. (2) be free from.

waillit, (adj.) choice.

wair, (1) were. (2) wild. (3) endure, pass, spend.

waist, (adj., v.) desolate.

wait, (1) know (also **wate**); **I ~,** indeed. (2) watch (v.); **-ing,** hunting (n.).

waith, (n.) hunting.

wald, would, will, wished; **as quha ~,** as if one were to.

walk, awake, watch over; **-ryfe,** alert.

wall, (n.) wave.

wallowit, (p.p.) withered, wasted away.

wam(b)e, womb, belly.

wammillis, is perturbed.

wan, (1) got (to), went. (2) dark, dull, pale.

wand, rod; **under the ~,** in rural parts.

wane, (1) dwelling-place, region. (2) **gude ~,** in good number.

wanhope, (n.) despair.

wanrufe, restless.

want, be missing, lack.

wantoun, healthful, unheeding, proud; **-lie,** luxuriously; **wantones,** wilfulness, golden days.

wappinnis, teeth.

war, wer, (1) worse. (2) ready, careful; **-lie,** warily. (3) were, would be.

wariand, unstable.

warisoun, (n.) reward.

wark, werk, wirk, (n., v.) act, work.

warld, ward, world, state of affairs.

warne, inform.

warrand, (n., v.) warrant.

warsche, pallid, sickly-looking.

warwolff, large wolf.

waryit, cursed.

watche, watcher.

watter-caill, meatless broth.

wax, wox(e), became (big).

wayis, method.

wecht, weight.

wedder, (1) weather. (2) wether.

weid, (1) garments. (2) weed (n.).

weil, joy.

weill, we(i)le, carefully, certainly, finely, fittingly, indeed, quite, safely, very, well; **~ lang,** over a long period; **~ wer,** it would be good for.

weir, (1) defend. (2) flit away, wear. (3) contention, war. (4) doubt, fear.

we(i)rd, destiny, fate, lot.

weit, wet (n., adj., v.), rain (n.)

well, pool, stream.

welterand, rolling, tossing, ungainly; **welterit,** reversed.

wend, pass, gone, went.

wene, believe, expect; *pa.t.* **we(i)nd.**

weryis, desists.

wesche, wash.

wicht, (1) creature. (2) rich, strong, tough, vigorous.

widderit, stale, faded.

will, (1) desire (*n.*, *v.*), prompt (*v.*), determination, inclination; **at ~,** in one's desires. (2) uncertain; **~ off ane gude reid,** at one's wits' end; **wilsum,** bewildering, drear, lonely.

win, gain (*n.*, *v.*), escape (*v.*), learn, procure.

wink, close the eyes, blink.

wirrie, harass; *pa.t.*, *p.p.* **wer(r)yit.**

wirschip, (mark of) honour.

wisk, quick movement.

wist, expected, realized, knew.

wit, (1) know. (2) wisdom, reason-(ing), senses, mind; **-ie,** learned, wise.

with, against, among, at, by, from.

withgang, liberty.

wo, sorrow(ful); **-full,** disastrous.

wo(i)d, wo(u)de, (1) arrogant, de-mented, surging. (2) forest.

woik, watched, lay awake.

woir out, fluttered.

woll, wool.

womenting, (*n.*) sorrow.

wonder, extremely.

worth, (1) value, fitting (*adj.*). (2) be, become, betide, come to; **weill ~,** quite, just, a blessing on; *pa.t.* **worthit,** *p.p.* **worthin.**

woundis, defilement.

wra(i)k, (1) punishment, revenge. (2) goods, possessions.

wraith, vex, wrath.

wrang(o)us, evil, illegal.

wrappit, (1) enveloped. (2) thrown.

wreik, avenge; *p.p.* **wrokkin.**

wrewche, (*adj.*) troubled.

wrinkis, wiles, tricks.

writ(e), Scripture, document.

wrocht, (*p.p.*) created.

wryte, write (about); *pa.t.* **wrait, wrate.**

wryth, contort, turn away.

wy, creature, person.

wyde, thickly.

wy(i)s, way, fashion.

wyle, stratagem.

wyn, dwell; **winning,** abiding (*n.*).

wynd, (*v.*) guide.

wyte, (*n.*, *v.*) blame.

yaa, ye(a), indeed.

yeid, yude, went.

yeild, (*v.*) reward.

yet, gate.

yeu, you.

ying, young.

yone, (that) one.

yow, ewe.

yo(w)uth(t), youth, **-heid,** youths, state of youthfulness.

Yule, Yule (as a time of merry-making).

ythand, busy, assiduous.